Lecture Notes in Computer Science 2819

Edited by G. Goos, J. Hartmanis, and J. van Leeuwen

T0232061

Springer

Berlin
Heidelberg
New York
Hong Kong
London
Milan
Paris
Tokyo

Boualem Benatallah   Ming-Chien Shan (Eds.)

Technologies for E-Services

4th International Workshop, TES 2003
Berlin, Germany, September 7-8, 2003
Proceedings

 Springer

Series Editors

Gerhard Goos, Karlsruhe University, Germany
Juris Hartmanis, Cornell University, NY, USA
Jan van Leeuwen, Utrecht University, The Netherlands

Volume Editors

Boualem Benatallah
The University of New South Wales
School of Computer Science and Engineering
Sydney 2052, Australia
E-mail: boualem@cse.unsw.edu.au

Ming-Chien Shan
Hewlett Packard Laboratories
1501 Page Mill Road, Palo Alto, CA 94304, USA
E-mail: ming-chien_shan@hp.com

Cataloging-in-Publication Data applied for

A catalog record for this book is available from the Library of Congress.

Bibliographic information published by Die Deutsche Bibliothek
Die Deutsche Bibliothek lists this publication in the Deutsche Nationalbibliografie;
detailed bibliographic data is available in the Internet at <http://dnb.ddb.de>.

CR Subject Classification (1998): H.2, H.4, C.2, H.3, J.1, K.4.4, I.2.11, J.1

ISSN 0302-9743
ISBN 3-540-20052-5 Springer-Verlag Berlin Heidelberg New York

Springer-Verlag Berlin Heidelberg New York
a member of BertelsmannSpringer Science+Business Media GmbH

http://www.springer.de

© Springer-Verlag Berlin Heidelberg 2003
Printed in Germany

Typesetting: Camera-ready by author, data conversion by PTP-Berlin GmbH
Printed on acid-free paper   SPIN: 10953570   06/3142   5 4 3 2 1 0

Preface

E-services, and in particular Web services, are emerging as a promising technology for the effective automation of application integration across networks and organizations. The basic technological infrastructure for e-services is structured around three major standards: SOAP, WSDL, and UDDI. These standards provide building blocks for service description, discovery, and interaction. E-service technologies have clearly influenced positively the development of integrated systems by providing programmatic access to e-services through SOAP, WSDL, and UDDI. E-services are evolving toward being able to solve critical integration issues including security, transactions, collaborative processes management, semantic aspects, and seamless integration with existing middleware infrastructures.

VLDB-TES 2003 was the fourth workshop in a successful series of annual workshops on technologies for E-services, held in conjunction with the VLDB conference. The objective of VLDB-TES 2003 was to bring together researchers, practitioners, and users to exchange new ideas, developments, and experiences on issues related to E-services. VLDB-TES 2003 took place in Berlin, Germany. It featured the presentation of 16 regular papers. In addition to the presentation of research papers, the workshop included two invited talks and a panel discussion.

We would like to thank the authors for submitting their papers to the workshop, the members of the program committee, and the external reviewers for the tremendous job they did in reviewing the submitted papers. Special thanks go Helen Paik and Quan Z. Sheng for all their help with the logistics of the review process. We are grateful to Fabio Casati for all his help and guidance with all aspects of the workshop. We also thank Helen Paik and Sara Comai who served as the publicity co-chairs and Axel Marten who organized and planned the local arrangements.

July 2003

Boualem Benatallah
Ming-Chien Shan

Organization

Workshop Officers

General Chair
Ming-Chien Shan, Hewlett-Packard, USA
shan@hpl.hp.com

Program Chair
Boualem Benatallah, University of New South Wales, Sydney, Australia
boualem@cse.unsw.edu.au

Local Arrangements Chair
Axel Marten, Humboldt University, Berlin
artens@informatik.hu-berlin.de

Publicity Co-chairs
Sara Comai, Politecnico di Milano, Italy
comai@elet.polimi.it
Hye-young Helen Paik, University of New South Wales, Sydney, Australia
hpaik@cse.unsw.edu.au

Program Committee

Dave Abel, CSIRO, Australia
Gustavo Alonso, ETH Zurich, Switzerland
Jean Bacon, Cambridge University, UK
Martin Bichler, Technical University of Munich, Germany
Athman Bouguettaya, Virginia Tech., USA
Christoph Bussler, Oracle Corp., USA
Fabio Casati, Hewlett-Packard, USA
Jen-Yao Chung, IBM, USA
Umesh Dayal, Hewlett-Packard, USA
Asuman Dogac, Middle East Technical University, Turkey
Marlon Dumas, Queensland University of Technology, Australia
Dan Fishman, Avaya Labs., USA
Mariagrazia Fugini, Politecnico di Milano, Italy
Dimitrios Georgakopoulos, Telcordia, USA
Claude Godard, INRIA-LORIA, France
Mei Hsu, Commerce One, USA
Eleanna Kafeza, Hong Kong University of Science and Technology, China
Alfons Kemper, University of Passau, Germany
Wolfgang Klas, University of Vienna, Austria

Frank Leymann, IBM, Germany
Christoph Liebig, SAP, USA
Heiko Ludwig, IBM, USA
Zakaria Maamar, Zayed University, Dubai, United Arab Emirates
Ann Hee Hiong Ngu, Southwest Texas State University, USA
Mike Papazoglou, Tilburg University, The Netherlands
Barbara Pernici, Politechnico di Milano, Italy
Krithi Ramamritham, IIT Bombay, India
Stefan Tai, IBM, USA
Farouk Toumani, LIMOS, France
Aphroditi Tsalgatidou, University of Athens, Greece
Steve Vinoski, IONA, USA
Hartmut Vogler, SAP Research Lab, USA
Jian Yang, Tilburg University, The Netherlands
Yanchun Zhang, University of Southern Queensland, Australia
Lizhu Zhou, Tsing-Hua University, China

Additional Referees

Tariq A. Al-Naeem	Markus Keidl	Stefan Seltzsam
George Athanasopoulos	Patrick Kellert	Quan Z. Sheng
Jan Camenisch	Piyush Maheshwari	Edgar Weippl
Malu Castellanos	Brahim Medjahed	Utz Westermann
Qiming Chen	Bart Orriens	Moe Wynn
Andrzej Cichocki	Helen Paik	Liangzhao Zeng
Rachid Hamadi	Thomi Pilioura	Sonja Zillner
Birgit Hofreiter	Pierluigi Plebani	
Christian Huemer	Fethi Rabhi	

Table of Contents

On Web Services Aggregation

Rania Khalaf[1] and Frank Leymann[2]

[1] IBM TJ Watson Research Center, Hawthorne, NY 10532, USA
rkhalaf@us.ibm.com
[2] IBM Software Group, Boeblingen, Germany
ley1@de.ibm.com

Abstract. The Web services framework is enabling applications from different providers to be offered as services that can be used and composed in a loosely-coupled manner. Subsequently, the aggregation of services to form composite applications and maximize reuse is key. While choreography has received the most attention, services often need to be aggregated in a much less constrained manner. As a number of different mechanisms emerge to create these aggregations, their relation to each other and to prior work is useful when deciding how to create an aggregation, as well as in extending the models themselves and proposing new ones. In this paper, we discuss Web services aggregation by presenting a first-step classification based on the approaches taken by the different proposed aggregation techniques. Finally, a number of models are presented that are created from combinations of the above.

Keywords. business process modeling, composition, aggregation, web services.

1 Introduction

Web services [10,20] offer an XML-based framework that embodies the concepts of the Service–Oriented Computing (SoC) paradigm, created as a result of the movement away from the tight integration previously required for distributed IT offerings that cross enterprise boundaries. In the SoC model, applications from different providers are offered as services that can be used, composed, and coordinated in a loosely-coupled manner.

The Web services framework consists of an extensible, modular stack of open XML-standards that enable an application to expose its functionality in a machine–readable, implementation–neutral description such that it may be discovered, bound to, and interacted with possibly over a number of different protocols regardless of its location in the network. This environment is therefore intrinsically heterogeneous, distributed, and dynamic.

With a viable service model in place, the aggregation of services to provide composite applications and maximize reuse becomes key. For example, service aggregators may reuse services that have already been created, or offer new services formed by choreographing interactions with available services offered by other providers. Although Web services overlay on top of existing IT technologies, the Web services environment is more dynamic and loosely coupled.

B. Benatallah and M.-C. Shan (Eds.): TES 2003, LNCS 2819, pp. 1–13, 2003.

In comparing agents and components, [18] notes that agents concentrate on dynamicity and components concentrate on composability. Web services need both, making their aggregation models of particular interest.

Choreography-based composition has taken the forefront when considering aggregation in Web services. However, other less-structured aggregation models exist. As multiple languages and mechanisms are proposed, understanding their relation to each other and to prior composition and aggregation models is useful when deciding how to create an aggregation, as well as in extending the models themselves and proposing new ones.

In this paper, we study prevalent aggregation mechanisms by creating a classification that groups them based on their approach and applicability. The aim of this classification is two-fold. First, it distills the space by grouping aggregation mechanisms based on their design goal, allowing one to step back from the plethora of acronyms, specifications, and systems. Second, it begins identifying primitive aggregation techniques, allowing one to reason about useful combinations.

We present each of the approaches in the classification and discuss future work. Finally, a number of models created from combinations of the above are presented.

2   Background: Defining Web Services

Before discussing aggregation, we provide an overview of the functional description of a Web service, usually provided by the Web Services Description Language (WSDL)[8]. WSDL embodies the Web services principle separating the abstract functionality of a service from its mappings to deployed implementations, thereby enabling an abstract component to be implemented by multiple code artifacts and deployed using different communication protocols and programming models.

In WSDL, the abstract part consists of one or more "portTypes", constituting the service's interface. PortTypes specify supported operations and their input and/or output message structures. These may then be used by third parties aggregating compo-nents or by client code invoking operations.

The concrete part of a WSDL definition consists of bindings, ports, and services. A binding is a mapping of a portType to an available transport protocol and data encoding format. A port provides the location of a physical endpoint that implements a portType using one of the available bindings. A service is a collection of ports.

The aggregation mechanisms covered in the rest of this paper, in particular those performing type–based aggregation, will make extensive use of the WSDL definitions of their constituent services.

3   A Classification of Web Services Aggregation

For the focus of this paper, we define Web services aggregation as the combination of a set of Web services to achieve a common goal. An aggregation may be created both at the interface–level (agnostic to service implementations), or directly at the instance level. The former provides more flexibility in allowing late binding to actual deployed instances. We consider mechanisms whose purpose is the first–class creation of such aggregates.

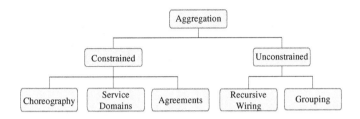

Fig. 1. Classification of Web Services Aggregation Models

The classification driving the discussion is illustrated in figure 1, and discussed in detail throughout the paper. The initial split depends on whether or not the aggregation is constrained. Unconstrained aggregation does not impose any control on the interactions between the services used or on the services that may be part of the aggregation. Approaches of this kind include simply grouping a set of services in one "bag" or defining an architectural setup through the use of join points and connectors.

On the other hand, constrained aggregation imposes constraints on the aggregated services, specifically regarding the functionality they must support and/or the interactions they may have with each other and with the aggregate itself. Three sub-categories are presented: choreography, service domains, and agreements.

This classification may be extended at each of the current leaves, and/or by adding higher level branches if significantly different models are proposed. For example, the choreography category can be further branched down based on the process meta–model used, including "calculus-based" [28], "state-chart based" [6], "graph-based" [16], and so on.

3.1   Unconstrained Aggregation

Grouping. Grouping simply provides a collection of services. Two cases are presented here, grouping of interfaces and grouping of instances.

– Interface Inheritance
  Multiple interface inheritance has been proposed for WSDL 1.2 in the form of portType inheritance. It introduces substitutability semantics at the instance level: An instance of a subtype in the inheritance hierarchy can be used wherever an instance of one of its supertypes can be used. Copy semantics apply at the specifications level as shown in figure 2, such that those of the supertypes are copied to the subtype. The implementation of the subtype provides a single endpoint with a single binding at which implementations

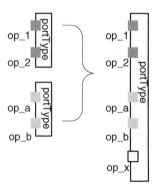

Fig. 2. Aggregating interfaces using portType inheritance

of all inherited operations are made available. This is different from service domains below.

While the area of multiple interface inheritance is relatively well understood due to prior experience in OOP, two issues have to be addressed that complicate the scenario for Web services: the lack of control over the portTypes being extended (they may be owned by a third-party) and the introduction of policies. The first leads to the problem of method signature clashes from methods coming from two different, inherited portTypes. Normally, one may be able to redefine or rename one of them, but those definitions may be out of the control of the user extending them. The second complication is the flexibility of the Web services quality of service framework, WS-Policy [3, 2]. Policies defining quality of service capabilities or requirements may be attached not only to the concrete part of the WSDL (part of the binding, or the port), but also to portTypes or operations within them. It is not yet clear what this would mean to multiple portType inheritance. The problems that could occur become clearer if one considers the following two cases: inheriting two operations with the same signature and different policies; inheriting a set of operations that may have conflicting policy requirements.

– Instance Grouping

An unstructured grouping of instances may be created to offer a number of related service instances together to a user. One example of its use is the creation of an aggregate as a collection of WSRP [15] portlets. Basically, a number of portlets of arbitrary functionality may be added to a portal that provides a unified access point to the user.

The WSRP specification enables portlets to be grouped into a portal, allowing a user to interact with them from a single location such as a Web page. While this approach is user-interface centric, it is one of the few examples of a pure grouping of instances. The container mediates the interaction between the user and the embedded services, but the portlets themselves are not connected to each other, and at the time of this writing, there was no way in WSRP to specify piping the output from one into the input of another as is done in "recursive wiring" below.

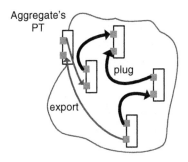

Fig. 3. Aggregation using Recursive Wiring

Recursive Wiring. One form of aggregation is to wire services together such that they may use each other's services. The aggregation created in this way may then itself be exposed as a service which can be wired and invoked. A simple example is a service composed of a chain of filters, where each filter is a Web service. Wiring occurs by connecting the output of the first filter to the input of the next and so on. The input of the first filter and the output of the last one may then be exposed on the aggregate.

This form of aggregation has been commonly used in component-based software engineering where component definitions include pluggable "ports", each port referring to an interface. Components are wired by binding input ports to output ports. The creation of compound components is done by binding an input port on an internal component to an input port on the created compound one, and similarly for output ports [23,25]. The wiring in these approaches is implicit, defined as part of the component definitions themselves. In Java, a similar approach is the use of event sources (output) and event listeners(input), with wiring occurring by adding one Bean as a listener to events from another. [13] presents a scripting language that makes the wiring first class. In [14], the focus is on making the connectors themselves first class, with an architecture created by combining components with connectors. Connectors are of different types, which specify the behavior of the interaction between the services they connect.

In Web services, WSFL's Global Models [16] define a variation on the recursive combination of components using explicitly defined connectors. In Global Models, directed "plug links" connect an output operation, op_{out} , from a portType of one service to the input operation, op_{in} , from a portType of another service. Message manipulations to match message types are enabled within the plug link definitions. "Dangling" operations may be exported to the boundary of the aggregation where they can be arranged in portTypes representing the interface of the aggregate, as illustrated in Figure 3.

WSFL's global model concept results in a recursive aggregation model at the interface (portType) level. External usage of operations of these portTypes will be delegated to the exporting operations. It can be perceived that the portTypes at the boundary of the aggregate are implemented by the corresponding exporting operations, i.e. the aggregation mechanism specifies an implementation of the operations via delegation. This exporting of operations enables recursive composition, similar to the creation of the compound components described earlier and to aggregation in COM [26].

The key differentiators between this model and those in the cited literature are that the wiring in Global Models is at the operation level, it does not require an exact mirror of the wired operations due to the ability to define message transformations, and most importantly it does not refer to instances of services but builds off of their abstract descriptions. The plug links may define a "locator", however, that defines how an instance may be located at runtime (for example, through a registry lookup).

3.2   Constrained Aggregation

Choreography. The wiring of services described above is based on the services themselves driving an instance of the aggregate. This is not sufficient for more complex cases such as those required in executing business functionality. In such situations, one needs to model a business process by choreographing the interactions with the services in the aggregate. The workflow and business process modeling mechanisms used in Web services fall under this category. Choreographies are constrained, proactive compositions that drive the interactions with the services they aggregate by defining execution semantics on a set of activities that perform these interactions. These semantics may be defined in a number of ways, such as connecting them with directed edges to form a DAG [21,16, 7], nesting them in compound activities with execution semantics [28], or using Petri Nets [17].

Web services choreography languages are based on the interfaces of the services, decoupled from specific service instances which may therefore be found and bound to during either the design, deployment [9], or execution phases of an aggregation. In [31,20], selection during execution enables the aggregate to meet (global) quality of service constraints. There are two main reasons for this: the dynamic nature of Service-Oriented Computing in which services and their requirements may change frequently, and the need to reuse business process logic across different implementations.

To illustrate, we describe one of the choreography mechanisms in more detail: The Business Process Execution Language for Web Services (BPEL4WS). The flow of control in BPEL4WS is defined using a combination of the aforementioned graph and calculus based approaches. A predefined set of simple activities is provided to: 1)perform Web services interactions: invoke operations on Web services, receive and reply to invocations on the process itself from the services it composes, and 2)provide additional functionality such as waiting, throwing faults, and manipulating data associated with the process. Control is defined using both (or either) directed control links and compound activities that impose, on the activities that are contained within them, semantics such as parallelism, sequencing, or non-deterministic choice. BPEL also defines compensation and fault handling mechanisms, [11].

Process PT

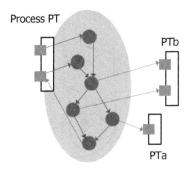

PTb

PTa

Fig. 4. Aggregating interfaces using choreography

BPEL4WS compositions are based purely on the interfaces of the composed services, that is, their abstract definitions in WSDL (portTypes, operations, and message types). From an architectural perspective, the resulting process is itself a Web service that can be exposed using WSDL definitions that define the portTypes it provides to clients. Additionally, the BPEL process also declares which portTypes it requires from each of the services it composes.

Mechanisms for binding service instances to a process are intentionally left up to the runtime and therefore out of the process definition. Dynamic binding is enabled through the definition of an activity that, when activated, copies a service reference from a received message (possibly from an invocation to a UDDI registry lookup or from a known service provider) into the runtime.

The "executable variant" of this semantics results in proactively driving the services as shown in figure 4. The "abstract interface variant" defines constraints in using the corresponding operations. The latter includes the degenerated case of a single portType, allowing one to specify ordering constraints in using the operations of that port type. Similarly, message exchange patterns (MEP) [1] between sets of portTypes can be defined via choreography.

In related work, semantic information is being used to enable the automatic creation of choreographies. For example, [24] presents a backwards chaining planner to automatically compose a set of Semantic Web services by working from a given goal.

Service Domains. A Service Domain is an aggregation formed by a set of implementations that complement (or compete) with each other to collectively implement a collection of portTypes. The service instances that may become part of this aggregate are constrained by the set of portTypes the aggregate includes, as illustrated in figure 5. The sum of the instances provides the implementation of the interfaces in the domain, with the domain dispatching each incoming call to the appropriate instance that can execute it. At the type level, a service domain SD is a set of portTypes, i.e. $SD = \{pT^1, ..., pT^n\}$. At the instance level a service domain sd is a collection of ports, i.e. $sd = \{p_1^1, ..., p_{k(1)}^1, p_1^n, ..., p_{k(n)}^n\}$. Here, each port $p_i^j \in sd$ is of portType $pT^j \in SD$.

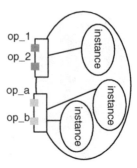

Fig. 5. Service Domains

The ports of a service domain *sd* may be provided by different service providers. An instance of a service domain is created by attaching ports for the aggregated portTypes to the instance. Different service providers may contribute ports for the same portType, and a given service provider may contribute ports of only a subset of the port types of the service domain.

A requestor is blind to the services constituting the aggregate, and picks a portType that he needs to interact with an instance of. A "hub" managing the instance of the service domain then selects a port of this portType from those made available to it by the different providers, and dispatches the call made by the requestor to it.

The next level of refinement of a service domain is the introduction of service level agreements (SLA) [22] to be used in the dispatching: Each portType of a service domain is associated with a set of SLAs. A provider that wants to contribute a port of a portType of the service domain registers with one of these SLAs, committing to the corresponding service level.

A requestor specifies a SLA with the service level he expects in his interactions with the ports of the instance of the service domain. The hub managing the instance of the service domain performs the choice underlying its dispatch decision based on matching SLAs and optimizing overall resource utilization. The owner of the hub specifies the rules to influence these choices.

This is similar to the aggregation model used in [27] and the *service communities* in [6], in which the service communities themselves are exposed as Web services.

Agreements. Agreement based aggregation is much more loosely constrained than choreographed aggregation. It is the creation of a distributed activity by the temporary grouping of a set of service instances, at the end of which a joint outcome is reached and possibly disseminated. This joint outcome is reached based on the members of the aggregation following a pre-defined set of protocols. Note that the portTypes of the services involved are not defined as part of this aggregation mechanism; instead, it relies purely on the ports (service endpoints) themselves.

One example is that of the sealed bid auction presented in [20]. Buyers and sellers are Web services following a certain coordination protocol and being coordinated by an auctioneer. At the end of the bidding period, the auctioneer decides who the winner of the bid is and informs both buyer and seller and the temporary collection of services ceases to exist.

The Web Services Coordination specification (WS–C for short)[4] is a realization of this approach. A distributed activity is a unit of computation that involves a set of services and at the end of which these services jointly agree on an outcome based on a coordination protocol. A coordination protocol consists of a set of messages and a specification of how these messages are to be exchanged. Coordination types then group a set of coordination protocols needed between the different services of a distributed activity. Additionally, methods are defined for registering participating services with coordinators. WS-C provides a pluggable framework for this form of aggregation, such that different and new coordination protocols may be used. The coordination protocols are defined separately, for example the WS-Transactions specification (WS–Tx for short)[5] describes two protocols for long-running transactions and for atomic activities.

WS–C has been considered in conjunction with WS–Tx. The use of this model will depend on the ease of introducing new protocols for different aggregations and additional real–world scenarios.

4   Instance Versus Interface Aggregation

The aggregation models discussed thus far aggregate either on the instances directly, such as is the case with service domains, or on the interfaces (WSDL portTypes) of the aggregated services. In the latter case, the binding to actual instances is done at some later point and is not the main concern of the aggregate's definition.

Table 6 summarizes the aggregation approaches defined above and shows corresponding Web services realization of these approaches. The level of granularity added to this table is the separation of aggregation concerned with instances from those concerned with interfaces.

5   Combined Aggregation Models

The categories defined above constitute different approaches to aggregation; however, useful patterns may be created by combining some of them together. The youth of the Web services technology means that such combinations are still in their very early stages. In this section, we describe a few possible combinations.

- *Choreography with Agreements:* The ability to coordinate multiple Web services extends naturally to coordinating both within and among aggregates. WS-Coordination (WS-C) was released in conjunction with BPEL4WS, along with WS-Transaction (WS-Tx), to be used either separately, or in tandem for more robust composition as described in [12]. The BPEL4WS specification contains an appendix on using WS-C/WS-Tx to coordinate nested scopes within a choreography.

how \ what		Types	Instances
Constrained	Choreography	BPEL4WS, MEPs	
	Service Domains	N/A	Service Domains, Service Communities
	Agreements	N/A	WS-Coordination
Unconstrained	Recursive Wiring	Global Models (WSFL)	
	Grouping	WSDL PortType Inheritance*	WSRP

*proposed, not part of current specification

Fig. 6. Summary of aggregation mechanisms

- *Choreographed Recursive Wiring*: The model of choreography presented in this paper has so far been from the perspective of the choreographing service. However, it is necessary to define global interaction choreographies that multiple partners may plug into. While recursive wiring allows plugging different services together, it does not restrict or define how they may interact - execution semantics are part of the implementations of the services. Outside of Web services, this requirement has been addressed in work on interorganizational workflow. The approaches used in the workflow literature map onto a combination of choreography and wiring: First, one must define the structure identifying the components and the channels of communication. This is similar to Global Models in section 3.1, but recursiveness is not addressed. Second, the literature defines interaction protocols either in terms of Petri Nets [30] or as sets of Message Sequence Charts [29,19].

  The realization of this combination will require further work in Web services, as BPEL4WS defines a protocol that drives an interaction instead of what is described here which is a protocol which defines how the different parties should drive the parts of the interaction that they are participating in.
- *Any Type-Based Aggregation with Service Domains:* Type-based aggregation mechanisms may refer to a service domain, restricting the choice of instances at runtime to the discretion of the domain. One example of this approach is used in [6] through its combination of choreography and service communities.
- *Recursive Wiring with Instance Grouping:* This combination results in instance based recursive composition, wiring together the instances that make up a grouping. For example, a set of portlets may be wired to pipe output from one portlet and into another.

6   Conclusion.

The area of Web services aggregations is seeing a large amount of activity as aggregation mechanisms are still evolving. Some are being extended and new ones created to enhance their capabilities. As multiple proposals emerge for aggregating Web services, it is important to understand where the mechanisms needed fit in and how they relate to existing approaches.

In this paper, we have discussed Web services aggregation by presenting a first–step classification based on the approaches taken by the different proposed aggregation techniques. The main commonality is that an aggregate is created to group a set of services in order to achieve a common goal. From there, we have shown an aggregation may be either constrained or unconstrained, depending on how much structure is needed to achieve the goal in question and on how independent the behavior of the constituent services may be from the composition itself. A choreography presents a composition-driven aggregation which defines control sequences of interactions with the aggregated services, whereas an aggregate created using recursive wiring does not care about sequencing. Instead it simply connects service interfaces together, so that once bound to instances the service instances drive their interactions along these connections. The ways in which aggregations may be formed is then further refined as shown in figure 1.

As the Web services model itself (WSDL, policy, etc) stabilizes, aggregation will become more central as it is a key capablity made more challenging by the distributed, dynamic, and heterogenuous nature of Web services. With the aim of clarification of aggregation models, and the youth of this technology, we have started with a small set of categories that identify the main areas as they stand today.

Ongoing work will reflect the effects of the evolution of core specifications, including WSDL, as well as the growth and adoption of Web services aggregation techniques. Refining and expanding the classification will consider both adding categories, and additional dimensions for existing categories, such as level and focus of constraints. We are also interested in identifying primitive aggregation mechanisms, and understanding the conditions under which they may or may not be combined

Acknowledgment. The authors acknowledge the contribution of comments on this paper with our colleagues at IBM, in particular, Ravi Konuru, Stefan Tai, and Francisco Curbera.

References

1. Web Services Message Exchange Patterns. Published online by W3C at http://www.w3.org/2002/ws/cg/2/07/meps.html, July 2002.
2. Web Services Policy Attachment (WS-PolicyAttachment). Published online by IBM, BEA, Microsoft, and SAP at http://www-106.ibm.com/developerworks/webservices/library/ws-polatt, 2002.
3. Web Services Policy Framework (WS-Policy Framework). Published online by IBM, BEA, and Microsoft at http://www-106.ibm.com/developerworks/webservices/library/ws-polfram, 2002.
4. WS-Coordination. Published online by IBM, BEA, and Microsoft at http://www-106.ibm.com/developerworks/library/ws-coor, 2002.

5. WS-Transaction. Published online by IBM, BEA, and Microsoft at
   http://www-106.ibm.com/developerworks/library/ws-transpec, 2002.
6. B. Benatallah, M. Dumas, and Z. Maamar. Definition and execution of composite
   web services: The self-serv project. *Data Engineering Bulletin*, 25(4), 2002.
7. Fabio Casati, Mehmet Sayal, and Ming-Chien Shan. Developing e-services for
   composing e-services. In *Proc. of CAiSE2001*, volume 2068 of *LNCS*, pages 171–
   186. Springer-Verlag, 2001.
8. Erik Christensen, Francisco Curbera, Greg Meredith, and Sanjiva Weerawarana.
   Web Services Description Language (WSDL) 1.1. Published online by W3C at
   http://www.w3.org/TR/wsdl, Mar 2001.
9. F. Curbera, M. Duftler, R. Khalaf, N. Mukhi, W. Nagy, and S. Weerawarana.
   BPWS4J. Published online by IBM at
   http://www.alphaworks.ibm.com/tech/bpws4j, Aug 2002.
10. Fancisco Curbera, Matthew Duftler, Rania Khalaf, William Nagy, Nirmal Mukhi,
    and Sanjiva Weerawarana. Unraveling the web services web: An introduction to
    SOAP, WSDL, and UDDI. *IEEE Internet Computing*, 6(2):86–93, 1 2002.
11. Francisco Curbera, Rania Khalaf, Frank Leymann, and Sanjiva Weerawarana. Ex-
    ception handling in the bpel4ws language. In *International Conference on Business
    Process Management(BPM2003)*, LNCS, Eindhoven, the Netherlands, June 2003.
    Springer.
12. Francisco Curbera, Rania Khalaf, Nirmal Mukhi, Stefan Tai, and S. Weerawarana.
    Web services, the next step: Robust service composition. *Communications of the
    ACM: Service Oriented Computing*, 10 2003. to appear.
13. Francisco Curbera, Sanjiva Weerawarana, and Matthew J. Duftler. On component
    composition languages. In *Proc. International Workshop on Component-Oriented
    Programming*, May 2000.
14. Eric M. Dashofy, Nenad Medvidovic, and Richard N. Taylor. Using off-the-shelf
    middleware to implement connectors in distributed software architectures. In *Proc.
    of International Conference on Software Engineering*, pages 3–12, Los Angeles,
    California, USA, May 1999.
15. A.L. Diaz, P. Fischer, C. Leue, and T. Schaeck. Web Services for Remote Portals
    (wsrp). Published online by IBM at
    http://www-106.ibm.com/developerworks/webservices/library/ws-wsrp/,
    January 2002.
16. Frank Leymann et. al. Web Services Flow Language (WSFL) 1.0. Published online
    by IBM at
    http://www-3.ibm.com/software/solutions/webservices/pdf/WSFL.pdf,
    May 2001.
17. Rachid Hamadi and Boualem Benatallah. A petri net-based model for web service
    composition. In *Proc. of the Australian Database Conference(ADC2003)*, Adelaide,
    Austaralia, 2003.
18. Denis Jouvin and Salima Hassas. Role delegation as multi-agent oriented dynamic
    composition. In *NetObjectDays*, 2002.
19. E. Kindler, A. Martens, and W. Reisig. Inter-operability of workflow applications.
    In W.M.P. van der Aalst, J. Desel, and A. Oberweis, editors, *Business Process
    Management: Models, Techniques, and Empirical Studies*, volume 1806 of *LNCS*,
    pages 235–253. Springer-Verlag, 2000.
20. Frank Leymann. Web services: Distributed applications without limits - an out-
    line. In *Proceedings, Database Systems for Business, Technology, and Web (BTW)*,
    LNCS. Springer-Verlag, Feb 2003.

21. Frank Leymann and Dieter Roller. *Production Workflow: Concepts and Techniques.* Prentice Hall, 2000.

22. H. Ludwig, A. Keller, A. Dan, R.P. King, and R. Franck. A service level agreement language for dynamic electronic services. *Journal of Electronic Commerce Research*, 3, mar 2003.

23. Jeff Magee, Andrew Tseng, and Jeff Kramer. Composing distributed objects in CORBA. In *3rd International Symposium on Autonomous Decentralized Systems (ISADS97)*, 1997.

24. Mithun Sheshagiri, Marie desJardins, and Tim Finin. A planner for composing services described in daml-s. In *Conf. on Autonomous Agents and Multi-Agent Systems(AAMAS03), Workshop on Web Services and Agent-based Engineering*, Melbourne, Australia, July 2003.

25. Vugranam C. Sreedhar. Mixin'up components. In *Proc. of the international conference on Software engineering (ICSE2002)*, Orlando, Florida, 2002.

26. Kevin Sullivan, Mark Marchukov, and John Socha. Analysis of a conflict between aggregation and interface negotiation in microsoft's component object model. *IEEE Transaction on Software Engineering*, 25(4), 1999.

27. Y.S. Tan, B. Topol, V. Vellanki, and J. Xing. Manage web services and grid services with service domain technology. Published online by IBM at http://www-106.ibm.com/developerworks/ibm/library/i-servicegrid/, 2002.

28. Satish Thatte. XLANG. Published online by Microsoft at http://www.gotdotnet.com/team/xml_wsspecs/xlang-c/default.htm, 2001.

29. W. van der Aalst. Interorganizational workflows: An approach based on message sequence charts and petri nets. *Systems Analysis - Modelling - Simulation*, 34(3):335–367, 1999.

30. W. van der Aalst and M. Weske. The p2p approach to interoganizational workflows. In *Proc. of CAiSE2001*, volume 2608 of *LNCS*, pages 140–156. Springer-Verlag, 2001.

31. Liangzhao Zeng, Boualem Bentallah, Marlon Dumas, Jayant Kalagnanam, and Quang Sheng. Quality driven web services composition. In *Proc. of WWW2003*, Budapest, Hungary, May 2003.

A Framework for Business Rule Driven Service Composition

Bart Orriëns, Jian Yang, and Mike. P. Papazoglou

Tilburg University, Infolab
PO Box 90153
5000 LE, Tilburg
Netherlands
{b.orriens,jian,mikep}@kub.nl

Abstract. One of the assumptions all the standards for web service composition (e.g. BPEL) make is that the business process is pre-defined. Obviously this assumption does not hold if business needs to accommodate changes in applications, technology, and organizational policies. We believe business processes can be dynamically built by composing web services if they are constructed based on and governed by business rules. In this paper we first analyze the basic elements in web service composition. Then we present a rule driven mechanism to govern and guide the process of service composition in terms of five broad composition phases spanning abstract definition, scheduling, construction, execution, and evolution to support on demand and on the fly business process generation.

1 Introduction

The platform neutral nature of web services creates the opportunity for corporate businesses to develop business processes by using and combining existing web services, possibly offered by different enterprizes. By selecting and combining most suitable and economical web services, business processes can be generated dynamically in the changing business environment. However the current composite web service development and management is very much a manual activity, which requires specific knowledge in advance and takes up much time and effort. This even applies to the applications that are being developed on the basis of available standards, such as BPEL4WS (BPEL for short) [3] and BPML [1]. Due to a vast service space to search, a variety of services to compare and match, and different ways to construct composed services service composition is simply too complex and too dynamic to handle manually. As such, we feel that the only alternative capable of facilitating dynamic service composition development and management is an automated process of service composition governed by rules and administrated by rule engines. Our conviction is that business rules can be used in the context of service composition to determine how the composition should be structured and scheduled, how the services and their providers should be selected, and how run time service binding should be conducted.

B. Benatallah and M.-C. Shan (Eds.): TES 2003, LNCS 2819, pp. 14–27, 2003.

In this a rule driven mechanism is used to steer the process of service composition in terms of five broad phases spanning *definition, scheduling, construction, execution,* and *evolution.* Based on these phases we analyze and classify business rules and determine how they impact service composition.

The paper is structured as followed: In section 2 we present a phase model for service composition and analyze the basic elements in a service composition. In section 3 we introduce the framework of business rule driven service composition. Section 4 discusses the related work. Finally we present our conclusions and discuss future research in section 5.

2   The Basis for Service Composition

In this section we first introduce a phased approach to service composition, based on which a rule based framework for service composition will be developed in section 3. We believe this approach helps to understand the issues and information needed in the process of service composition, and most importantly how business rules can be applied in each phase. Secondly we identify the basic elements in a service composition which lays a foundation for classifying business rules in section 3.

2.1   Service Composition Life-Cycle

This paper advocates a phased approach to service composition. The activities in this phased approach are collectively referred to as the *service composition life-cycle* [10]. The purpose of these activities, or phases, is to first describe services in the abstract and then to generate executable service processes from these abstract specifications, which can be controlled and governed by composition rules (will be discussed in section 3). In this approach five broad phases are distinguished spanning composition *definition, scheduling, construction, execution* and *evolution.* Here we focus on the first four phases, which we discuss as follows:

1. *Definition Phase.* The definition phase allows defining *abstractly* composite services. Composite service definitions employ WSDL in conjunction with a language for defining business processes by orchestrating web services, viz., BPEL. The difference between an abstract service composition and a concrete service composition lies in the fact that in the abstract definition, the structure, the actual services, and the service providers are not completed. The whole idea behind the phased approach and rule driven service composition is to start with an abstract definition and gradually make it concrete and executable.
2. *Scheduling Phase.* The scheduling phase is responsible for determining how and when services will run and preparing them for execution. The main purpose is to concretize the definition developed in the definition phase by correlating messages to express data dependencies, and synchronizing and prioritizing the execution of the constituent activities. Alternative composition schedules may be generated and presented to the application developer for selection

3. *Construction Phase.* The outcome of this phase is the construction of a concrete and unambiguous composition of services – out of a set of desirable or potentially available/matching constituent services – ready for execution.
4. *Execution Phase.* The execution phase implements composite service bindings on the basis of the scheduled service composition specifications and executes the services in question.

2.2   Service Composition Elements

In order to analyze how a service composition is developed through the phases outlined in the previous section, and how business rules can control and govern the process of service composition, we need to look at the basic elements and their properties in a service composition. By studying the current standards (e.g. BPEL, BPML) we can identify the following *composition elements:* **activity, control flow, condition, events, message, provider** and **role**. We discuss each composition element and their properties using examples as follows:

- **Activity** represents a well-defined business function. It has eight properties as illustrated in the following:

```
 Activity: (
name="flightActivity"
functionality="flightTicketBooking"
inputMessage="flightReservationData"
outputMessage="flightTicket"
performedBy="flightRole"
preConditions="(seatAvailableCondition)"
postConditions="(seatReservedCondition)"
impactEvents="(seatUnavailableError)"
)
```

  The above describes an activity named "flightActivity" that offers flight ticket booking functionality. As input this activity requires a message named "flightReservationData" (which is specified later). It generates the message "flightTicket" as output. Responsible for carrying out the activity is the role "flightRole". Optionally, activity execution can be constrained by conditions, e.g. "flightActivity" may only be carried out if "seatAvailableCondition" is true. Similarly its result is constrained by "seatReservedCondition". Lastly, this activity may be affected by events, e.g., "seatUnavailableError".
- **Condition** constrains the behavior of the composition. They can be used to guard activities, to enforce integrity constraints, and to control event occurrences. A condition has three properties: *name, argument,* and *predicates.*
- **Event** describes an occurrence during the process of service composition. An event is represented as follows:

```
Event: (
name="seatUnavailableError"
nature="seatUnavailable"
severity="unrecoverable"
conditions="seatUnavailableCondition"
source="flightRole"
signal="seatUnavailableSignal"
action="stopExecution"
)
```

It describes an event "seatUnavailableException", occurring when there are no seats available. The severity of this event is "unrecoverable" indicating that if it occurs, execution cannot continue. The other value for severity is "normal", indicating an event that affects, but does not disturb execution. The event is raised by the role "flightRole". This role can do so by sending the message "seatUnavailableSignal" as a signal. When such a message is received, the specified action is carried out, in this case to stop execution.

- **Flow:** it defines a block of activities and how they are connected. A flow is represented as for example:

```
Flow: (
name="SimpleTravelPlanFlow"
activities="(flightActivity,hotelActivity)"
pattern="sequential"
)
```

It shows a flow called "SimpleTravelPlanFlow", which groups two activities, named "flightActivity" and "hotelActivity", in a sequential pattern. The list of activities can contain both activities and flows. Furthermore, the order in which the activities will be carried out is the same as the order in which they are referenced in the list (of relevance in flows of a sequential nature). Besides sequential patterns iterative and parallel patterns are also supported.

- **Message:** it represents a container of information and has properties as: name, parts, dependencies, and integrity constraints.
- **Provider:** it describes a party offering concrete web services, which can be used at runtime to carry out activities. It specifies properties such as name, description, capabilities, cost, quality, URI, services, etc.
- **Role:** it provides an abstract description for a party that can participate in the composition. A role is specified as for example:

```
Role: (
name="flightRole"
type="airline"
rights"(showAvailableSeats,approveSeatReservation,cancelReservation)"
playedBy="KLM"
)
```

It describes a role named "flightRole". This role is of the type "airline" and is authorized to find and show available flights, approve seat reservations as well as cancel reservations. In this case the role is played by provider "KLM".

Now we can say that for an abstract service composition, some composition elements or some properties of the composition elements can be absent. On the other hand, for a concrete executable service composition, all the composition elements defined in this section and their properties have to be specified. We can start e.g. with an abstract service composition by specifying activities and constraints based on the user requirements, and leaving the **flow, message, providers** elements open. These unspecified elements and property values will be instantiated gradually with the help of business rules and more user inputs. As such the process of dynamic service composition becomes a matter of specifying composition elements and their property values. In the next section we demonstrate how this can be achieved by a business rule driven mechanism.

3   Business Rule Driven Service Composition

This section introduces a business rule driven framework for service composition, which is based on the phase approach discussed in the previous section. We shall firstly provide a business rule classification designed for service composition. Then we will demonstrate how the process of service composition generation is governed by the business rules. We use the following travel example for illustration:

1. Book a flight from New York to Vancouver. The departure date is July 15th, the return date August 22th. These dates are non-negotiable.
2. Reserve a hotel room.
3. Rent a car.

3.1   Business Rule Classification for Service Composition

There has been substantial work on business rule classification, e.g. in [9],[4],[7] and [5]. The problem with these classifications is that they cannot be applied to the service composition process. What we need is a classification that can guide this process by specifying the composition elements and property values.

Due to space limitation, we only illustrate the rules that are required in the *Definition* and *Scheduling* phase as follows:

– **Structure Rules:** structure rules govern how things are to be done in the composition. We further distinguish between *activity structure*, *activity dependency* and *event handling* rules. For example, an activity structure rule can look like (more examples can be found in Table 6):

```
AST: If (Activity: functionality="flightTicketBooking",
          Activity: functionality="hotelRoomReservation")
     Then (Flow: pattern="parallelWithSynchronization")
```

It says that if we have activities offering functionality such as flight ticket booking and hotel room reservation, they must be combined in a flow using a parallel with result synchronization pattern.
– **Data Rules:** data rules control the use of data in the composition, i.e., how messages are related to each other, what is the necessary input/output message for an activity. For example we can specify the required input message of activity "flightTicketBooking" as follows (for more examples see Table 7):

```
AIP: If (Activity: functionality="flightTicketBooking")
     Then (Message: input="(departureDate,returnDate,from,to)")
```

It specifies that if we have an activity for flight ticket booking, its input must contain a departure and return date, starting location and destination.
– **Constraint Rules:** constraint rules include *activity guardian*, *event control* and *message integrity* rules. For example a pre-condition for activity "flightTicketBooking" can be specified as follows (see Table 8 for more examples):

```
PRG: If (Activity: functionality="flightTicketBooking")
     Then (Condition: argument="seatsAvailable",predicate="=", value="true")
```

– **Resource Rules:** resource rules guide the use of resources in the composition in terms of selecting services, providers, and event raisers. For example we can specify the requirements of a role to carry out the activity "flightTicketBooking" as follows (more examples can be found in Table 9):

```
APE: If (Activity: functionality="flightTicketBooking")
     Then (Role: type="airline",rights="approveSeatReservation")
```

– **Exception Rules:** exception rules regulate the exceptional behavior of the composition. An example can be the rule below, which depicts that if we have an activity for flight ticket booking, it can be impacted by an event indicating that there are no seats available.

```
AIN: If (Activity: functionality="flightTicketBooking")
     Then (Event: nature="seatUnavailable")
```

3.2 Business Rule Driven Service Composition Framework

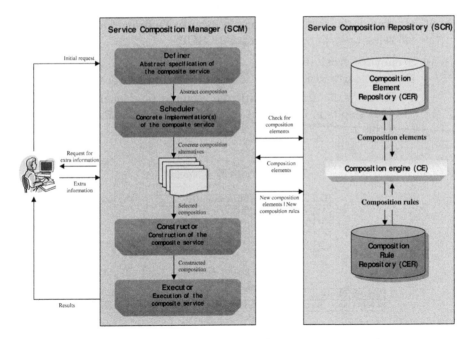

Fig. 1. Framework for business rule driven service composition

In the previous subsection we analyzed the different rules required to control and guide the service composition life cycle. Based on the resulting classification we define the business rule driven service composition framework. As shown in Fig. 1 it mainly consists of two components:

- **Service Composition Manager (SCM)** is responsible for assisting the user during the process of service composition. **SCM** interacts with **SCR** to drive this process spanning *Definition, Scheduling, Construction* and *Execution* phases.
- **Service Composition Repository (SCR)** is responsible for maintaining *composition elements* and *composition rules* that are used in the process of service composition. The composition elements and rules are maintained in the **Composition Element Repository (CER)** and the **Composition Rule Repository (CRR)** respectively, which is managed by the **Composition Engine (CE)**.

In the following we will walk through the travel example to explain how the framework works. We assume that the states of **CER** and **CRR** are as follows:
Composition Element Repository† (Table 1-5)
Composition Rule Repository (Table 6-10)
Now the process of developing a composite service can be described as follows:

1. The application developer (user) sends a request to **SCM** saying that he wants to book a flight, reserve a hotel room and rent a car.
2. **SCM** receives the request and passes it on to **Definer**. **Definer** performs the following tasks in collaboration with **SCR**:

   a) **Structure Activities**

   Definer starts with deriving a structure for the composition as follows:

   i. Retrieve the activities with the required functionality from **CER**. This results in adding `Activity1`, `Activity2` and `Activity3` (see Table 1).

Table 1. Activity elements

Label	Name	Functionality
Activity1	flight	flightTicketBooking
Activity2	hotel	hotelRoomReservation
Activity3	car	carRental
Activity4	stop	stopExecution

Table 2. Event elements

Label	Name	Nature	Severity
Event1	seatUnavailableException	seatUnavailable	unrecoverable

Table 3. Message elements

Label	Name	Parts
Message1	flightData	departureDate,returnDate,from,to
Message2	hotelBookingData	checkinDate,duration,roomType
Message3	carRentalData	period,carType,insurance
Message4	flightTicket	airline,leave,return,flightNr,seatNr
Message5	hotelConfirmation	hotelName,period,roomNr
Message6	carRentalApproval	carType,pickupLocation,pickupDate,period,dropOff
Message7	seatUnavailableSignal	faultCode,faultMessage

Table 4. Provider elements

Label	Name	Description	Capabilities	cost	quality
Provider1	KLM	Royal Dutch Airline	searchFlight,bookFlight	expensive	high
Provider2	MartinAir	Dutch Airline	searchFlight,bookFlight	cheap	average
Provider3	Hertz	Car Rental Company	rentCar	expensive	high
Provider4	Dollar	Car Rental Company2	rentCar	average	average
Provider5	HotelDirect	Hotels Worldwide	searchHotel,reserveRoom	cheap	average

Table 5. Role elements

Label	Name	Type	Rights
Role1	flightRole	airline	approveSeatReservation
Role2	hotelRole	hotelBroker	acceptBooking
Role3	carRole	carRentalCompany	

Table 6. Structure rules

Label	If	Then
AST1	Activity: funct="hotelRoomReservation", Activity: funct="carRental"	Flow: pattern="parallelWithSync"
ADP1	Activity: funct="flightTicketBooking", Activity: funct="hotelRoomReservation"	Flow: pattern="sequential"
ADP2	Activity: funct="flightTicketBooking", Activity: funct="carRental"	Flow: pattern="sequential"
EHA1	Event: nature="seatUnavailable"	Activity: functionality="stopExecution"

Table 7. Data rules

Label	If	Then
AIP1	Activity: funct="flightTicketBooking"	Message: parts="(departureDate,returnDate, from,to)"
AIP2	Activity: funct="hotelRoomReservation"	Message: parts="(checkinDate,duration)"
AIP3	Activity: funct="carRental"	Message: parts="(period)"
AOP1	Activity: funct="flightTicketBooking"	Message: parts="(leave,return,flightNr)"
AOP2	Activity: funct="hotelRoomReservation"	Message: parts="(hotelName,period)"
AOP3	Activity: funct="carRental"	Message: parts="(period,pickupLocation)"
MDP1	Message: part="checkinDate"	Message: part="leave"
ESI1	Event: nature="seatUnavailable"	Message: parts="(faultCode,faultMessage)"

Table 8. Constraint rules

Label	If	Then
ECO1	Event: nature="seatUnavailable"	Condition: argument="seatNr", predicate="=",value="-1"
MIT1	Message: part="departureDate"	Condition: predicate=">", value="currentDate"

Table 9. Resource rules

Label	If	Then
APE1	Activity: funct="flightTicketBooking"	Role: type="airline", rights="(approveSeatReservation)"
APE2	Activity: funct="hotelRoomReservation"	Role: type="hotelBroker", rights="(acceptBooking)"
APE3	Activity: funct="carRental"	Role: type="carRentalCompany", rights=""
RPL1	Role: type="airline",rights=""	Provider: capabilities=("bookFlight"), quality="high"
RPL2	Role: type="hotelBroker",rights=""	Provider: capabilities=("reserveRoom"), quality=>"average"
RPL3	Role: type="carEntalCompany",rights=""	Provider: capabilities=("rentCar"), cost<"expensive"
ERA1	Event: nature="seatUnavailable"	Role: type="airline",rights=""

Table 10. Exception rules

Label	If	Then
AIN1	Activity: functionality="flightTicketBooking"	Event: nature="seatUnavailable"

ii. Structure the activities. Applying `AST1` (from Table 6) to `Activity2` and `Activity3` results in adding a new flow `Flow1` (see specification below) to the composition definition, grouping these activities in a parallel with synchronization pattern. Then, applying `ADP1` and `ADP2` to `Activity1` and `Activity2`, and `Activity1` and `Activity3` respectively results in a new flow element `Flow2` (see specification below).

As a result we get a composition specification (please note that this specification is just for illustrative purposes, it is not the real syntax):

```
<composition>
 <structure> Activity1,Activity2,Activity3
 Flow1: (name="hotelCar",activities="(hotel,car)",pattern="parallelWithSync")
 Flow2: (name="travel",activities="(flight,hotelCar)",pattern="sequential")
 </structure>
</composition>
```

b) **Add Message Exchanging Behavior**

Next, **Definer** adds message exchanging behavior, as follows:

i. Determine the input of the activities. Applying `AIP1`, `AIP2`, and `AIP3` (from Table 7) to `Activity1`, `Activity2`, and `Activity3` results in adding `Message1`, `Message2`, and `Message3` (see Table 3) respectively. Also, references to these messages are added as values of 'inputMessage' properties of `Activity1`, `Activity2`, and `Activity3`.

ii. Determine the output of the activities. Applying `AOP1`,`AOP2`, and `AOP3` to `Activity1`, `Activity2`, and `Activity3` results in adding `Message4`, `Message5`, and `Message6`. Also, references to these messages are added as values of 'outputMessage' properties of `Activity1`, `Activity2`, and `Activity3`.

iii. Depict any message dependencies. Applying `MDP1` (from Table 7) to `Message2` and `Message4` results in adding dependency `Dependency1` (see specification below). Also, a reference to `Dependency1` is added as value of `dependencies` property of `Message2`.

As a result we get (only changed elements and properties are shown)

```
<composition>
  <structure>
  Activity1: (inputMessage="flightData",outputMessage="flightTicket")
  Activity2: (inputMessage="hotelBookingData",outputMessage="hotelConfirmation")
  Activity3: (inputMessage="carRentalData",outputMessage="carRentalApproval")
  </structure>
  <data> Message2: (dependencies="(departureDateEqualsCheckinDate)"),
  Dependency1: (name="departureDateEqualsCheckinDate",source="flightTicket.leave",
              target="hotelRoomBookingData.checkinDate",type="=") </data>
</composition>
```

c) **Assign Participants**

Then, **Definer** determines the participants that are to carry out the activities. Applying APE1, APE2, and APE3 to Activity1, Activity2, Activity3 results in adding Role1, Role2 and Role3. Also, references to these roles are made in the 'performedBy property of Activity1, Activity2, and Activity3. As a result we get (only changed elements and properties are shown)

```
<composition>
  <structure>
   Activity1: (performedBy="flightRole"),
   Activity2: (performedBy="hotelRole"),
   Activity3: (performedBy="carRole")
  </structure>
  <resource> Role1,Role2,Role3 </resource>
</composition>
```

d) **Define Event Handling Behavior**

Subsequently, **Definer** derives event handling behavior. This is done as followed:

  i. Determine which events may impact the activities. Applying AIN1 (from Table 10) to Activity1 results in adding Event1 (see Table 2).

  ii. Find out who can raise Event1. Applying ERA1 (from Table 9) results in adding Role1. Also, a reference to Role1 is made in the source property of Event1.

  iii. Check which information is needed to raise Event1 by applying ESI1 (from Table 7) results in adding Message7. Also, a reference to Message7 is made in the signal property of Event1.

  iv. Deduce how Event1 is to be handled. Applying EHA1 (from Table 9) results in adding Activity4. Also, a reference to Activity4 is made in the action property of Event1.

As a result we get (only changed elements and properties are shown)

```
<composition>
  <structure>
   Activity1: (impactEvents="(seatUnavailableException)")
  </structure>
  <data>
   Message7
  </data>
  <exception>
   Event1: (source="flightRole",signal="seatUnavailableSignal",action="stop")
  </exception>
</composition>
```

e) **Determine Constraints**

Finally, **Definer** determines the constraints for the composition. This can be achieved either by getting the constraints (such as pre-condition, post-condition) from **CRR**, or asking the user (such as data constraints). As an example we can have (only changed elements and properties are shown)

```
<composition>
  <structure>
   Activity1: (postConditions="(departureDateCondition,arrivalDateCondition)")
  </structure>
  <data>
   Message1: (integrityConstraints="(departureDateGreaterThanCurrentDate)")
  </data>
  <exception>
   Event1: (conditions="(seatReservedCondition)")
  </exception>
  <constraint>
   Condition1: (name="departureDateCondition",argument="flightTicket.departureDate",
                predicate="=", value="15-07-2003")
   Condition2: (name="arrivalDateCondition",argument="flightTicket.arrivalDate",
                predicate="=", value="22-08-2003")
   Condition3: (name="validDepartureDate",argument="flightData.departureDate",
                predicate="=", value="currentDate")
   Condition4: (name="seatReserved",argument="flightTicket.seatNr",
                predicate="!=", value="-1")
  </constraint>
</composition>
```

3. Next, to concretize the composition **Scheduler** collaborates with **SCR** to select providers that will implement the roles. For the travel composition RPL1, RPL2, and RPL3 (from Table 9) can be applied to Role1, Role2, and Role3 respectively, which results in adding Provider2, Provider5, and Provider4. Also, references to these providers are made in the playedBy property of Role1, Role2, and Role3. As a result we get (note: only changed elements and attributes are shown)

```
<composition>
  <resource>
   Role1: (playedBy="KLM"),
   Role2: (playedBy="HotelDirect"),
   Role3: (playedBy="Dollar"),
   Provider2,Provider5,Provider4
  </resource>
</composition>
```

4. Step 3 may be repeated several times to obtain a set of alternatives. If the user opts to do so, he is subsequently asked to select one. If not, this step is skipped.
5. Subsequently, **Constructor** generates executable software to ready the constituent services in the selected, concrete composition for execution.
6. Lastly, **Executor** asks the user to provide the input, required for execution. Subsequently, **Executor** executes the composition and presents the results to the user.

Please note not every composition needs to go through every step discussed above. If all the composition elements are already in **CER**, constructing an executable service composition is just a matter of matching and retrieving elements and assembling them. As such, once many (or all) rules relevant for a composition have been specified in **CRR** the knowledge in these rules can be utilized to automatically develop a composition ready for execution, thus reducing the time and effort involved. This sets our approach apart from current approaches where new compositions usually have to be developed from scratch.

Also, please observe that in this section we illustrated the basics of our approach, i.e., how to develop a service composition based on composition elements and composition rules, in conjunction with the phase approach. Due to space limitation, other issues such as verification, rule conflict resolution, etc. were not discussed.

4   Related Work

Most work in service composition has focused on using work flows either as a engine for distributed activity coordination or as a tool to model and define service composition. Representative work is described in [2] where the authors discuss the development of a platform specifying and enacting composite services in the context of a workflow engine. The eFlow system provides a number of features that support service specification and management, including a simple composition language, events and exception handling.

The workflow community has recently paid attention to configurable or extensible workflow systems which present some overlaps with the ideas reported in the above. For example, work on flexible workflows has focused on dynamic process modification [8]. In this publication workflow changes are specified by transformation rules composed of a source schema, a destination schema and of conditions. The workflow system checks for parts of the process that are isomorphic with the source schema and replaces them with the destination schema for all instances for which the conditions are satisfied.

The approach described in [6] allows for automatic process adaptation. The authors present a workflow model that contains a placeholder activity, which is an abstract activity replaced at run-time with a concrete activity type. This concrete activity must have the same input and output parameter types as those defined as part of the placeholder. In addition, the model allows to specify a selection policy to indicate which activity should be executed.

In [11] authors developed an agent-based cross-enterprise Workflow Management System (WFMS) which can integrate business processes on user's demand. Based on users' requirements, the integration agent contacts the discovery agent to locate appropriate service agents, then negotiates with the service agents about task executions. Authors in [12] proposed a dynamic workflow system that is capable of dynamic composition and modification of running workflows by using a business rule inference engine. However these two approaches are more of the focus of dynamic process execution and management.

Our approach is very different from the existing work in terms of supporting composition of web services dynamically in the following manner:

- We propose an integrated approach towards service composition, which covers the entire service composition life-cycle abstract service definition, scheduling, construction and execution.
- Instead of starting from a service composition specification, we construct a concrete service composition specification from the basic *composition ele-*

ments using *composition rules*, reducing the time and effort involved in the development of compositions.

- Business rules are classified based on the requirements of service composition life-cycle. We analyze the types of rules required for each phase and demonstrate how they can be used to drive the service composition process.

5   Conclusions and Future Research

It is clear that current standards in service composition, such as BPEL, are not capable of dealing with the complex and dynamic nature of developing and managing composite web services to realize business processes. With a vast service space to search, a variety of services to compare and match, and different ways to construct composed services, manual specification of compositions is impossible. The challenge is therefore to provide a solution in which dynamic service composition development and management is facilitated in an automated fashion. We argue that our approach not only makes service composition more flexible and dynamic compared to current standards, but also reduces time and effort involved in composition development and management. The work presented here is at its very initial stage. In the future we will investigate into issues such as rule specification, architectural aspects of the rule system including a rule engine that links rule specifications with the generation of composite service specifications, and a change management sub-system that manages the evolution of business rules and service specifications.

References

1. Business Process Modelling Initiative; "Business Process Modeling Language", June 24, 2002, http://www.bpmi.org
2. F. Casati, S. Ilnicki, L. Jin, V. Krishnamoorthy, M.C. Shan. Adaptive and Dynamic Service Composition in eFlow, *HP Lab. Techn. Report, HPL-2000-39*.
3. F. Curbera, Y. Goland, J. Klein, F. Leymann, D. Roller, S. Thatte, S. Weerawarana; "Business Process Execution Language for Web Services", July 31, 2002, http://www-106.ibm.com/developerworks/webservices/library/ws-bpel/
4. Business Rules Group; "Defining business rules, what are they really?", July 2000, http://www.brcommunity.com
5. C.J. Date; "What Not How: The Business Rule Approach to Application Development", Addison & Wesley Longman Inc, 2000
6. D. Georgakopoulos, H. Schuster, D. Baker, and A. Cichocki. Managing Escalation of Collaboration Processes in Crisis Mitigation Situations. Proceedings of ICDE 2000, San Diego, CA, USA, 2000.
7. B. von Halle; "Business rules applied: Building Better Systems Using the Business Rule Approach", Wiley & Sons, 2002
8. G. Joeris and O. Herzog. Managing Evolving Workflow Specifications with Schema Versioning and Migration Rules. TZI Technical Report 15, University of Bremen, 1999.
9. R. Veryard; "Rule Based Development", CBDi Journal, July/August 2002

10. J. Yang, M.P. Papazoglou; "Service Component for Managing Service Composition Life-Cycle", Information Systems, June, Elsevier, 2003
11. Liangzhao Zeng, Boualem Benatallah, and Anne H. H. Ngu, "On Demand Business-to-Business Integration", CooPIS01, Trento, 2001.
12. Liangzhao Zeng, David Flaxer, Henry Chang, Jun-Jang Jeng, "PLM$_{flow}$-Dynamic Business Process Composition and Execution by Rule Inference", TES2002, Hong Kong, 2002.

Context-Aware Composition of *E*-services *

L. Baresi[1], D. Bianchini[2], V. De Antonellis[2], M.G. Fugini[1], B. Pernici[1], and P. Plebani[1]

[1] Politecnico di Milano – Department of Electronics and Information Science
{baresi,fugini,pernici,plebani}@elet.polimi.it
[2] Università di Brescia – Dipartimento di Elettronica per l'Automazione
{bianchini,deantonellis}@ing.unibs.it

Abstract. Composition of *E*-services in a multichannel environment requires taking into account the constraints imposed by the context: user profiles, geographical locations, available channels, and usable devices.

In this paper, we propose an approach for context-aware composition of *E*-services based on an abstract description of both *E*-services and context. *E*-services are described in terms of functionality and quality of service. The context describes the channels that can be used to access *E*-services. The paper proposes adaptation rules as the means to allow the composition and dynamically select *E*-service channels according to the constraints posed by available architectures and application-level requirements. Composition and adaptation rules are exemplified on a simple case for emergency management.

1 Introduction

Nowadays, users are greatly interested in easily accessing a wide variety of services through different channels [10,12]. This means that *E*-services can be accessed using different devices (e.g., PCs, laptops, palmtops, cell-phones, TV sets), but also different network technologies and application protocols. For example, the same service could be delivered via call centers, the Web, or message-based systems like SMS. In particular, nomadic users want to access services from their current locations and with the best possible performance. As a consequence, the need emerges for the design of networks and services that are highly flexible and adaptive, capable of exploiting available resources in an optimal way and with different levels of quality of service.

The Italian MAIS (Multichannel Adaptive Information Systems) project [6] aims to create an enabling platform, a methodology, and design tools for the development of distributed information systems based on *E*-services and with significant adaptability features.

Adaptive information systems span different research areas. For example, the simplest way towards adaptation is through transcoding [2]. As to profiles and context information, we can mention the WWRF (Wireless World Research Forum) [16], the Cameleon project [5], and the CC/PP (Composite Capabilities/Preferences Profile) initiative of the W3C *device independence working group* [15]. Gu et al. [11] present

---

* This work has been partially supported by the Italian MIUR FIRB MAIS (Multichannel Adaptative Information Systems) Project.

B. Benatallah and M.-C. Shan (Eds.): TES 2003, LNCS 2819, pp. 28–41, 2003.
© Springer-Verlag Berlin Heidelberg 2003

a precise model for quality of service and also propose rules to support the negotiation phase. But also, the UWA project studied and proposed *customization rules* [7] to describe and constrain the adaptability of ubiquitous Web applications. Finally, composition is addressed in [13], where they use DAML-S and coloured Petri nets to reason on *E*-service composition.

The goal of this paper is to define a modeling framework for adaptive information systems based on *E*-services. We aim at separating the aspects at application and technological levels and at providing a basis for formalizing contracts between *E*-service providers and the user.

In the proposed modeling approach, *E*-services are defined by means of two complementary perspectives: the request perspective, which provides an abstract model of the context where the *E*-service is requested and executed, and the provisioning perspective, which models available *E*-services in terms of their functional description and composition. Both perspectives consider proper characteristics of quality of service to allow *E*-service negotiation in terms of user requests, channels used in the interaction, and constraints from the *E*-service provider. These negotiation policies are coded in adaptation rules. The two perspectives and adaptation rules form the basis for context-aware composition of *E*-services that is able to dynamically select *E*-service channels according to the constraints posed by available architectures and application-level requirements. In particular, adaptation rules allow us to dynamically adapt the execution flow of our services – described as workflows – according to the characterization of the selected channel.

The paper is organized as follows. Section 2 presents the reference example used to illustrate the proposed approach. Section 3 shows the two modeling perspectives, while Section 4 discusses the application of the approach to the reference example. Section 5 and Section 6 address the specification of quality of service and adaptation rules, respectively. Finally, Section 7 introduces the MAIS platform and Section 8 concludes the paper.

2   *E*-service Model

In this paper we present two different modeling perspectives related to the *provisioning* and *request* of *E*-services. The provisioning perspective specifies who provides the *E*-service, what the *E*-service does and how to invoke its functionality, according to the available quality of service. The request perspective specifies who requires the *E*-service, i.e., the actor, who wants to have a certain level of quality for the required *E*-service, has a particular user profile, and operates in a particular *context*.

In the MAIS project, we use UML (Unified Modeling Language) [14] as modeling language because of its expressiveness.

2.1   *E*-service Provisioning

Figure 1 shows the components used to model an *E*-service with respect to the E-*service provisioning perspective*.

An *EService* is described by means of a *name* that identifies it, a short textual *description*, a service *category* (such as, for example, *commercial service* or *information service*), and an aggregation of three types of elements:

– a *Channel*, on which the *E*-service is provided. To pursue adaptativity, an *E*-service can be provided through one or more channels and an association class *CQuality-Dimension* represents the quality of the *E*-service with respect to the channel used. There can exist several parameters to express the quality of service, for instance: response time, channel availability, usability, accessibility, integrity, bandwidth, reliability, and price;

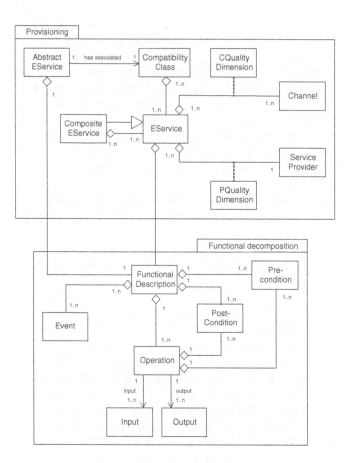

Fig. 1. Service provisioning perspective

– one or more *ServiceProviders*, each of them described by a *name* and standard address information. An association class *PQualityDimension* expresses the quality parameters guaranteed by the service provider: for example, data reliability, provisioning time, service availability, price;

– a *FunctionalDescription* that describes the operational aspects of the *E*-service.

The *FunctionalDescription* – inspired by WSDL [3] – is a set of *Operations*, with a *name* and a short textual *description* about "what the operation does":

– Each operation requires one or more *Inputs* and gives back one or more *Outputs*; input and output parameters are described by a *name* and a *value*;
– Each operation is associated with a set of *PreConditions* and *PostConditions* that predicate on the *Inputs* and *Outputs* of the operation. The former must be verified before the execution of the operation, while the latter must be satisfied after the execution. Pre- and post-conditions can also be defined on whole services;
– External *Events* are used to model actions that are asynchronous with respect to the normal flow of the *E*-service. Each event has a *name* that identifies it and a *type* such as *temporal event, data event* and so on: for instance, a *temporal event* is a timeout that occurs during the execution of an operation. Events must be managed through appropriate rules.

E-services can be composed in a recursive manner to create *CompositeEServices* (similarly to BPEL4WS [8]). Composite *E*-services are described through workflows, where component *E*-services are connected by means of control constructs [4].

Moreover, *E*-services are grouped into *CompatibilityClasses* for substitutability purposes. A compatibility class is associated with an *AbstractEService*, that is the *E*-service required in a process execution expressed in terms of the functionality it provides. A compatibility class groups, on the basis of predefined "similarity" criteria performed through comparison between functional descriptions [9], *E*-services that are able to substitute each other in satisfying the considered abstract service. When an *E*-service during the execution of some tasks is not available anymore, it can be automatically substituted by another *E*-service that belongs to the same compatibility class and that offers at least the same functionality. An *E*-service can belong to more than one compatibility class at the same time.

2.2 *E*-service Request

Figure 2 presents the elements that define our *service request perspective*. An *Actor* issues requests for *EServices*, already defined in Section 2.1, with a given *Quality Level*. In a simplified setting, *Quality Level* indicators could be: speed, availability, security, conformity to standards, and price. More thorough descriptions should be used in real cases. The actual quality of service with which the service is supplied comes from the negotiation of this *Quality Level* with that supplied by the provider (i.e., *PQuality Dimension* in Figure 1).

Each *Actor* has a *Profile*, defined as a set of *User Preferences*. Since *User Preference* is abstract, the *Profile* can contain a *Role*, which identifies the role played by the actor while using the application, its *Expertise* on the application, and a set of *Generic Preferences* to add application-specific characterizations to the profile. The hypothesis is that *Role* or *Expertise* define the minimum profile, which can always be enriched with further information: *Generic Preference* has a *name* and *value* to let the designer render and "quantify" any property. The additional requirement that a *Profile* must have at most

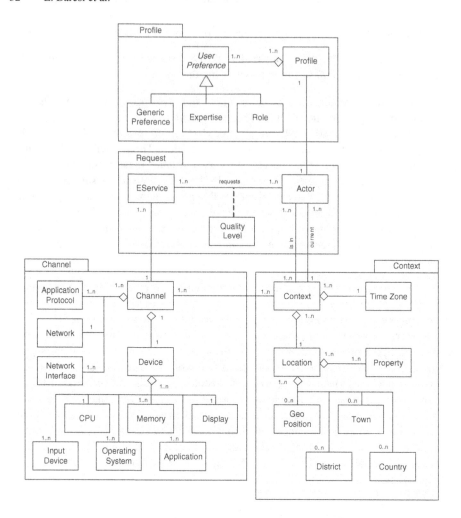

Fig. 2. Service request perspective

one *Role* and one *Expertise* is not shown here, but can be easily added by means of an OCL constraint[1].

We assume that an *Actor is in* some *Contexts* at the same time, but only one of these is his *current Context*. The latter identifies the channels that can be used to supply required services, while the former define the back-up options, that is, the set of available *Contexts* – and thus channels – in which the user can be moved to recover from problems with his current channel.

A *Context* is characterized by a *Location* and a *Time Zone*. *Location* can be zero or more *Geo Positions*, i.e., latitudes and longitudes, *Districts*, e.g., special-interest areas, *Towns*, and *Countries*. Moreover, a *Location* can be associated with a set of *Properties*:

---

[1] OCL (Object Constraint Language) is the constraint language supplied with UML [14].

a general-purpose mechanism to add further information to the context description. For instance, we could use a *Property* to specify weather conditions. *Time Zone* describes the *Context* with respect to its time information, i.e., its offset from Greenwich mean time, and the daylight saving time.

The user *requests* a *Service* on a given *Channel*. As soon as this *Channel* becomes unavailable, the *Actor* can switch to a new *Channel* among those associated with his *current Context*. The choice is even wider since the *Actor* can change *Context* and thus the set of available channels.

A *Channel* is characterized by one *Device*, one *Network*, one or more *Network Interfaces*, and one or more *Application Protocols*. A *Device* comprises one *CPU*, one or more *Input Devices*, one *Display*, and one or more *Memories*. These hardware components are described through the usual characteristics: for instance, a *Display* is defined by means of its size and number of colors. Besides specifying the hardware on board, we also define the software with which it is equipped: one ore more *Operating Systems* and one or more *Applications*. *Network* defines the network as a *name* and a *bandwith*, *Network Interfaces* define how the *Device* can connect to the *Network* (e.g., Ethernet, WI-FI), and *Application Protocols* specify the application protocols that can be used: for instance, HTTP, SOAP, SMTP.

3   Reference Example

The MAIS project defines sample domains to test multichannel adaptive applications. In this section, we present an example in the *emergency management* domain, where we have to deal with interventions for territorial emergencies due to hydro-geological events or sanitary emergencies (e.g., due to car accidents). In particular, we consider the *collection and diffusion of information at fixed stations* to deliver on-line traffic information to travelers, policemen, firemen, highway operators, and tele-control centers.

This activity implies rapidity of service provisioning and urgency. We assume that provisioning sites are fixed stations spread on wide areas and endowed with small-sized computing facilities (e.g., PCs). Data collection is managed by operators and users on the territory via mobile stations, smart phones, GSM, and radio systems. The fixed stations coordinate the information flow from and to mobile stations, operate data processing, such as check and cross analysis of received data, and distribute information back to reachable mobile users, and also to the other fixed stations.

Given the distributed nature of the domain, GSM/SMS and mobile channels play a key role. The strategy, in this context, is to maximize the availability of information on these channels and minimize the delay in redistributing collected critical information.

The scenario considers that fixed stations act as coordinators and mobile stations (e.g., travelers as well as police cars) collect data on local traffic and forward them to the closest, and reachable, fixed station. Fixed stations receive these data, check them for accuracy and timeliness, and process them with weather information and statistical data available on site.

Considering composed *E*-services modeled as workflows, whose steps are operations or *E*-services, the composed service *Collection and diffusion of information at fixed stations* can be modeled as the *cooperation* of two services (Figure 3): an *E*-service

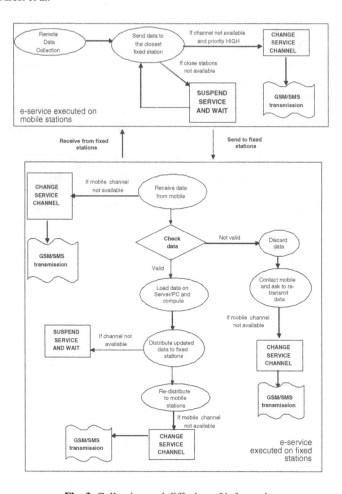

Fig. 3. Collection and diffusion of information

to collect data, which is executed on mobile stations, and an *E*-service to process and re-transmit data, which is executed on fixed stations.

Both services are modeled as workflows and include *channel switches*. The cooperation between the two services is modeled through message exchange with conditions. Each service starts executing as soon as it receives a *start* event. Service requests are processed within the given context, but if a message is urgent and the current channel is not available, the workflow schema specifies a channel switch. Urgency (i.e., priority) is modeled through a condition in the workflow.

We specify explicitly those channel switches that are visible to the user and may involve a change in the process composition logic. As shown in the example, service/channel switches can occur basically because of:

1. E-*service Characteristics*: these are inherent to the workflow, hence statically identifiable in the design phase. An example is the condition of no close stations available

for data transmission on Internet-based channels. In this case, the service can be suspended; alternatively, if the message is urgent, it can be simplified and sent on a different channel (e.g., SMS). It is a design choice to decide the conditions that can lead to adaptation actions.

2. *Channel Status*: these are parameters that depend on provisioning and can vary over time. For instance, system workload, speed, bandwidth, and price – our *PQuality-Dimensions* in Figure 1 – can make the *E*-service be deviated on a different channel during its execution. At design time, we must foresee both important events, to capture significant changes of the current channel, and the ways to react to these changes.

Summarizing, besides conditions, the schema for a composed service must be augmented with *adaptation rules* to specify how to adjust the execution flow at run-time. These rules, presented in Section 5, predicate in terms of parameters bound to the quality of service and available context. Adaptation actions include: suspend, alternatives in the workflow, channel switch, and request for channel upgrade.

4   QoS Specification

The reference example highlights situations in which channel availability influences process execution. In this paper, we focus on adaptivity related to quality of service parameters. As described above, we take in account two perspectives: *E*-service request and *E*-service provisioning. In the same way we define the quality of service following such two standpoints. We define a set of basic *quality dimensions* that characterize the service being provided on a given channel and requests for quality levels in service requests. Quality of service dimensions are grouped in quality of service parameters related to the provider (*PQualityDimension*) and quality of service parameters related to the provisioning on a given channel by a given provider (*CQualityDimension*) as shown in Figure 1.

Consistently to the models presented in Section 2, we can represent such characteristics using XML:

```
<Service name="sendData">
  <Provider name="provider1">
    ...
    <PQualityDimensions>
      <ProvisioningTime unit="s">10</ProvisioningTime>
      <ServiceAvailability hoursperday=24 daysperweek=7>90%</ServiceAvailability>
      <Price currency="USD">100</Price>
    </PQualityDimensions>
  </Provider>

  <Channels>
    <Channel name="PDA/HTTP/GPRS">
      <Device>PDA</Device>
      <ApplicationProtocol>HTTP</ApplicationProtocol>
      <Network>GPRS</Network>
      <NetworkInterface>ModemGPRS</NetworkInterface>
      <CQualityDimensions>
        <Bandwidth unit="Kbps" min=56.6 max=113.2/>
        <ChannelAvailability hoursperday=24 daysperweek=7>99%</ChannelAvailability>
        <Price model="flatrate" currency="USD">100</Price>
      </CQualityDimensions>
    </Channel>
```

```
<Channel name="Phone/HTTP/UMTS">
  <Device>Phone</Device>
  <ApplicationProtocol>HTTP</ApplicationProtocol>
  <Network>UMTS</Network>
  <NetworkInterface>UMTSModem</NetworkInterface>
  <CQualityDimensions>
    <Bandwidth unit="Kbps" min=50 max=1024/>
    <ChannelAvailability hoursperday=24 daysperweek=7>99%</ChannelAvailability>
    <Price model="per minutes" currency="USD">0.30</Price>
  </CQualityDimensions>
</Channel>

<Channel name="PDA/WAP/GPRS">
  <Device>PDA</Device>
  <ApplicationProtocol>WAP</ApplicationProtocol>
  <Network>GPRS</Network>
  <NetworkInterface>ModemGPRS</NetworkInterface>
  <CQualityDimensions>
    <Bandwidth unit="Kbps" min=28.3 max=56.6/>
    <ChannelAvailability hoursperday=24 daysperweek=7>96%</ChannelAvailability>
    <Price model="per minutes" currency="USD">0.30</Price>
  </CQualityDimensions>
</Channel>
</Channels>
</Service>
```

In this case, we consider service *sendData*, which sends data to the fixed stations. The provider assures its provisioning with a `ProvisioningTime` equal to at most 10 seconds, `ServiceAvailability` equal to 90% 24 hours 7 days a week, and a price of 100 USD. We also suppose that it can be used through three wireless channels: a PDA which uses (i) HTTP or (ii) WAP over GPRS and (ii) a SmartPhone which communicates via HTTP over UMTS. These three channels provide different performances and availability degrees described by `Bandwidth` and `Availability`.

From a user perspective, the quality of service can be defined as a set of *quality levels* that depend on either the basic quality dimensions presented above or dimensions that capture the status of the system. In the first case, the actor that uses the service knows the quality features and is able to negotiate the more appropriate quality level. In the second case the system informs the actor that some aspects of the system can be observed. For example, let us consider the following dimensions:

```
<QualityLevels>
  <Dimension name="Speed">
    <Level name="very high">
      <Bandwidth>
        <Condition type="greaterThan" unit="Kbps">512</Condition>
      </Bandwidth>
      <ProvisioningTime>
        <Condition type="lessThan" unit="s">2</Condition>
      </ProvisioningTime>
    </Level>
    <Level name="high">
      <Bandwidth>
        <Condition type="between" unit="Kbps">
          <min>60</min><max>512</max>
        </Condition>
      </Bandwidth>
      <ProvisioningTime>
        <Condition type="between" unit="s">
          <min>2</min><max>4</max>
        </Condition>
      </ProvisioningTime>
```

```
      </Level>
      ...
  </Dimension>

  <Dimension name="Availability">
    <Level name="very high">
      <ChannelAvailability>
        <Condition type="greaterThan" dimension="hourperday">10</Condition>
        <Condition type="greaterThan" dimension="dayperweek">6</Condition>
        <Condition type="greaterThan" dimension="percent">99</Condition>
      </ChannelAvailability>
    </Level>
  </Dimension>
</QualityLevels>
```

The actor can negotiate the `Speed` and `Availability` of the service. Thus, after the negotiation phase, the actor selects, for each *offered* quality dimension, the required level. During the execution of the process which involves *E*-service *sendData*, the execution system has to ensure that the quality does not assume a rate lower than the negotiated level.

5   Adaptation Rules

In an adaptive context, *E*-service composition has to handle critical situations. Due to *E*-service failures or insufficient quality of service, the execution could consider service changes or reconfigurations. The first case has already been studied in [9]: We analyze the functional aspects of the *E*-service to discover a similar one that can substitute the former. *E*-service substitutability and similarity are tackled by considering the compatibility classes introduced above.

The second case is analyzed in this paper. Service provisioning still occurs, but using a different channel, that is, by changing one of its components: device, network, application protocol, or network interface. Additional *E*-services might be invoked to handle aspects related to the reconfiguration.

To disclose those critical situations that require service reconfiguration, we suppose that a system can monitor the execution and reveal any modification about the quality dimensions considered during the negotiation phase. Thus, following the event-condition-action paradigm [1], we define *adaptation rules* to specify how the service reconfiguration has to occur. Such rules are associated with the workflow schema.

In our reference example, we consider a critical situation that refers to a communication breakdown due to a service or channel unavailability while the service is sending data to a fixed station using a SmartPhone over UMTS. In particular, since priority is high, if the service becomes unavailable, the service itself will must be changed. For instance, we could select a different service provider: After a negotiation phase, we would decide a new quality level. On the contrary, if the channel fails, the system can decide to change the communication channel by selecting a new transmission protocol like GPRS. In our approach, we define events to notify significant changes on quality dimensions. For instance:

```
<Events>
  <Event type="ChangeSpeedEvent">
    <Conditions>
```

```
        <Predicate dimension="Speed" condition="lessthan">
          <value>high</value>
        </Predicate>
      </Conditions>
      <Actions>
        <Action type="changeDevice"/>
        <Action type="eventActivation">ChangeDeviceEvent</action>
      </Actions>
    </Event>

    <Event type="ServiceNotAccessibleEvent">
      <Conditions>
        <Predicate dimension="Availability" condition="true">
        </Predicate>
      </Conditions>
      <Actions>
        <Action type="changeChannel"/>
        <Action type="eventActivation">ChangeChannelEvent</action>
      </Actions>
    </Event>

    <Event type="ChangeChannelEvent">
        <Action type="notification">The channel is changed</action>
    </Event>
<Events>
```

Event `ServiceNotAccessible` occurs when the communication breakdowns. In such a situation, if `Availability` is true, we impose a channel switch, because we need to find another means to deliver the service. If `Availability` is false, we must switch to another service (this is not shown in the rule). The two rules are applied to an excerpt of our running example in Figure 4 (the *E*-service on mobile stations). `ChangeSpeed` can be triggered when sending data to the closest fixed station (because the speed drops down drastically), while `ServiceNotAccessible` is triggered when we discover that the channel is not available, but we want to send our data with high priority. To maintain a consistent environment, every service reconfiguration generates an event to inform all active services and the user about the new status.

6   MAIS Architecture

The e-service composition and selection approach presented in the previous sections is based on the adaptive architecture that we are developing in the MAIS project. This architecture assumes adaptivity at various levels, as shown in Figure 6. As we discussed

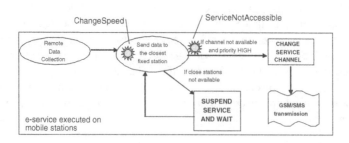

Fig. 4. Adaptation rules in our example

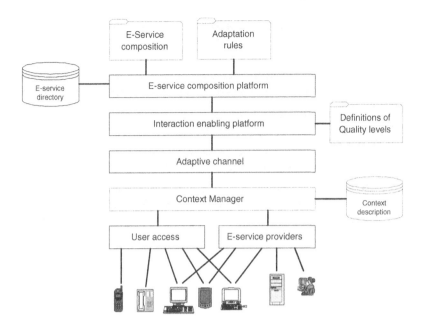

Fig. 5. MAIS Architecture

in Section 2, services may be accessed by different types of devices, provided using different technological channels, and networks may present different levels of quality of service. All information about networks, devices, and service providers is supplied as *Context description* used by the *Context manager*. The architecture is reflective to provide functionality to access context information, and to control channel configurations, according to suitable parameters.

The *Interaction enabling platform* uses the *Definitions of Quality levels* illustrated in Section 4 to transform quality of service requests at the E-*service composition platform* into requests in technological terms to the *Adaptive channels* used by the application. Initially, such transformations are to be obtained by mapping application level rules into technological constraints; negotiation of parameters at different levels in the *Interaction enabling platform* will be considered at later phases in the project.

E-services are stored in an E-*service directory*, representing the characteristics of e-services in terms of provided functionality and possible channels for their provisioning. The *E*-service directory provides functionality for retrieving *E*-services to enable a dynamic composition of processes according to the characteristics of the user requests and context information. The directory being realized extends the *E*-service registry developed in the VISPO project [4]. This registry stores *E*-service information in terms of descriptors derived from WSDL abstract specifications and allows retrieval and adaptation of e-services to a given composition schema on the basis of a domain ontology.

7   Conclusions and Future Work

The paper analyzes context-aware composition of *E*-services and discusses the MAIS approach for a flexible and channel-dependent composition of services. We propose to separate the characteristics of *E*-service provisioning and user contexts, for *E*-service requests, and we propose two separate models to describe them.

We also discuss *adaptation rules* for mapping user level requirements into technological constraints. These rules allow for the composition of *E*-service specifications based on context information. In this way, we define flexible processes that are able to provide and access services which are adequate to the context available to the user.

The MAIS project is developing an adaptive approach that addresses both technology (e.g., networks, devices, micro-databases) and composition and enabling platforms to manage and control context information and to allow context-aware dynamic composition.

References

1. F. Casati, S. Ceri, S. Paraboschi, and G. Pozzi. *Database Support for Workflow Management: the WIDE Project*, chapter Active Rule Support. Kluwer Academics Publishers, 1999.
2. Y. Chen, W.Y Ma, and H.J. Zhang. Detecting web page structure for adaptive viewing on small form factor devices. In ACM press, editor, *Proceedings of WWW 2003*, 2003.
3. E. Christensen, F. Curbera, G. Meredith, and S. Weerawarana. Web Services Description Language (WSDL) 1.1. www.w3.org/TR/2001/NOTE-wsdl-2001_0315, March 2001.
4. E. Colombo, V. De Antonellis, C. Francalanci, M. Mecella, M. Melchiori, B. Pernici, and P. Plebani. Cooperative information systems in virtual districts:the vispo approach. *IEEE Bulletin on Data Engineering*, 2002.
5. Cameleon Consortium. Cameleon web site. giove.cnuce.cnr.it/cameleon.html.
6. MAIS Consortium. Mais: Multichannel adaptive information systems. *black.elet.polimi.it/mais/*.
7. UWA Consortium. UWA web site. www.uwaproject.org.
8. F. Curbera, Y. Goland, J. Klein, F. Leymann, D. Roller, S. Thatte, and S. Weerawarana. Business Process Execution Language for Web Services, version 1.0. www.ibm.com/developerworks/library/ws-bpel/, July 2002.
9. V. De Antonellis, M. Melchiori, and P. Plebani. An Approach toWeb Service compatibility in cooperative processes. In *Proc. IEEE SAINT2003 of Int. Workshop SOC, Orlando, Florida, USA*, 2003.
10. A. Maurino et al. Studio delle caratteristiche dei canali. Technical report, Politecnico di Milano, 2003. In Italian.
11. X. Gu, K. Nahrstedt, W. Yuan, D.Wichadakul, and D. Xu". An xml-based quality of service enabling language for the web. Technical Report UIUCDCS-R-2001-2212, University of Illinois at Urbana-Champaign - Computer Science Department, 2001.
12. J. Krogstie, K. Lyytinen, A. Opdahl, B. Pernici, K. Siau, and K. Smolander. Mobile information system–research challengers on the conceptual and logical level. *International Journal of Mobile Communication, special issue on Modeling Mobile Information Systems: Conceptual and Methodological issues., 2003*.
13. S. Narayanan and S.A. McIlraith:. Simulation, verification and automated composition of web services. In *Proceedings of WWW 2002*, pages 77–88, 2002.

14. Object Modeling Language (OMG). UML Unified Modeling Language – Version 1.5. `www.omg.org/technology/documents/formal/uml.html`, 2003.
15. W3C. Composite capabilities/preferences profile. `www.w3.org/Mobile/CCPP/`.
16. WWRF. Book of visions 2001. `www.wireless-world-research.org/`.

A Quality-Aware Approach to Web Services Procurement *

Octavio Martín-Díaz, Antonio Ruiz-Cortés, David Benavides, Amador Durán, and
Miguel Toro

Dpto. de Lenguajes y Sistemas Informáticos
E.T.S. de Ingeniería Informática, Universidad de Sevilla
41012 Sevilla, España, Spain
Phone: +34 95 455 3871   Fax: +34 95 455 7139
{octavio,aruiz,amador,mtoro}@lsi.us.es, benavides@us.es

Abstract. Web services bring programmers a new way to develop advanced
applications able to integrate any group of services on the Internet into a single
solution. Web services procurement (WSP) is focussed on the acquisition of web
services, including some complex tasks such as the specification of demands,
the search for available offers, and the best choice selection. Although the
technology to support them already exists, there are only a few approaches
wherein quality-of-service in demands and offers is taken into account, in
addition to functionality. In this paper, we present some implementation
issues on a quality-aware approach to WSP, whose solution is mainly based on
using mathematical constraints to define quality-of-service in demands and offers.

Keywords: software procurement, web services, quality-of-service.

1   Introduction

The incredible successfulness of the Internet world has paved the way for a sub-industry
devoted to developing and consuming web services, which is being considered as the
core of the next-generation Internet. Web services bring programmers a new way to
develop advanced applications which can integrate any group of services on the Internet
into a single solution. It may involve, possibly, the use of web services provided by
different organisations, cooperating in complex collaborations. Thus, there is a need of
agreements in order to establish the obligations to both sides, i.e. customers which use
web services, and providers which supply them.

Moreover, if we want to have a competitive technology based on web services, then
one of challenges to be solved is quality-of-service owned by them [30]. Therefore, these
agreements should include not only functional, but also quality-of-service obligations.
All available web services may not be appropriate, only those fulfilling the demands
on quality-of-service. Federated systems [2], cross-organisational workflows [13,15]

---

* Supported by the Spanish Interministerial Commission on Science and the Spanish Ministry
of Science and Technology under grants TIC2000-1106-C02-01, FIT-150100-2001-78, and
PCB-02-001.

B. Benatallah and M.-C. Shan (Eds.): TES 2003, LNCS 2819, pp. 42–53, 2003.

and multi-organisational web-based systems [5,23] are several examples of this kind of systems.

In this context, software procurement [9,10] becomes web services procurement (WSP): an activity focussed on the acquisition of web services which are required by a web-service-based system. In general, typical tasks involved in WSP are: i) the specification of demands, ii) the search for available offers, and iii) the best choice selection. Thus, WSP is a critical activity for current developers because the great number of available offers and quality-of-service parameters which can be involved in these tasks. Nowadays, there is a great effort from industry in supporting WSP-related tasks. However, most of approaches are based on functionality, and there are only a few which allow a limited expressiveness when specifying quality-of-service in demands and offers. Usually, some of their drawbacks are: i) specification of quality-of-service is only based on single quality-of-service parameters involved in simple expressions, or ii) specification of quality-of-service in offers is based on pairs parameter/value, or iii) unavailability of a solver able to process (some of) expressions, or iv) no optimization of search processes, or others.

In this paper, we present some implementation issues on a quality-aware approach for WSP. The proposed solution is based on using mathematical constraints to specify, in a declarative way, quality-of-service in demands and offers of web services. This allows a great deal of expressiveness and makes possible the implementation of WSP-related tasks by means of solving constraint satisfaction problems (CSP). Currently, we are working on a prototype which makes use of available technology: i) XML is used to specify quality-of-service in demands and offers, following the XML schema corresponding to QRL [23,27], the language we have proposed for specifying quality requirements, ii) XSLT is used to transform XML documents into constraint satisfaction problems, and iii) ILOG's OPL Studio is the constraint solver.

The rest of this paper is structured as follows. First, Section 2 introduces the notion of web service procurement with a case of study. Next, Section 3 shows the use of mathematical constraints to specify quality-of-service, and implementation of WSP-related tasks by means of CSP. Then, Section 4 describes some implementation issues of the prototype, remarking on web services we have built so far. Finally, Section 5 reviews the related work, giving a brief comparative of existing approaches, and Section 6 will summarise the presented work and the immediate future.

2   WSP in a Nutshell

As introduced above, WSP is focussed on the acquisition of web services which are required by a web-service-based system. As an example, consider that someone is interested in setting up a web portal devoted to video broadcasting, so that it offers a catalogue of videos, and the same functionality just as a domestic video player. In order to achieve such goal, the system should include a service for streaming video through the Internet, a service for managing catalogues and keeping them up-to-date, and a service for managing virtual shops. Thus, the web portal becomes a composed service that integrates web services, possibly provided by other organisations. As well, the agreements for using these services should be established having their quality-of-service taken into account, including both the original demand and the selected offer.

Figure 1 shows a fragment of the components view of the multi-organisational web-based system which corresponds to this portal. The IVideoServer interface abstracts those operations that a component delivering video on demand should implement in order to be incorporated into the system. There are several notes attached to every architectural fragment. They are written in QRL (Quality Requirements Language) [23,27], a language we have designed for specifying quality-of-service. A first note is associated with the IVideoServer interface: it states the demand for quality-of-service to be guaranteed by a web service which implements this interface so that it can be eventually used by the system. Remaining notes are associated to web services: they state the offer of quality-of-service which their providers guarantee when delivering video on demand.

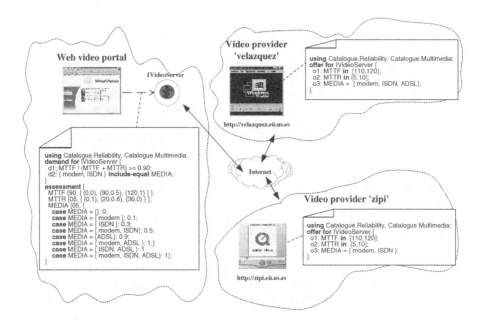

Fig. 1. A components view of a video web portal.

In this case, the involved quality-of-service parameters are Mean Time To Failure (MTTF), Mean Time To Repair (MTTR), and Media Support (MEDIA). Whenever a new offer or demand is submitted to the system, it needs to be checked for consistency, that is to say, whether or not it contains inner contradictions. If we read both demand and offers in Figure 1, we will verify that they all are consistent. On the other hand, whenever new consistent demands on web services are submitted to the system, it needs to search those available offers in conformance with them. An offer is conformant to a demand if all quality-of-service values guaranteed by the offer fulfill the demand. If we read all the offers in Figure 1, we will verify they all are conformant to the demand which is needed to be subcontracted by the system.

Moreover, as different offers can be conformant to a given demand the best offer should be selected. This selection is based on assessment criteria which customers can attach to demands, containing their assessments regarding with values that quality-of-service parameters can take, together with their preferences among them. In this way, a web-service-based application is said to be optimum when it is composed of a set of web services so that their offers maximise the assessment criteria from a customer's point of view. These systems are also very flexible, because web services can be exchanged without unnecessary stops whenever new demands and offers are submitted, and/or better offers are found. According to assessment criteria included in Figure 1, provider velazquez is the best offer: both offers velazquez and zipi own the same values for MTTF and MTTR, but the first offers a better media support because it includes ADSL, which has a better assessment from the customer's viewpoint.

3   Supporting WSP with Constraint Programming

The core of the solution relies on the specification of quality-of-service in demands and offers by means of mathematical constraints. In this way, it is achieved a greater deal of expressiveness, and subsequent checking of properties, such as consistency and conformance, and computing of utility assessment of offers, can be implemented as a constraint satisfaction problem (CSP) [11,14,20]. A CSP is composed of a set of variables, each of which is given a domain which specifies the values it can take, and a set of constraints on values they can take in a concrete context. A CSP is said to be satisfiable whenever there exists (at least) one solution, i.e. all the variables can be given a value so that the constraints are fulfilled as a whole. In general, CSP-based modelling is quite simple and intuitive (in most cases) in the context of problems which we are dealing with.

3.1   Consistency and Conformance

The consistency of every demand or offer which is submitted to the system needs to be checked, i.e., to compute whether or not the corresponding CSP, composed of all the mathematical constraints which are included in it, is satisfiable. In Figure 1, we can verify all CSP corresponding to demand and offers are satisfiable, so they all are consistent.

On the other hand, the conformance of an offer (by a provider) to a demand (from a customer) also needs to be checked, i.e., we are interested in determining whether or not each and every solution to the CSP corresponding to the offer is also a solution to the CSP corresponding to the demand. Formally [20]:

$$conformance(\omega, \delta) \Leftrightarrow sat(c_\omega \wedge \neg c_\delta) = false$$

where ω is the offer and c_ω its corresponding CSP, δ is the demand and c_δ its corresponding CSP, and sat is a function that we identify with the constraint solver we are using. It can be applied on a constraint c so that it returns one of the following results: $true$, if c is satisfiable, $false$ if not, and $\perp$ if the constraint solver cannot determine whether c is satisfiable or not. In Figure 1, we can verify both offers are conformant to the demand.

3.2 Optimality

As described above, it is possible to have several offers which are conformant to a demand for a web service. Therefore, a selection mechanism to choice the optimum service is needed. This selection is carried out according to the assessment criteria the customer includes in his or her demand. These criteria are given by means of utility functions [8, 18,22] which, in general, have the signature $\mathcal{U} : \pi \rightarrow [0, 1]$, where π is the measuring domain of a quality-of-service parameter. In this way, the customer can define his/her assessment criteria regarding with a parameter by means of an utility function which assigns an utility assessment (ranging from 0 to 1) to every value it can take, so the greater the assessment, the better the consideration of the customer. Therefore, utility functions allow the establishment of an objective criteria, given by customers, in order to select the offers which better fulfill the demands. Figure 2 shows several utility functions corresponding to the demand in Figure 1.

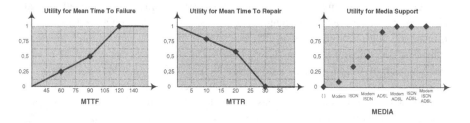

Fig. 2. Utility functions for $MTTF$, $MTTR$, and $MEDIA$.

Moreover, we are not usually interested in utility functions with regard to lonely quality-of-service parameters, but on maximising the global assessment of offers in order to select the best one, being these offers conformant to the demand. Nevertheless, we can not compute the maximum utility assessment of offers when comparing them, because offers are guaranteeing the complete range, not only a particular quality-of-service value. Therefore, we compare the minimum utility assessments of offers. Formally:

$$\omega_S = \omega \in \Omega_\delta \cdot \ \forall \omega_i \in \Omega_\delta - \{\omega\} \ \mathcal{U}^\delta(\omega) \geq \mathcal{U}^\delta(\omega_i)$$

where ω and ω_i stand for offers in the set Ω_δ of conformant offers to the demand δ, and ω_S represents the selected offer. The utility function $\mathcal{U}^\delta(\omega)$ of an offer ω according to assessment criteria in demand δ is expressed as an optimization problem:

$$\mathcal{U}^\delta(\omega) = \min_{subject\ to\ c_\omega} \ \sum_{\pi \in c_\omega} w_\pi^\delta U^\delta(\pi)$$

where π represents a quality-of-service parameter which is involved in the offer's CSP c_ω, and $U^\delta(\pi)$ its utility function, and w_π^δ its assigned weight, according to assessment criteria in demand δ. On the other hand, weights are needed to express that a quality-of-service parameter is preferred to another.

In Figure 1, since both offers are conformant to the demand, we will have to compute their utility assessments in order to compare them. In this way, both offers own $U(MTTF = 110) = 0.83$ and $U(MTTR = 10) = 0.8$, the velazquez offer owns $U(MEDIA) = 1$, and the zipi offer owns $U(MEDIA) = 0.5$. Therefore, utility assessment of velazquez is $0.9 * 0.83 + 0.05 * 0.04 + 0.05 * 1 = 0.84$, and utility assessment of zipi is $0.9 * 0.83 + 0.05 * 0.04 + 0.05 * 0.5 = 0.815$, so the best offer is velazquez.

4 Implementation Issues

4.1 Overview of the Prototype's Architecture

Currently, we are developing a prototype of the framework for management and execution of multi-organisational web-based systems. A preliminary version of the prototype is available at the web page http://www.lsi.us.es/ octavio, which shows some prepared examples using the web services which have been implemented so far. In fact, they will constitute the kernel of a future run-time framework whose architecture has been already defined and published in other works [21,24,28]. A components view of its architecture is shown in Figure 3.

Fig. 3. Architecture of the prototype's run-time framework.

One of design decisions we have made is to deploy all components as web applications and web services, so that the framework itself can be properly considered just as another multi-organisational web-based system:

– The CSP Solver web service is a wrapper to access the actual component which provides the solver for processing the incoming CSP. It provides the services IsSatisfiable() which it returns whether the CSP passed as a parameter is satisfiable or not, and getUtilityAssessment() which it computes the utility assessment of the optimization problem passed as a parameter.
– The Quality Trader web service provides the checkForConsistency(), checkForConformance(), and searchForBestSelection() services. All these functions have a similar operation: they take the involved demands and offers written in XML as parameters, the they invoke the appropriate XSLT transformations in order to generate automatically the corresponding CSP, which is processed by the CSP solver to get the result, which is finally returned.

4.2   XML Schemas for QRL

We have decided to adopt XML as the language for exchanging QRL-based quality-of-service specifications, so we have defined several XML schemas corresponding to abstract semantics of QRL language. We have defined up to 291 elements in all, for the time being, so that any QRL-based document can be written in XML with no loss of original expressiveness.

```
using Catalogue.Reliability, Catalogue.Multimedia;
demand for IVideoServer {
    d1: MTTF / (MTTF + MTTR) >= 0.90;
    d2: { modem, ISDN } include-equal MEDIA;
}
assessment {
    MTTF {90, { (0,0), (90,0.5), (120,1) } };
    MTTR {05, { (0,1), (20,0.6), (30,0) } };
    MEDIA {05, {
        case MEDIA = {}: 0;
        case MEDIA = { modem }: 0.1;
        case MEDIA = { ISDN }: 0.3;
        case MEDIA = { modem, ISDN}: 0.5;
        case MEDIA = {ADSL}: 0.9;
        case MEDIA = { modem, ADSL }: 1;}
        case MEDIA = { ISDN, ADSL }: 1;
        case MEDIA = { modem, ISDN, ADSL}: 1};
}
```

```xml
<?xml version="1.0" encoding="utf-8" ?>
<QRL-Core-QualityDoc
        xmlns:qrl="http://oztabio/Qrl-Xml-Opl/Qrl-Core.xsd">
    <Catalogues>
        ...
    <Requirements>
        <Requirement>
            <Identifier>d1</Identifier>
            <ComplexConstraint>
                <BasicConstraint>
                    <GreaterOrEqualThanConstraint>
                    <Arithmetic>
                        <LeftOp><Division>
                            <DividendOp><ArithmeticVariable> ...
                            <Addition>
                                <Operand><ArithmeticVariable> ...
                                <Operand><ArithmeticVariable>

            <RightOp><ArithmeticValue>

        ...
    </Requirement>
    <Requirement>
            <Identifier>d2</Identifier>
            <ComplexConstraint>
                <BasicConstraint>
                    <IncludeOrEqualConstraint>
                    <Set>

    </Requirement>
    </Requirements>
    <AssessmentCriteria>
        <UtilityFunction>
            <QualityAttribute>MTTF</QualityAttribute>
            <Weight>90</Weight>
            <Function><Piecewise>
                <Point><QualityValue>...<Valuation>...

    </UtilityFunction>

    <UtilityFunction>
            <QualityAttribute>MEDIA</QualityAttribute>
            <Weight>5</Weight>
            <Function><Casewise>
                <Case>
                    <QualityValue><ComplexConstraint> ...
                    <Valuation>

                <Case>
                    <QualityValue><ComplexConstraint> ...
                    <Valuation>

    </Casewise></Function>
    </UtilityFunction>
    </AssessmentCriteria>
</QRL-Core-QualityDoc>
```

Fig. 4. An example of a QRL-based demand written in XML.

As an example, Figure 4 shows partially a demand written in XML. The QRL-Core-QualityDoc XML-element is the root of specification, which includes names of catalogues which are being used and the requirements. Each requirement is given an identifier and a constraint. In turn, a constraint is expressed with a ComplexConstraint XML-element, which is the root of all mathematical constraints available in QRL, including logic, comparison, assignment, and arithmetic operators. Finally, the AssessmentCriteria XML-element is the root of specification of assessment criteria. Each inner UtilityFunction XML-element contains the name of a quality-of-service parameter and its weight of preference, and its proper specification.

4.3   CSP Solver: ILOG's OPL Studio

The CSP solver which we have used is ILOG's OPL Studio [16]. Its language OPL (OPtimization Language) is easy to use, so we have considered it for solving the CSP corresponding to WSP-related tasks, such as checking of consistency and conformance, and best choice selection. An OPL model contains a CSP, and it is basically composed of a section for declaring variables, a maximise/minimise section to include an optimization function, and a section which includes the set of constraints.

```
range TYPE_MTTF 0..9999;
var TYPE_MTTF MTTF;

range TYPE_MTTR 0..9999;
var TYPE_MTTR MTTR;

enum TYPE_MEDIA
        {MEDIA_modem,MEDIA_ISDN,MEDIA_ADSL};
var int MEDIA[TYPE_MEDIA] in 0..1;

// IF SATISFIABLE, DEMAND IS CONSISTENT

solve {
  ( (MTTF * 100) / (MTTF + MTTR) >= 90 )
  &
  ( MEDIA[MEDIA_modem]=1 & MEDIA[MEDIA_ISDN]=1);
};
```

a) OPL model for consistency.

```
enum TYPE_MEDIA
        { MEDIA_modem,MEDIA_ISDN,MEDIA_ADSL};
var int MEDIA[TYPE_MEDIA] in 0..1;

range TYPE_TTF 0..120;
var TYPE_TTF TTF_MEAN;

range TYPE_TTR 0..30;
var TYPE_TTR TTR_MEAN;

// IF NO SATISFIABLE, THE OFFER IS CONFORMANT
// TO DEMAND

solve {
  ( // VELAZQUEZ'S IVIDEOSERVER OFFER
    (110 <= TTF_MEAN <= 120)
  & (5 < TTR_MEAN <= 10)
  & ( MEDIA[MEDIA_modem] = 1
    & MEDIA[MEDIA_ISDN] = 1
      & MEDIA[MEDIA_ADSL] = 1) )
  &
  not( // IVIDEOSERVER DEMAND
      ( (TTF_MEAN * 100) / (TTF_MEAN+TTR_MEAN) >= 90 )
    & MEDIA[MEDIA_ISDN] = 1
        & MEDIA[MEDIA_modem] = 1) );
};
```

b) OPL model for conformance.

```
enum TYPE_MEDIA { MEDIA_modem,MEDIA_ISDN,MEDIA_ADSL};
var int MEDIA[TYPE_MEDIA] in 0..1;
var int UTILITY_MEDIA_VALUE in 0..111;

range TYPE_MTTF 0..120;
var TYPE_MTTF MTTF;

range TYPE_MTTR 0..30;
var TYPE_MTTR MTTR;

minimize
  0.90 * piecewise{0.55->90;1.67->120;0} MTTF+
  0.05 * (100 - piecewise{2->20;6->30;0} MTTR) +
  0.05 * piecewise{1->1;3.22->10;20->11;0.45->100;10->101;0}
                UTILITY_MEDIA_VALUE

subject to {
  UTILITY_MEDIA_VALUE
    = sum(AUX_MEDIA in TYPE_MEDIA)
        MEDIA[AUX_MEDIA] * pow(10,ord(AUX_MEDIA));

  // VELAZQUEZ'S IVIDEOSERVER OFFER
  ( 110 <= MTTF <= 120
   & 5 < MTTR <= 10
   & MEDIA[MEDIA_modem] = 1
     & MEDIA[MEDIA_ISDN] = 1 & MEDIA[MEDIA_ADSL] = 1 );
};
```

c) OPL model for computing the utility assessment.

Fig. 5. OPL models for consistency, conformance, and utility assessment.

Nevertheless, although the OPL solver has demonstrated to be a good CSP solver, it presents some drawbacks, but none of them have demonstrated to be definitely un-avoidable. These weaknesses have slightly restricted the original expressiveness of our solution, and made some implementation aspects harder as well. Figure 5 shows several examples of OPL models, referred to examples of Figure 1, according to definitions in Section 3: a) consistency of a demand, b) conformance of velazquez's offer to a demand, and c) computing the utility assessment of velazquez's offer with regard to a demand.

4.4   XSLT Transformations to OPL Models

XSLT (eXtensible Stylesheet Language Transformations) describes rules by means of templates for transforming an XML source into any arbitrary result. These transformations are not trivial at all, since XML schemas of QRL and structure of OPL models are very different:

```
<?xml version="1.0" encoding="utf-8" ?>
<Qrl-Conformance
       xmlns:qrl="http://oztabio/Qrl-Xml-Opl/Qrl-Core.xsd">
  <Catalogues></Catalogues>
  <Attributes></Attributes>
  <TheOffer></TheOffer>
  <TheDemand></TheDemand>
</Qrl-Conformance>
```

Fig. 6. An XML template devoted to XSLT transformations.

Figure 6 shows the template which is needed to invoke our XSLT transformations. In general, a new XML document is created in order to get together the involved demand, offer and used catalogues. As we have used the ILOG's OPL Studio tool as the CSP solver, we have defined several XSLT transformations to get the OPL model which contains the appropriate CSP for checking the consistency and conformance, and computing the utility assessment.

5   Related Work

Several tools provide all necessary elements to implement, search and invoke web services using the current technology. However, these approaches have been focussed on functionality to be provided by web services, but not on quality-of-service. On the other hand, there are only a few proposals which allow a limited expressiveness to specify quality-of-service offered by/demanded from web services, such as *DARPA Agent Markup Language plus Services* (DAML+S) [3], *Web Services Outsourcing Manager* (WSOM) [6], and *UDDI extension* (UDDIe) [29]. In general, these proposals do not allow a symmetric way to specify quality-of-service, because demands are usually specified with a greater deal of expressiveness than offers, and in most of cases specification of quality-of-service in offers is only based on pairs parameter/value, but not any more complex expression. Figure 7 shows a comparative among current quality-aware approaches to WSP.

Currently, there are two approaches (as far as we know) which allow a greater deal of expressiveness when specifying quality-of-service in demands and offers, such as HP's *Matchmaking Engine* (MME) [12], which is based on the DAML semantic web language [4], and *Web Services Matchmaking Engine/Web Service Level Agreement* (WSME/WSLA) [15,17,19], which is an enhancement of the CORBA/ODP trader service and it has been integrated into IBM's *Web Services ToolKit* (WSTK) [7]. The former owns a great deal of expressiveness due to the use of the semantic web language DAML, but there is currently no Description Logic's solver able to process some of most complex

The Reference Model	Static View: The Lexicon					Dynamic View: The Process Model
	Stakeholders	Quality-of-Service Documents	Catalogues, Parameters & Measures			
			Data Structuring	Customer's	Provider's	
IBM's WSME MME	Providers Costumers	Advertisements Queries Agreements	Data Dictionary: pre-def. basic types sequences records	Name-Value Pair Properties Static/Dynamic Binding Scripts for Rule-based Reqs.		Advertisement/Submission Query/Submission Matchmaking Selecting Providers' Offers
HP's MME Service	Advertisers Requestors	Service Offers & Requests	DAML+OIL Ontology: datatypes and types subsumption	Composition Single-Parameter Constraints on Parameters of Service (expandable)		Advertising Querying Browsing
UDDIe	Providers Consumers	Publishing Inquiry	Blue Pages	Single-Par. Constraints on Properties (Qualifiers)	Name-Value Pair Properties	Publishing Search and Discovery
QRL	Providers Costumers	Demands Offers Agreements	Catalogues: pre-def. basic types catalogue extension basic and derived p.	Composition Multiple-Parameter Constraints on Parameters of Service		Creating Catalogues Offers Submission Demands Submission Matchmaking

Fig. 7. Comparative of quality-aware approaches to WSP.

expressions which can be specified. The latter also owns a great deal of expressiveness: its specification is based on using rules written in a scripting language, wherein offers and demands are absolutely symmetric from both viewpoints: the demand can impose conditions on the offer, and viceversa. However, their results are the lists of all conformant offers to a demand but there is no optimization of searches.

6   Conclusions and Future Work

In this paper, we have presented some of implementation issues of our quality-aware approach to WSP. The proposed solution is based on using mathematical constraints in order to specify quality-of-service in demands and offers, so we have achieved a lot of interesting properties. First, it owns a great deal of expressiveness, including multiple parameters and non-linear expressions involving quality-of-service parameters. As the same expressiveness is allowed to specify quality-of-service in demands and offers, our approach can be said to be symmetric. As well, our approach includes the possibility to express the assessment criteria which is very important to select the best choice according to a demand.

We have developed a prototype of the run-time framework for management and execution of multi-organisational web-based systems. This prototype includes a quality trader web service as the main component, which offers services such as checking for consistency and conformance, and searching for the best choice. Of course, this web service is a cornerstone of the framework's kernel, which will be available in the near future. Among the main characteristics of implementation, we have used the QRL language to specify quality-of-service, and XML to specify QRL-based documents, the definition of XSLT transformations to get the appropriate CSP for carrying out the WSP-related tasks, and the use of a constraint solver as ILOG's OPL Studio. At the moment of writing this paper, readers who are interested in our proposal can have an overview of our prototype in the web page http://www.lsi.us.es/ octavio.

Regarding with future work, we want to point out that our approach can be extended in several ways in order to include new characteristics: temporality clauses in constraints, negotiation clauses to improve the flexibility of the model whenever no solution can be initially found, and importance and soft clauses in order to enlarge the solution space of the search. In fact, definition of temporality and negotiation are currently in study [25, 26], so we are beginning the first phases of improvements of our prototype to include them.

Finally, the integration of our model on the current technology is also one of our pending work. We are aware of the uselessness of our approach if we do not have a working prototype integrated with any of them, such as UDDI or similar. In this way, our quality trader will be a component leveled at the top of a pyramid wherein lower levels would be devoted to functional-aspects of WSP [1]. This stage of development is currently starting, but we hope to have a completely functional prototype in the very near future.

References

1. A. Beugnard, J-M. Jézéquiel, N. Plouzeau, and D. Watkins. Making components contract aware. *IEEE Computer*, pages 38–45, July 1999.
2. P. Bhoj, S. Shingal, and S. Chutani. SLA management in federated environments. *Computer Networks*, 35: 5–24, 2001.
3. DAML+S Coalition. DAML+S: Semantic markup for web services. In *Proc. of the Int'l Semantic Web Working Symposium SWWS01*, 2001.
4. Joint US/EU Agent Markup Language Committee. DARPA Agent Markup Language. Technical report, US's DARPA Defense Advance Research Projects Agency and EU's IST Information Society Technologies, 2000. http://www.daml.org.
5. R. Corchuelo, A. Ruiz-Cortés, J. Mühlbacher, and J.D. García-Consuegra. Object-oriented business solutions. In *Chapter 18 of ECOOP'2001 Workshop Reader, LNCS 2323*, pages 184–200. Springer-Verlag, 2001.
6. IBM International Business Machines Corporation. Web Services Outsourcing Manager overview (WSOM), 2002. http://www.ibm.com.
7. IBM International Business Machines Corporation. Web Services ToolKit (WSTK), 2002. http://www.ibm.com.
8. J.J. Dujmovic. A Method for Evaluation and Selection of Complex Hardware and Software Systems. In *Proceedings of the 22nd International Conference for the Resource Management and Performance Evaluation of Enterprise Computing Systems*, volume 1, pages 368–378, 1996.
9. B. Farbey and A. Finkelstein. Software acquisition: a business strategy analysis. In *Proc. of the Requirements Engineering (RE'01)*. IEEE Computer Society Press, 2001.
10. A. Finkelstein and G. Spanoudakis. Software package requirements and procurement. In *Proc. of the 8th Int'l IEEE Workshop on Software Specification and Design (IWSSD'96)*. IEEE Press, 1996.
11. E.C. Freuder and M. Wallace. Science and substance: A challenge to software engineers. *Constraints IEEE Intelligent Systems*, 2000.
12. J. González-Castillo, D. Trastour, and C. Bartolini. Description logics for matchmaking of services. Technical Report HPL-2001-265, Hewlett-Packard, 2001.
13. P. Grefen, K. Aberer, Y. Hoffner, and H. Ludwig. CrossFlow: Cross-organizational workflow management in dynamic virtual enterprises. *International Journal of Computer Systems Science & Engineering*, 15(5): 277–290, 2000.

14. P. Hentenryck and V. Saraswat. Strategic directions in constraint programming. *ACM Computing Surveys*, 28(4), December 1996.
15. Y. Hoffner, S. Field, P. Grefen, and H. Ludwig. Contract-driven creation and operation of virtual enterprises. *Computer Networks*, (37): 111–136, 2001.
16. ILOG. OPL Studio. `http://www.ilog.fr`.
17. A. Keller and H. Ludwig. The WSLA framework: Specifying and monitoring service level agreements for web services. Technical Report RC22456 (W0205-171), IBM International Business Machines Corporation, 2002.
18. J. Koistinen and A. Seetharaman. Worth–based multi-category quality–of–service negotiation in distributed object infrastructures. In *Proceedings of the Second International Enterprise Distributed Object Computing Workshop (EDOC'98)*, La Jolla, USA, 1998.
19. H. Ludwig, A. Keller, A. Dan, and R.P. King. A service level agreement language for dynamic electronic services. Technical Report RC22316 (W0201-112), IBM International Business Machines Corporation, 2002.
20. K. Marriot and P.J. Stuckey. *Programming with Constraints: An Introduction*. The MIT Press, 1998.
21. O. Martín-Díaz, A. Ruiz-Cortés, R. Corchuelo, and A. Durán. A Management and Execution Environment for Multi-Organisational Web-based Systems. In *ZOCO: Métodos y Herramientas para el Comercio Electrónico*, pages 79–88, San Lorenzo del Escorial, Spain, 2002.
22. L. Olsina, D. Godoy, G. Lafuente, and G. Rossi. Specifying Quality Characteristics and Attributes for Websites. In *Proceedings of the Web Engineering Workshop, in conjunction with 21st International Conference on Software Engineering (ICSE)*, pages 84–93, May 1999.
23. A. Ruiz-Cortés. *A Semi-qualitative Approach to Automated Treatment of Quality Requirements (in Spanish)*. PhD thesis, E.T.S. de Ingeniería Informática. Dpto. de Lenguajes y Sistemas Informáticos. Universidad de Sevilla, 2002.
24. A. Ruiz-Cortés, R. Corchuelo, and A. Durán. An automated approach to quality-aware web applications. In *Enterprise Information Systems IV*, pages 237–242. Kluwer Academic Publishers, 2003.
25. A. Ruiz-Cortés, R. Corchuelo, A. Durán, and M. Toro. Enhancing Win–Win requirements negotiation model. In *Applied Requirements Engineering*. Catedral, 2002.
26. A. Ruiz-Cortés, R. Corchuelo, A. Durán, and M. Toro. Automated negotiation of quality requirements. In *VII Jornadas de Ingeniería del Software y Bases de Datos (JISBD'02)*, 2002.
27. A. Ruiz-Cortés, A. Durán, R. Corchuelo, and M. Toro. Specification of Quality Requirements in Multi-Organisational Web-based Systems (in Spanish). In *Sextas Jornadas de Ingeniería del Software y Bases de Datos JISBD'01*, pages 615–629, Almagro, Spain, 2001.
28. A. Ruiz-Cortés, R. Corchuelo, A. Duran, and M. Toro. Automated support for quality requirements in web-services-based systems. In *Proc. of the 8th IEEE Workshop on Future Trends of Distributed Computing Systems (FTDCS'2001)*, Bologna, Italy, 2001. IEEE Press.
29. A. ShaikhAli, R. Al-Ali O. Rana, and D. Walker. UDDIe: An extended registry for web services. In *Proc. of the IEEE Int'l Workshop on Service Oriented Computing: Models, Architectures and Applications at SAINT Conference*. IEEE Press, January 2003.
30. Gerhard Weikum. The Web in 2010: Challenges and opportunities for database research. *Lecture Notes in Computer Science n° 2000*, 2001.

Towards a Context-Aware Service Directory

Christos Doulkeridis, Efstratios Valavanis, and Michalis Vazirgiannis

Database Systems Laboratory
Department of Informatics
Athens University of Economics and Business (AUEB)
10434 Athens, Greece
{cdoulk,valavani,mvazirg}@aueb.gr

Abstract. Advances in the areas of mobile computing and web services lead to new scenarios of use and innovative applications. Our approach involves mobile devices that act not only as requestors of data, but as data providers as well, providing access to their data through web services. Context plays an important role in such a scenario, when used to improve existing service discovery mechanisms, by finding the most appropriate service conforming to the search criteria. In this paper we propose a context-aware service directory and we investigate the process of service discovery with respect to contextual information. We adopt the MOEM model for representing contextual information within the service directory and we try to improve the performance of searching. Furthermore, we deal with issues related to the temporal dimension of context, namely prediction of service availability. We also present some preliminary experimental results concerning the search costs.

Keywords: service directory, service discovery, context-aware computing, mobile computing, web services

1 Introduction and Motivation

Nowadays mobile computing comes into the everyday life more and more. Mobile devices, like 3G cellular phones, personal digital assistants (PDAs), digital cameras, laptops, keep getting widely accepted and their usage has become a commodity. As a result, a number of possible scenarios of use are presented every day. In contrast to desktop applications, mobile applications are characterized by dynamic changes of the actors' environment and the restrictions imposed by the size and capabilities of the actual devices [1]. Device and user context can provide valuable information that assists applications to adapt to the needs of specific situations, reducing the waste of resources and offering perspectives for the design of novel context-aware applications [2].

Mobile and pervasive systems make extensive use of heterogeneous data residing on diverse devices. This results in a dynamic system, which comprises numerous mobile information resources, e.g. databases, file repositories, media, etc. Accessing mobile data through web services offers two major advantages: it hides the heterogeneous nature of data scattered around the world, and it

B. Benatallah and M.-C. Shan (Eds.): TES 2003, LNCS 2819, pp. 54–65, 2003.

provides a globally accepted, well-defined interface for data access. In such a dynamically evolving environment, service discovery plays a critical role in the system functionality.

The majority of web service architectures use service directories, i.e. registries of service descriptions, which facilitate service discovery based on parameters. However, when the entities involved (providers and requestors) are static, there exist alternative means of communication, such as direct connection or through an FTP server or even a Web site. In the case of more dynamic architectures, the role of a service directory is crucial, since it is responsible for enabling the discovery of available services by taking into account several parameters such as: location of the service, hosting device capabilities, type of the returned results.

Obviously a context-aware service directory would facilitate service discovery and increase its precision. So far, discovery mechanisms focus either on exact matching based on some service attribute or on semantic service discovery (more ambitious approaches). We argue that using the context of devices and services will make the existing methods more efficient. Thus, we argue in favor of a service directory that can answer queries like the following ones:

- "Which services (or devices) are available in location L at time T?"
- "Which services return results that the requestor device can represent?"
- "Which services were available at timestamp T?"
- "Which services are published by user U and by his device D?"

The innovative part of our work is embedding contextual information within a service directory, thus creating a context-based index for efficient retrieval of services. The contribution of our work is the enhancement of service discovery by taking into account the available contextual information.

The rest of the paper is organized as follows. In section 2, we present our approach for a context-aware service directory and we describe the process of searching in detail. In section 3, we examine the temporal domain by predicting service availability. In section 4, some preliminary experimental results are presented. Section 5 is about the related work, and finally section 6 concludes the paper.

2   Context-Awareness in the Service Directory

Recent surveys on context-aware computing, such as [1], recognize that:

- Only a few types of context (usually *location*) are actually used by applications, either because it is hard to collect and represent more complex types of context or because it is considered useless.
- Context histories are rarely used.
- Applications should tend to minimize user distraction [2] by avoiding to prompt the user to provide contextual information explicitly.

Regarding these points, our approach provides a context representation model capable of handling any type of contextual information, as long as this can be described in terms of key-value pairs. Keys are called *dimensions* and they can take one or more discrete values, or they can range over a specific domain. We also explore context histories and we describe a couple of interesting use cases. Moreover, our approach deals with any number of context types, as we will show in the following sections. At the same time, we try to respect the user's reluctance of providing information to the system.

We argue that context plays an important role in service discovery, as an additional set of criteria that enables locating the most suitable service, after having found the appropriate service category semantically [6]. Defining a global context model that applies to all services is both complicated and imposes several useless dimensions. Therefore we define context per service category.

In the following subsections, we will focus on a service category that includes file-sharing services, in order to demonstrate the feasibility of our approach. It is needless to say that the results of our study can be applied in any service category that is included within the service directory. The only obstacle is discovering the most interesting context dimensions for each service category.

2.1   Data Model

In order to introduce a context-aware service directory, we adopt a representation model that is capable of holding information presenting different facets under different contexts. We exploit this property and we represent service categories as multidimensional entities. Context is used to differentiate services that belong to the same service category.

Intuitively, the service directory is represented by a Multidimensional OEM graph [3], modelling services as atomic nodes (i.e. leaves of the graph). In fact every service category is represented by an (degenerate) (see 2.4) MOEM graph, which stores services in its leaves and uses multidimensional entities to differentiate these services based on the contextual information under which they hold.

We will show the usage of an MOEM graph as a service directory through an example. Figure 1 shows (part of) a service directory that represents file-sharing services. The graph comprises two kinds of nodes: rectangular nodes, called *multidimensional nodes*, represent multidimensional entities that present different facets under different contexts, whereas circular nodes, representing entities, are called *atomic* or *context nodes*, depending on whether they are leaves of the graph or not. Atomic nodes are able to hold some kind of data and in our approach they represent web services. There are also two kinds of edges: *context* and *entity edges*. Context edges are represented by thick lines and they define the contexts (represented by labels called *explicit contexts*) under which the services hold. Entity edges are plain edges that represent relations between entities.

In figure 1, the file-sharing service category is further analyzed in four subcategories, namely *document retrieval, image retrieval, audio retrieval* and *video-sharing* services. The actual services that belong to each of these (semantic) categories are distinguished by means of context. For example, services represented

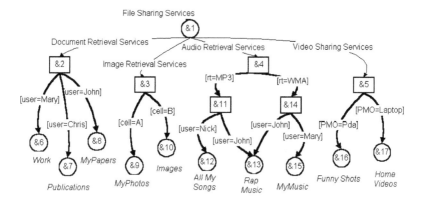

Fig. 1. An MOEM graph representing (part of) a service directory.

by nodes &6, &7 and &8 return documents, but they belong to different users. In a similar way, two image retrieval services are registered in the directory: service &9, which is located in cell A, and service &10, located in cell B (assuming a cell-based space model). We also notice that different dimensions of context can apply to the same services. This is the case with services &12, &13 and &15, which belong to different users and return different types of files (dimension: rt - return type). Service &12 returns MP3 files and service &15 returns files in WMA format, whereas service &13 returns both types of files. Finally, differentiating video-sharing services &16 and &17 is accomplished through the dimension PMO (Primary Mobile Object) [6] that defines the type of the device providing the service. Service &16 resides on a PDA, whereas service &17 on a laptop.

2.2   Searching for Services

Having explained the role of the MOEM graph as a model for representing a service directory, it is important to elucidate the service discovery mechanism. We introduce a breadth first search algorithm to traverse the graph and to spot the services that match the search criteria. This algorithm takes as input the identifier of the root and a context specifier, which is a syntactical construct representing the context under which the search is performed.

Intuitively, we note that a path starting from the root must exist for every service that is supposed to belong to the result set of the search. This path should only consist of context edges with explicit contexts consistent with the context specifier representing the search criteria.

The algorithm starts its execution from the root of the graph, and examines all edges that depart from the root. For each of these edges, its explicit context is compared to the context specifier, which determines the context under which the search is performed, and if their *intersection* [3] is equal to the *empty context* [-] [3], then the subgraph pointed by this edge is ignored. Alternatively, the node (pointed by the edge) is kept for further processing. When the algorithm finds an atomic node, this node represents a service that is in accordance with the search criteria, and it will be included in the search results. The algorithm ensures that only the atomic nodes, which should be returned, will be examined.

SEARCH ALGORITHM

```
INPUT:   nRoot        // the identifier of the root
         strContext   // context specifier describing the context
OUTPUT: SelNodes      // list with the ids of the selected services
SEARCH ALGORITHM:
STEP1: Mark node (&nRoot), and add it to queue
STEP2: While the queue is not empty...
  STEP2(A): Get the next node (&n) from the queue
  STEP2(B): If (&n) is an atomic node, add it to SelNodes,
  and go to STEP2
  STEP2(C): Get all edges that start from (&n) and put
  them in a list
  STEP2(D): While the list is not empty...
    STEP2(D)(i): Take the next edge from the list
    STEP2(D)(ii): If the intersection of the explicit context of
    the edge and strContext, is different than the empty set, and
    if the node (&p) pointed by the edge is not marked, then add
    (&p) to the queue and mark (&p)
    STEP2(D)(iii): Remove the edge from the list
    STEP2(D)(iv): Go to STEP 2(D)
  STEP2(E): Go to STEP 2
STEP3: Return SelNodes
```

For example, consider the query: "Find all services provided by user B", which is issued at the service directory depicted in figure 2(a). The context specifier representing the query is: [user=B]. It is easy to understand that applying the search algorithm on the graph, returns service &12. Note that the subgraph with node &5 as its root, is completely excluded from the search, since it holds under the context [user=A], thus not conforming to [user=B].

2.3 Improving Search

We argue that the same graph can be represented by numerous equivalent graphs, by simply changing the hierarchy of the dimensions that define context. We will show that the time required to perform a search depends on the morphology of the graph that represents the service directory.

Assume that context is defined for document retrieval services by means of the following dimensions: PMO, user, and rt - Return Type. We summarize the contextual information in a table, called *State Table*.

We will construct an MOEM graph that represents the information held in the *state table*, with the help of a construction algorithm. Let us choose the

Table 1. State Table

PMO	User	Return Type	Service
PDA	A	pdf	&10
Laptop	A	pdf,ps	&11
Laptop	B	ps	&12

dimensions with respect to their order on the *state table*, i.e. at first dimension *PMO*, then *User*, and finally *rt* (return type). Consider the root (&1) of the graph depicted in figure 2(a). In order to apply the algorithm on the *state table*, we start with service &10, and we create and then draw the path under which the service holds, namely: *PDA* → *A* → *pdf* → *&10*. Similarly, for service &11 we create two paths: *Laptop* → *A* → *pdf* → *&11*, and *Laptop* → *A* → *ps* → *&11*. At last, the path that is produced for service &12 is: *Laptop* → *B* → *ps* → *&12*. The graph that is constructed by these paths is depicted in fig. 2(a).

CONSTRUCTION ALGORITHM

```
INPUT: State Table (ST)
OUTPUT: MOEM graph (G) representing the service directory
CONSTRUCTION ALGORITHM:
(foreach service in ST) begin  // i.e. each line of the state table
  - create all possible paths to the service
  - draw the produced paths on G (if a subpath of a path
  already exists, extend it to point to the specific service)
end
```

Let us now try to construct an equivalent graph. This graph is depicted in fig. 2(b), which is constructed by selecting the dimensions with a different order. At first, we choose dimension *rt*, then *User*, and finally *PMO*. Applying the construction algorithm, results in the following paths: *pdf* → *A* → *PDA* → *&10* (for service &10), *pdf* → *A* → *Laptop* → *&11* and *ps* → *A* → *Laptop* → *&11* (for service &11), and *ps* → *B* → *Laptop* → *&12* (for service &12).

Regarding search performance, we claim that search is faster when the queries concern dimensions that are closer to the root. In many cases we can optimize service search by restructuring the directory. Performance is improved due to a reduction of the number of nodes and edges examined by the algorithm.

For example, consider the query: *"find all services that return documents of type pdf"*, which is issued against each of the graphs depicted in fig. 2(a) and fig. 2(b). When the search algorithm is applied to the graph in fig. 2(a), the following nodes will be examined: &1, &2, &3, &4, &5, &6, &10, &11, as well as all the edges of the graph, and it will finally retrieve nodes &10 and &11. The same algorithm applied on the graph in fig. 2(b) would examine the nodes: &1, &2, &4, &10, &11, as well as five (5) from the total nine (9) edges, and would retrieve nodes &10 and &11, too. Obviously, when the query is issued against the graph in fig. 2(b), the performance of the search is improved, and the difference is significant even in the case of graphs of relatively small size.

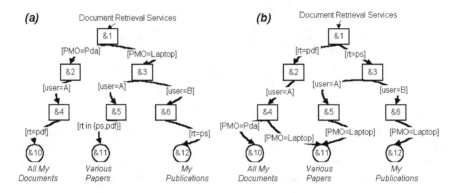

Fig. 2. Two equivalent graphs holding contextual information.

2.4   Complexity Analysis

This section examines the space requirements and time complexity that characterize the service directory. Our aim is twofold: first, to identify the search cost, and second, to determine the space cost induced by this structure.

We can make some interesting observations based on the description of the graph. First, the MOEM graph is actually a degenerate MOEM graph, since it is mainly constructed by successive context edges that point either to multidimensional nodes or to atomic nodes representing the actual services. There are practically no entity edges (except from those defining service categories) and the only context nodes that exist in the structure are those that represent the available services in the directory. Moreover, the morphology of the graph is similar to a tree, with the only difference that there can exist leaves, which belong to different subtrees (i.e. service nodes pointed by more than one edge, like service &11 in fig. 2(b)). Based on these observations, we find that the graph presents several similarities with multiple way (m-way) search trees. This point will be clarified by the analysis that follows.

Consider a service directory that contains n services, and k dimensions (defining the context). Assume that each dimension can take up to m distinct values. Further on, let us assume a 'complete' graph, i.e. m edges starting from every node, which is the worst-case scenario both in terms of space and time complexity. If we think of the graph as a tree, then its height is:

$$h = k + 1$$

since k is the number of dimensions and each level corresponds to context edges describing one dimension. The fan-out of the tree is equal to the number of values m that a dimension can take, so:

$$fo = m$$

which is the number of edges starting from a node. The number of nodes for a complete tree of height h and fan-out m is:

$$N_m(h) = 1 + m + m^2 + .. + m^k = O(m^k)$$

The mean value of the number of node accesses for a successful search (for exactly one service, i.e. node) is:

$$E = m/2 * k + 1 = O(mk)$$

since $m/2$ is the mean value of outcoming edge comparisons in each node in order to find the edge that matches the search criteria, and the search is performed in k levels. When searching for all services that hold under a specific context:

$$E = m/2 * k + n_i = O(mk + n_i)$$

with $n_i \leq n$ representing the number of services under this context. Generally:

$$\Sigma n_i = n, \ i = 1..m^k$$

and if a uniform distribution is presumed, then:

$$n_i = n/m^k$$

3   Temporal Aspects of Context and Its Applications

This section deals with issues that arise when the temporal domain is examined. So far, we have avoided explicit references to the temporal dimension within the service directory, for this dimension distinguishes itself from the usual dimensions of context. This is, mainly, due to the fact that the frequency of modifications concerning time is expected to be enormous compared to other dimensions, since the latter are usually not affected by frequent changes. In addition to that, when temporal information is taken into account, some interesting applications and some new scenarios of use come up, that highlight its distinguishing nature.

The basic motivation of this part of our work is to predict the availability of services, in terms of time and geographical space, i.e. when and where a service is expected to be available in the future. In many cases this could be achieved using the current state or a sequence of states of the device hosting the service. By analyzing the past behavior of a user, we claim that it is possible to discover interesting patterns, thus allowing the prediction of future appearances of devices, and therefore the prediction of service availability.

We try to exploit the fact that service availability is directly dependent on regular habits of users offering services. For example, consider the case of a user that provides access to his services only when he is at work, from Monday to Friday during working hours. A request, for such a service, issued at night would normally get no results, whereas in our case the requestor would be informed that the service will probably be available the next morning. We are in favor of a system that returns approximate results, rather than no results at all.

In [4], the authors show that MOEM is capable of representing temporal changes in semistructured databases. We take advantage of this property of MOEM to maintain time-dependent information about services and their availability. We will explain the usage of such a graph in our case with the help of an example.

Figure 3(a) shows the initial state of the MOEM graph that keeps information about the PMOs, within the boundaries of a single cell, and about the services they publish. At timestamp t=start, only one PMO, named A,

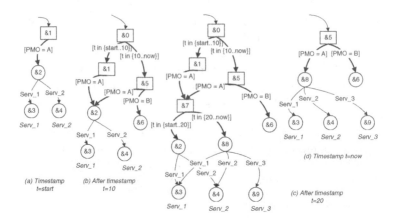

Fig. 3. The service directory describing the devices and the services published, at various time instances.

is registered and it publishes two services: `Serv1` and `Serv2`. At timestamp `t=10`, a new PMO named B, which provides no services, enters the cell and is registered in the system (fig. 3(b)). A new multidimensional node with id &0 is created, which groups together nodes &2 and &6 that represent the registered PMOs in the cell before and after `t=10` respectively. Notice that the new PMO is accessible from the root, only for timestamps before `t=10`. Then, at `t=20`, PMO A publishes a new service: `Serv3`(fig. 3(c)). A new multidimensional node with id &7 replaces node &2, and points to node &2 that represents the services published before `t=20`, and to node &8 that encapsulates all published services after `t=20`. Finally, fig. 3(d) shows a snapshot of the current state of the directory, containing both PMOs and all the services they publish.

ALGORITHM: DISCOVERING THE ONLINE TIME INTERVALS

```
STEP1: Find all context edges with explicit context [PMO=X], since
they point to the PMO in question
STEP2: For each of these edges...
  STEP2(A): Find all starting nodes (father nodes)
  STEP2(B): Find all context edges pointing to these nodes
  STEP2(C): Extract the time intervals from these edges
STEP3: Accumulate all intervals, apply pattern-matching techniques
```

In order to predict the future behavior of services, we need to accumulate the time intervals they were available, and try to apply pattern-matching techniques on them. We present a simple, case-specific algorithm for extracting the time intervals from the directory. The algorithm takes as input a specific PMO and finds all the related time intervals. The algorithm results in a time interval (or a union of time intervals), which is kept for every service, showing the expected time of availability for each service.

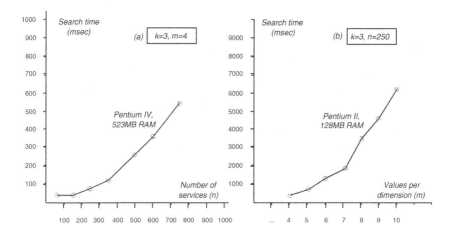

Fig. 4. Time required for service retrieval for:(a)k=3, m=4, and for various numbers (n) of services, (b)k=3, n=250, and for various numbers of values for dimensions (m).

4   Experimental Results

We have performed a series of experiments concerning service lookup with respect to contextual information. Given a graph (of varying size) representing the service directory, we measured the time required to find *all services* that hold under the specified context. All experiments are performed in main memory.

Figure 4(a) shows the results when context is defined by k=3 dimensions, with each dimension ranging over m=4 discrete values. Figure 4(b) depicts the results produced from a directory that contains n=250 services that hold under k=3 dimensions of context. The number of values m (i.e. the fan-out of the graph) that each dimension can take is shown on the X-axis.

The charts show the linear relationship between the required search time and (a) the number of services n, (b) the number of values per dimension m. Notice that this is in accordance with our complexity analysis (see 2.4), which shows that the search time exhibits a linear relationship with m, k, and n, when we search for all services holding under a specified context.

5   Related Work

Some protocols support exclusively directory-less operation, based on multicasting (like UPnP [14,19] and HP Cooltown [16]), in which all the participants can advertise or request service from each other in an ad-hoc manner. Others use service repositories (Jini lookup tables, SLP Directory Agents or Salutation SLMs [14,15,17,18]). Service discovery is usually based on service types and attributes not taking context into account, except Cooltown. However, Cooltown's [16] concept of context is rather informal with descriptions that can be unstructured web pages.

The UDDI specification [20] provides a model used to describe services and facilitate service and business discovery. The discovery mechanism adopted is still at an immature level, and service classification is based on *tModels*, which present certain limitations. The ebXML approach [21] shares some common features with UDDI, but goes a step further by trying to introduce an infrastructure for business-to-business communication. The data model treats all entities as objects, thus providing a generic model. Nevertheless, discovery mechanisms are rather limited and categorization is achieved through the use of *Slots*, a similar concept to *tModels*. Like UDDI, the ebXML specification does not address issues like mobility of services, semantic discovery and context-awareness.

The most popular model for representing raw contextual data are key-value pairs [8] and arbitrary annotations (tags) [9]. Object-oriented approaches [10,13] model real world entities as objects with types, names, capabilities and properties to allow computer systems to share and use the user's perceptions of the real world (location, time, environmental condition). This approach is quite powerful, but involves an important overhead for constructing the objects. Finally, logic-based models [11] keep context data as facts in rule-based systems. Nearly all of these approaches use their own ad-hoc data structures to model contextual data. This results in many islands of contextual information that work well as stand-alone entities, but hinder communication and exchange of information.

The data formats used to model contextual information should be independent of any requirements concerning hardware, programming language or operating system [7]. Our approach for storing contextual information is based on the use of the MOEM model, which is a generic model that fulfills such requirements. Furthermore, in our case, exchanging information regarding context (just like in the case of stick-e notes [12]) is supported with the use of MXML [5], a markup language that incorporates the notion of context in XML.

6   Conclusions and Future Work

In this paper, we presented a context-aware service directory, we explained the process of searching for services based on contextual information, and we presented some preliminary experimental results. We also discussed about prediction of service availability. The innovative part of our work is creating a context-based index for efficient service retrieval and our contribution is the enhancement of service discovery by taking into account the available contextual information.

Our future work will focus on the synchronization and communication of distributed context-aware service directories, and we will try to define formally the notion of context regarding services. We also intend to exploit context-awareness in order to improve existing service discovery mechanisms.

References

1. G. Chen and D. Kotz *A Survey of Context-Aware Mobile Computing Research.* Dartmouth Computer Science Technical Report TR2000-381.
2. M. Satyanarayanan *Pervasive Computing: Vision and Challenges.* IEEE Personal Communications, August 2001.

3. Y. Stavrakas and M. Gergatsoulis. *Multidimensional Semistructured Data: Representing Context-dependent Information on the Web*. In Proc. of the 14th Int. Conf. on Advanced Information Systems Engineering (CAISE'02), Toronto, Canada, May 2002.

4. Y. Stavrakas, M. Gergatsoulis, C. Doulkeridis and V. Zafeiris. *Accomodating Changes in Semistructured Databases Using Multidimensional OEM*. In Proc. of the 6th East European Conference, Advances in Databases and Information Systems (ADBIS'02), Bratislava, Slovakia, September 2002.

5. Y. Stavrakas, M. Gergatsoulis, and P. Rondogiannis. *Multidimensional XML*. In the Proceedings of the Third International Workshop, Distributed Communities on the Web, DCW 2000, Quebec City, Canada, June 19–21, 2000, pp.100–109.

6. E. Valavanis, C. Ververidis, M. Vazirgiannis, G. C. Polyzos, K. Norvag. *MobiShare: Sharing Context-Dependent Data and Services from Mobile Sources*. To appear in the Proceedings 2003 IEEE/WIC International Conference on Web Intelligence, WI2003, Halifax, Canada, October 13–17, 2003.

7. J. Hong and J. Landay. *An Infrastructure Approach to Context-Aware Computing*. Human-Computer Interaction, 16: 287–303, 2001.

8. G.M. Voelker and B.N. Bershad. *Mobisaic: An Information System for a Mobile Wireless Computing Environment*. In Proceedings of IEEE Workshop on Mobile Computing Systems and Applications, pages 185–190, Santa-Cruz, California, December 1994. IEEE Computer Society Press.

9. P.J. Brown, J.D. Bovey and X.Chen. *Context-aware Applications: from the Laboratory to the Marketplace*. IEEE Personal Communications, 4(5): 58–64, October 1997.

10. N. Davies, K. Cheverst, K. Mitchell and A. Friday. *Caches in the Air: Disseminating Tourist Information in the GUIDE System*. In Proceedings of the Second IEEE Workshop on Mobile Computing Systems and Applications, New Orleans, Louisiana, February 1999. IEEE Computer Society Press.

11. J. Bacon, J. Bates and D. Halls. *Location-oriented Multimedia*. IEEE Personal Communications, 4(5): 48–57, October 1997.

12. J. Pascoe. *The Stick-e note Architecture: Extendind the Interface Beyond the User*. In Proccedings of the 1997 International Conference on Intelligent User Interfaces, pp. 261–264, Orlando, FL, January 1997, ACM Press.

13. A. Harter, A. Hopper, P. Steggles, A. Ward, and P. Webster. *The Anatomy of a Context-Aware Application*. In Wireless Networks 8(2-3): 187–197, 2002.

14. S. Helal, C. Lee. *Protocols for Service Discovery in Dynamic and Mobile Networks*. International Journal of Computing Research, vol.22, no.1, pp. 1–12, 2002.

15. E. Guttman. *Service Location Protocol: Automatic Discovery of IP Network Services*. IEEE Internet Computing, 3(4): 71–80, 1999.

16. T. Kindberg, et al. *People, Places, Things: Web Presence for the Real World*. Technical Report HPL-2000-16, Internet and Mobile Systems Laboratory, HP Laboratories Palo Alto, February, 2000.

17. Salutation Consortium, http://www.salutation.org/, 2003.

18. Sun Microsystems Inc. Jini Network Technologies, http://www.sun.com/jini/, 2003.

19. Universal Plug and Play (UPnP), http://www.upnp.org/

20. UDDI *The UDDI Technical White Paper*, http://www.uddi.org

21. ebXML, http://www.ebxml.org

User-Facing Web Service Development: A Case for a Product-Line Approach

Oscar Diaz, Salvador Trujillo, and Iker Azpeitia

EKIN Group. University of the Basque Country
PO Box: 649, 20080, San Sebastian, Spain
Phone: + 34 943 018 064
{oscar,struji,iker}@si.ehu.es

Abstract. Web service technology has proved its way as a function integration enabler. The next step is to achieve application integration whereby one application is made available within the context of a consumer application, and this can also include the interface. This is the aim of the WSRP initiative, sponsored by OASIS. This initiative is standardizing the notion of Portlet as a user-facing, presentation-oriented Web Service, intended to simplify the creation of distributed interactive applications. One of the challenges is how to cope with the extent and heterogeneity of the diverse aspects that are now being encapsulated by the Web Service. And how variability requirements can be addressed. To this end, this paper proposes a product-line approach. As a first step, this work focuses on the feature model, i.e. a model that provides an abstract and concise syntax for expressing commonality and variability when addressing Portlet development. As the encapsulation of the presentation layer is what distinguishes a Portlet from a traditional Web Service, the paper focuses on presentation, personalization and consumer-platform requirements. The aim is to facilitate the construction and adaptation of future WSRP Portlets to the specificities of the consumer application. This endeavour aims at leveraging Web service technology as an application-integration enabler.

1 Introduction

Smooth and seamless system integration is a main requirement to deliver the so-called extended enterprise. Web service technology delivers significant promise for achieving such a smooth integration. However, the traditional use of Web services has not yet delivered its full potential. Web service standards facilitate the sharing of the business logic, and suggest that Web service consumers should write a new presentation layer on top of the business logic. A common pattern of usage is for the consumer collecting some parameters via an input form. Within the form, an *http* request might support a call to the Web service which, in turn, renders some data back. The presentation of this data is also left to the consumer and results in the presentation layer being hard coded in each application requesting this Web service.

This scenario illustrates the traditional use of Web services as a function-integration technology whereby one application programmatically invokes code that lies in another application. But this is not enough. True application integration results from making one

B. Benatallah and M.-C. Shan (Eds.): TES 2003, LNCS 2819, pp. 66–77, 2003.

application available within the context of another, and this can also include the user interface [22]. Microsoft OLE objects are a case in point. For example, this technology allows embedding an Excel spreadsheet directly into a Word document through simply dragging. Once embedded, you can work on the spreadsheet *from* the Word document as if you were within Excel.

This scenario is far from being achieved in a Web setting. As an example, consider the portal of a car dealer. The portal provides an eCatalogue with car models, and offers cars currently on sale at the dealership. Now, considers that Ford has such an eCatalogue as an HTML-supported application. This application encapsulates both the functionality (e.g. access to Ford's database) and most important, the presentation layer. Issues such as the layout or navigation strategies to browse the eCatalogue have been carefully thought by Ford's developers. Using current technology, the car dealer does not have any satisfactory response for integrating Ford's eCatalogue. Using a simple hypertext link from the dealer's site to Ford's permits to "re-use" the presentation layer, *but at the cost of losing the control over the end customer, and probable usability mismatches between the calling site and the called site.* Web clipping tools, currently available in main Portal IDE providers such as Oracle Portals or IBM's Web Sphere do not help too much, neither. Clipping would only permit to integrate the doorway of the Ford's eCatalogue into the dealer's site. However, once this doorway is crossed, the customer abandons the dealer's portal, and moves to the Ford's site. No integration remains.

For Web services to be an application-integration technology, user-interface requirements should be considered. Web services currently lack a mechanism to encapsulate a user interface, which is key to being able to package an application and embed it into another application. These issues are currently being tackled by an OASIS initiative, the *Web Services for Remote Portals* (WSRP) Technical Committee[1]. Hereafter, the term *"Portlet"* is used to refer to *an application* being hosted by Web Services. The duties of these services include markup generation (e.g. XHTML) as well as processing interactions with that markup. The generated markup can then be framed within a third-party application (e.g. a portal).

However, seamless integration frequently requires adapting/configuring the components to be integrated. This is indeed the case for Portlets. The notion of ubiquitousness indicates the extent to which a Portlet can be seamlessly integrated into distinct utilization context. Integrating Portlets into a consumer application is more than merely invoking these services, or arranging their outputs together (also called *side-by-side* integration).

We argue that ubiquity demands for Portlets are going to be even more stringent than for other kinds of software components due to both the coarse-grained nature of Portlets, and the criticality of the functions being encapsulated by the Portlet. Effective presentation logic has been shown to be a source of competitive advantage, and hence, Portlet consumers will be specially demanding on adapting the syndicated service to their own criteria. Ubiquity is thus, a main quality factor that compels the Portlet designer to consider a wide-range of potential utilization contexts. The usefulness of a Portlet will largely stem from its capacity to be tailored to distinct settings.

The premise of this work is that the size, complexity and diversity of the aspects to be considered during Portlet construction and configuration, demands a product-

---

[1] WSRP version 1.0 has been delivered in April, 2003.

line approach. That is, the heterogeneity of the utilization contexts where the Portlet will have to function, demands an analysis of the commonality and variability of the distinct scenarios to be supported, and how this variability is going to be upheld in a cost-effective manner. Software product-line techniques serve precisely this purpose. Product lines develop an architecture and a set of reusable assets well suited to express and efficiently implement the different members of a family of related applications. To do this, a reuse-oriented analysis of the domain is conducted whose outcome includes a *feature model [6]*. This model provides an abstract and concise syntax for expressing commonality and variability in the domain. It helps not only to assess the reusability of an existing product line but it is also helpful in understanding the variability of a product during the development of a product-line architecture.

This paper provides some insights into a feature model. The aim is to facilitate the construction and adaptation of future WSRP Portlets to the specificities of the consumer application. This endeavour aims at promoting Web service technology to a full application-integration enabler.

The rest of the paper is structured as follows. Section 2 illustrates the notion of Portlet. Section 3 argues about the use of a product-line approach to Portlet development. This implies the existence of a feature model that identifies the commonality and variability of the different scenarios to be tackled by the Portlet product-line. As the encapsulation of the presentation layer is what distinguishes a Portlet from a traditional Web Service, the paper focuses on presentation, personalization and consumer-platform requirements. These are the topics of sections 4, 5 and 6, respectively. Finally, conclusions are given.

2   Illustrating the Notion of WSRP Portlets

Web service standards facilitate the sharing of the business logic, and suggest that Web service consumers should write a new presentation layer on top of the business logic. As an example, consider an airline company such as *jetFlight*. This company could make available part of its assets via Web services. In this way, an API could be offered that includes at least two operations, *flightSearch* and *flightBook*. The former takes the data of the flight (e.g. the departure airport, the arrival airport, the date, and so on) as an input, and returns an XML document with the flights matching the selected criteria. The operation *flightBook* takes the date, the flight and the seats to be booked, and returns the so-called e-ticket. Using these two operations, a consumer application can recreate the screenshots of figure 1. First, the Web application collects the flight parameters via an input form. Within the form, an *http* request might support a call to the *flightSearch* operation which, in turn, renders a set of flights whose presentation is left to the client application. This list of references is presented together with an input button that leads to the invocation of the second operation, i.e. *flightBook*. The document returned (e.g. the e-ticket) is rendered next in accordance to the customer presentation instructions. This example illustrates the traditional approach where all the presentation layer is left to the consumer application.

But the presentation layer is one of the most critical but also cumbersome and time-consuming software to be created. As the previous example highlights, the reconstruction of the screenshots not only involves aesthetic aspects, but also leaves to the client application the recomposition of the workflow among the API's operations, and the maintenance

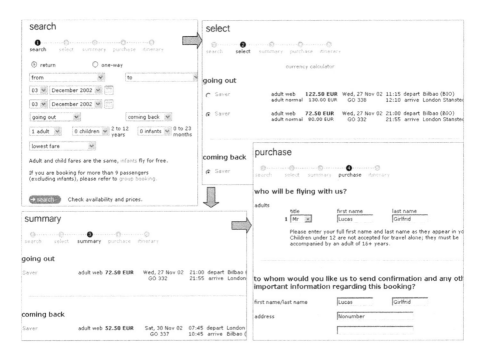

Fig. 1. flightSearch Operation screenshots

of the session state (e.g. keeping the parameters among operation calls). And such work-flow can be quite complex, indeed. Therefore, an API-based approach as the one provided by traditional Web services, falls short for complex interactive applications whose flow spans several Web pages.

The solution is to encapsulate the whole application, presentation-layer included, as a Web Service. In this way, not only can the business logic be reused but presentation layer as well. This is the approach fueled by the *Web Services for Remote Portals* (WSRP) initiative [15]. This working group, hosted by OASIS, strives to provide an alternative to data-centric Web services and simple XML APIs. These Web Services, referred in the WSRP document as Portlets, are then user-facing and presentation-oriented, intended to simplify the creation of distributed interactive applications.

Let's go back to our sample application but now using a Portlet approach. The whole application for booking flights is now offered as a WSRP Web Service. The previous screenshot sequence can be seen as distinct states of a single, coarse-grained operation. Traditional Web Service technology is used (i.e. WSDL, UDDI and SOAP). The only requirement is that the output document should be based on an XML-based markup language (e.g. XHTML). This output document is then framed by the consumer application. "Only remains" agreeing on a common protocol between the consumer and the producer. Standardizing this protocol is precisely the endeavour of the WSRP working group.

As with any other component technology, the benefits of Portlets largely rest on the extent to which they can be reused. While traditional operation-base data-oriented Web Services can be readily used in diverse contexts, application-based user-facing Portlets should carefully foresee the different scenarios where they can be deployed. Going back to our sample problem, what if the Portlet markup is going to be rendered in a mobile phone? What if the consumer application has already set the departure airport, should this parameter still be prompted to the user? What if the consumer application wants to use the Portlet just as a timetable for flights but suppressing the possibility of booking the flight? What if the rendering space left to display the Portlet is not the full-page but a more reduced slot? Configuration mechanisms are needed for the portlet to cater for the specifics of the consumer application.

From this standpoint, Portlet development resembles the creation of a *set* of similar products rather than a single product. We then advocate for a product-line approach to Portlet development.

3   From Components to Product Lines

Web services have been considered as the natural consequence in the reuse succession containing classes, components, and finally, Web services. This succession is at least valid in the tendency to larger level of granularity and higher interoperability. But, increasing granularity and interoperability poses more stringent demands on how to cope with variability. Component-based development does not give yet a satisfactory solution. If any variation is involved, it is usually accomplished by writing code, and the variants are most likely maintained separately. Component-based development alone also lacks the technical and organizational management aspects that are so important to the success of variability in a software product [3]. This drawback can be minimized for fine-grained and rigid Web Services. However as the size and variability requirements of Web Services increases, proper product-line strategies should be deployed. And this is the case for Portlets.

By encapsulating also the presentation layer, Portlets do not only gain in size but also new variability challenges need to be tackled. Different consumers can demand different configurations, ranging from the transport protocol being used, to the payment mode or the layout required. And these variations should be deployed and maintained under stringent time and budget constraints.

This calls for a product-line approach to Portlet development. A software product line is "a set of software-intensive systems sharing a common, managed set of features that satisfy the specific needs of a particular market segment or mission and that are developed from a common set of core assets in a prescribed way. Software product lines give you economies of scope, which means that you take economic advantage of the fact that many of your products are very similar not by accident, but because you planned in that way" [3].

A product-line strategy comprises the development of an architecture and a set of reusable assets well suited to express and efficiently implement the different members of a family of related software products [12]. The difference between those products can be discussed in terms of features. Consequently, a software product line must support variability for those features that tend to differ from product to product.

A feature can be conceived as a construct used to group related requirements [1]. Similar understanding is presented in [13] where it is stated that "constructing a feature set is the first step of interpreting and ordering the requirements. In the process of constructing a feature set, the first design decisions about the future system are already taken".

Features have been categorized as mandatory, optional, variant [14] and external [11]. The definition and examples that follow are taken from [13]:

- Mandatory Features. These are the features that identify a product. E.g. the ability to type in a message and send it to the SMTP server is essential for an email client application.
- Optional Features. These are features that, when enabled, add some value to the core features of a product. A good example of an optional feature for an email client is the ability to add a signature to each message. It is in no way an essential feature and not all users will use it but it is nice to have it in the product.
- Variant Features. A variant feature is an abstraction for a set of related features (optional or mandatory). An example of a variant feature for the email client might be the editor used for typing in messages. Some email clients offer the feature of having a user configurable editor.
- External Features. These are features offered by the target platform of the system. E.g. in an email client, the ability to make TCP connections to another computer is essential but not part of the client. Instead the functionality for TCP connections is typically part of the OS on which the client runs.

The requirements involved during Portlet development can be first arranged along the following mandatory features:

- **Business_Logic**. This feature comprises the set of requirements that focuses on the functionality of the application. The aim is to identify the main functional modules and their variations. The variants are application-specific. The novelty of the Portlet approach does not rest here.
- **Service_Model**. Portlets are services, and hence, they might need to address concerns such as how to bill for the service, how to register to the service, and the like. These requirements are the same regardless of the Web Service supporting a traditional service or a user-facing one. A general model for service is outside the scope of this paper. The DAML-S consortium is striving to find an ontology for service description [4]. As for non-functional requirements, an outline of the complexity of the endeavour can be found in [10].
- **Presentation**. This feature addresses rendering and layout requirements.
- **Personalization**. Being "user-facing", Portlets might need to adapt to distinct user profiles. After all, personalization is seen as one of the main differences between traditional software and Web applications.
- **Consumer_Platform**. This feature attempts to describe the technological environment of the Portlet's consumer.

The first two features are not specific to Portlets and then, fall outside the scope of this paper. Figure 2 outlines the main variants for the rest of the features, using the UML stereotypes introduced in [2] [2].

4   Presentation Requirements

By encapsulating also the presentation layer, a feature model for Portlets must address variability on the requirements about how the service is rendered. These requirements can be arranged as follows.

Output_Device Requirements. It indicates the device used to render the markup of the Portlet. In this sense, it is an external feature that influences the markup to be generated by the Portlet. This feature can in turn be split as follows

- *Markup_Type*. It is a mandatory feature that indicates which markup standards will be supported. Common variants include *HTML*, *WML20*, or *VoiceXML*,
- *User_Agent*. A mandatory feature of the agents to be used to render the markup document. Possible alternatives are *Netscape702*, *msie60*, or *nokia7650*.

Window_State Requirements. Rendering-wise, a Portlet might need to be visualized side-by-side with other Portlets. This implies that the space available for Portlet rendering might not be the full page but a region of the page. The size available will have an impact on deciding how much information to render in the generated markup. This aspect is already considered in current Portlet technology. The WSRP [15] standard considers the following variants:

- *normal*, which indicates the Portlet is likely sharing the aggregated page with other Portlets,
- *minimized*, which states that the Portlet should not render visible markup, but is free to include non-visible data such as JavaScript or hidden forms,
- *maximized*, where the Portlet is likely the only Portlet being rendered in the aggregated page, or that the Portlet has more space compared to other Portlets in the aggregated page,
- *solo,* which indicates the Portlet is the only Portlet being rendered in the aggregated page.

Interaction Requirements. A main part of the presentation is the set of interactions that the Portlet will conduct with the user to fulfill the service. In [5], the notion of "interactive lifecycle" is introduced to surface to the Consumer the visible process flow of

---

[2] Although not addressed in this paper, feature combinations can be restricted via constraints. For instance, the Feature Description Language [18], introduces the following constraints: A1 requires A2: if feature A1 is present, then feature A2 should also be present; A1 excludes A2: if feature A1 is present, then feature A2 should not be present. A Portlet instance is then defined by making a feature selection which is valid with respect to the feature description (which includes the constraints). In this way, developing and maintaining a feature description for an existing Portlet product line, gives a clear understanding of the variability allowed for the distinct Portlet instances. This model can be used not only during product instantiation, but also when discussing the design of the product-line.

the Portlet. Interactions are classified as *"requesting"*, *"rendering"* and *"contingency"* based on the interaction's purpose, namely, requesting a parameter, rendering a result-ing, or overcoming an unsatisfactory situation (e.g. an empty result), respectively. An interaction can be qualified as "overridable" whereby the default *realization* (i.e. the one

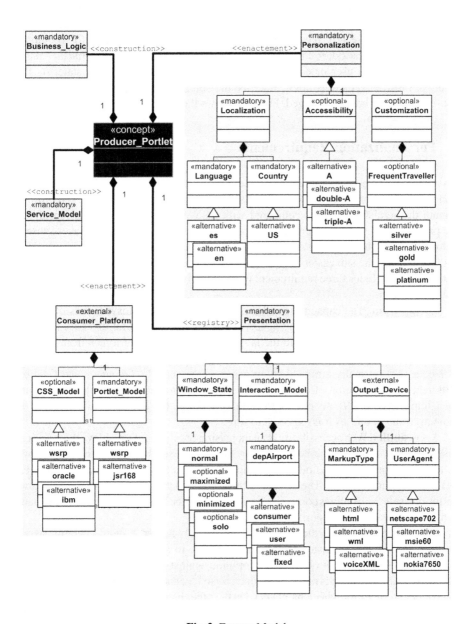

Fig. 2. Feature Model

given by the Provider) of the interaction can be substituted by a realization given by the Consumer.

As an example of the usage of these feature, consider the *departureAirport* parameter of the *flightBooking* Portlet. A standard scenario would be to prompt this parameter directly to the user. However, the Portlet analyst can also consider the scenario where this parameter is already available as part of the consumer's state -e.g. due to previous interactions with other Portlets. In this case, the *departureAirport* can flow from the consumer's state to the Portlet without enquiring the final-user. Another situation is for this parameter to take a fixed value. If the Portlet is integrated into a portal for a company headquartered in Madrid, it could make sense to fix this parameter to *"Madrid"* rather than prompting the user or collecting this parameter from the portal's state. As this example illustrates, there is not a "one-fits-all" solution, but it largely depends on the consumer setting being envisaged. Figure 2 shows these three options.

5   Personalization Requirements

Personalization has been defined as "providing special treatment in the form of information and applications matched to a visitor's interests, roles, and needs" [7]. It represents a main distinguishing feature compared with no-Web applications. By encapsulating the presentation layer, Portlet designers should also consider whether it makes sense to tailor the Portlet to distinct user needs. Two common reasons for personalizing a Web site are to make the site easier to use and to increase sales. This notion is multi-faceted but basically includes three requirement types, namely, **Localization**, **Accessibility** and **Customization**.

Localization. The capacity to tailor one Web site to the idiosyncrasies of a given culture is becoming an increasing concern. The aspects of cultural diversity that need specific support are not limited to the language but to a range of topics from date and calendar issues to letter written figures or telephone numbers. These aspects known as locales, are normally arranged along two features, namely, *Language* and *Country*. Different standardization efforts are being conducted to set the possible variants and their implications [8,9]. As part of its requirement list, the Portlet should indicate the languages and countries it is expected to support.

Accessibility. Web accessibility is an increasing requirement to achieve the e-society. A set of recommendation has been issued by the Web Accessibility Initiative [19], known as the Web Content Accessibility Guidelines (WCAG) that are considered by the EU as the facto standard [20]. The WCAG 1.0 recommendation divides its rules into three "priority levels" and defines corresponding "conformance levels" (A, AA, AAA). Variants can then use the same categorization.

An interesting issue in the scope of this work is whether it should be emphasized the goal of making "mainstream" products suitable to all people, instead of separate versions for people with disabilities. The opinion against special arrangements is probably mainly aimed against arrangements that create "second-class" access, comparable to backdoor entrances for wheelchairs [17]. On the other hand, the one-fits-all solution also find resistance by the opinion that making pages accessible makes them dull, boring, and unimaginative visually, up (or down) to thinking that they'll be "black text on grey background" (in all presentations). Moreover, there are still serious problems in combining accessibility and good visual design. In theory, authors are supposed to make pages accessible and use style sheets to suggest visual appearance. In practice, there are hard problems, largely due to a huge number of errors (bugs) in browsers' support to style sheets. Moreover, there are relatively few examples of sites that combine accessibility and visually attractive design [17].

Customization. A Portlet's output can need to be customized to distinct user categories. Those requirements can then be stated in terms of the distinct profiles to be supported, deferring for a late stage whether this customization is manual or automatic, and in this latter case, the data and tracing requirements that the personalization mechanism requires. For our sample problem, the designer can consider three different traveller categories based on the frequency of the travels. This decision should be based on whether this categorization is meaningful to enhance the usability of the markup generated by the Portlet (e.g. frequent travellers can be bored by a too verbose interface while this approach can be useful for occasional users) or increase the revenue of the Portlet (e.g. cross-selling can be segmented by the same criterion).

6   Consumer_Platform Requirements

This external feature strives to identify variability at the consumer side as they will probably influence the implementation of the Portlet. So far, two aspects have been identified, the *CSS_Model* and the *Portlet_Model*.

CSS_Model. An optional feature that indicates which CSS (Cascading Style Sheet) vocabulary is used [21]. Because the portal aggregates the markup fragments produced by distinct Portlets into a single page, some rules and limitations are needed to ensure the coherence of the resulting page to be displayed to the end-user. By using a common CSS style sheet, a uniform final page can be obtained regardless of the origin of the Portlet. This CSS introduces a set of terms to describe fonts (e.g. *wsia-font*), messages (e.g. *wsia-msg-alert*), sections (e.g. *wsia-section-header*), forms (e.g. *wsia-form-button*) or menus (e.g. *wsia-menu-caption*). The examples have been taken for those provided by the WSRP standard. However, this standard is still far from being widely adopted. At the time of this writing, the current situation is characterized by each portal IDE vendor using its own vocabulary. Therefore, possible variants include *WSRP_Compliant*, *Oracle_Compliant*, *WebSphere_Compliant* and so on. If this feature is not specified, the Portlet producer will deliver the markup with no CSS tags.

Portlet_Model. The lack of interoperability in the Portlet market is the driving force behind the WSRP initiative. Although the notion of Portlet is widely supported among IDE players, the lack of a common model makes very costly to migrate Portlets among distinct portal platforms. Currently, each vendor has its own Portlet API. To complicate things further, another standard exists for J2EE platforms, namely, the JSR168 recommendation [16]. Hence, and waiting for which standard will prevail, the designer should indicate the Portlet models to be supported.

7   Conclusions

Current practices imply custom programming to create a user interface tier for each new Web service, resulting in set-up and maintenance efforts that render business initiatives cost prohibitive as the number of components increases. The transition from function-based Web Services to application-based Web Service will alleviate most of these problems by encapsulating the presentation layer as well as the function flow of the application within the Service itself. In this way, the consumer application is relieved from these burdens, the user-facing Web Service can be easily integrated using "plug-and-play" techniques.

However, this scenario alleviates the problems of the integrating application at the cost of adding presentation concerns to the integrated application, the Portlet. This paper introduces a set of additional concerns a Portlet designer has to face. Our contention is that a product line can be used to face the increasing complexity of building user-facing Web Services. As a first argument, the paper presents a feature model that illustrates the complexity and heterogeneity of the variants to be considered. In this way, a Portlet product (i.e. a Portlet ready to be "integrated" into a consumer application) is an instantiation of the product line. It is important to notice that if a consumer requires a variation not contemplated in the feature model, the associated product line will not accommodate this requirement.

The good news is that some of these features are common to most Portlets. This permits these features to be moved out of the Portlet realm to a Portlet framework. Multilingual requirements are a case in point. Rather than each Portlet having to face the challenge of handling different language, a framework can be in place that does the work for you. An IBM effort is currently being conducted to offer a similar mechanism for Web sites [23]. But, we do not see any main objection for this approach to be extrapolated to the Portlet arena. Unfortunately, this approach can only be achieved where the impact of the variant on the Portlet implementation can be generalized, regardless of the Portlet semantics.

The next logical follow-on to this work includes to obtain an architecture and its variation points that can accommodate the requirements expressed in the feature model.

Acknowledgements. This work was partially supported by the Spanish Science and Technology Ministry (MCYT) under contract TIC2002-01442. Salvador Trujillo enjoys a doctoral grant for the MCYT. Our gratitude to Juan Jose Rodriguez, Iñaki Paz and Felipe Ibañez for their valuable comments while preparing this manuscript. Also thanks are given to the anonymous referees for their advices to improve the legibility of this paper.

References

1. J. Bosch. *Design & Use of Software Architectures – Adopting and Evolving a Product Line Approach.* Addison-Wesley, 2000.
2. M. Claus. Modelling Variability with UML. In *Proceedings of theThirdInternational Symposium on Generative and Component-Based Software Engineering*, 2001.

3. P. Clemence and L.M. Northrop. *Software Product Lines – Practices and Patterns*. Addison-Wesley, 2002.
4. DAML. DARPA Agent Markup Language Services (DAML-S) Version 0.9 Beta, 2003. http://www.daml.org/services/.
5. O. Diaz and J. J. Rodriguez. Portlet Syndication: Raising Ubiquity Concerns. *Submitted to ACM Transactions on Internet Technology*, 2003.
6. M.L. Griss. Implementing Product Line Features with Component Reuse. In *Proceedings of theSixthInternational Conference on Software Reuse*, 2000.
7. IBM. Web Site Personalization, 2000. http://www7b.software.ibm.com/wsdd/library/ techarticles/hvws/personalize.html.
8. ISO. Codes for the Representation of Names of Countries (ISO 3166), 1997. http://www.din.de/gremien/nas/nabd/iso3166ma/codlstp1/en_listp1.html.
9. ISO. Codes for the Representation of Names of Languages (ISO 639-2), 1998. http://lcweb.loc.gov/standards/iso639-2/langcodes.html.
10. D. Edmond J. O'Sullivan and H.M. ter Hofstede. What's in a Service? Towards an Accurate Description of Non-Functional Service Properties. *Distributed and Parallel Databases*, 12(2/3):117–133, September 2002.
11. J. Bosch J. van Gurp and M. Svahnberg. On The Notion of Variability in Software Product Lines. In *Proceedings of WICSA 2001*, 2001.
12. K.C. Kang. FORM: A feature-oriented reuse method with domain specific architectures. *Annals of Software Engineering*, 5: 345–355, 1998.
13. J. van Gurp M. Svahnberg and J. Bosch. A Taxonomy of Variability Realization Techniques. *Submitted to ACM*, 2002.
14. J. Favaro M.L. Griss and M. d'Alessandro. Integrating Feature Modeling with the RSEB. In *Proceedings of theFourthInternational Conference on Software Reuse*, pages 76–85, Vancouver, BC, Canada, 1998.
15. OASIS. Web Service for Remote Portals (WSRP) Version 1.0, 2003. http://www.oasis-open.org/commitees/wsrp/.
16. JCP (Java Community Process). Java Specification Request for portlet API. http://www.jcp.org/en/jsr/detail?id=168.
17. Diffuse Project. Guide to Web Accessibility and Design for All. http://www.diffuse.org/accessibility.html.
18. A. van Deursen and P. Klint. Domain-Specific Language Design Requires Feature Descriptions. *Journal of Computing and Information Technology*, 10(1), 2002.
19. W3C. Web Accessibility Initiative. http://www.w3.org/WAI/.
20. W3C. Web Content Accessibility Guidelines (WCAG) Version 1.0, May 1999. http://www.w3.org/TR/WAI-WEBCONTENT/.
21. W3C. Cascading Style Sheets (CSS), 2001. http://www.w3.org/Style/CSS/.
22. S. Wong. Web Services: The Next Evolution of Application Integration, 2001. http://e-serv.ebizq.net/wbs/wong_1.html.
23. Xiao Hui Zhu. Web Services Globalization Model, 2003. http://www-106.ibm.com/developerworks/webservices/library/ws-global/.

A Contract Model to Deploy and Control Cooperative Processes

Olivier Perrin and Claude Godart

LORIA – INRIA – UMR 7503
BP 239, F-54506 Vandoeuvre-lès-Nancy Cedex, France
{olivier.perrin,claude.godart}@loria.fr

Abstract. In a virtual enterprise context, business process interoperability and cooperative process enactment are important in order to achieve a common objective despite the distribution in space, time and organizations. A contract is a facility that allows for deploying cross-organizational processes, monitoring and enforcing the composition and the enactment of these processes both inside and outside the organization's boundaries. This paper presents a contract model for describing clauses that address business interactions, for deploying cross-organizational activities (called *synchronization points*) and for enforcing and controling policies through the use of ECA rules. A contract is an XML document that allows for describing how process Web services cooperate and how *synchronization points* enforce contract clauses.

1 Introduction

Business pressures (margin erosion, rising customer expectations, development costs, time-based competition...) are placing increased emphasis on how organizations operate and interoperate with other enterprises to achieve a common business goal using cross-organizational and cooperative processes [6]. In this paper, we detail how we use contracts in order to deploy synchronization points that help cooperative interactions to take place simply and how contracts help to enforce obligations of cooperative processes by partners.

A contract is an agreement between two or more partners, defining the set of obligations and rewards in a business process [4]. The definition of *e-contract* is a hot topic within the Web services context. [1] have proposed a classification of all the steps that are needed to define such a contract. If we refer to this classification, we locate our work in the post-contractual (settlement) phase called the *"Contract fulfillement"* contract execution, execution monitoring, re-negotiation and contract settlement evaluation.

In particular, our contract model has the following objectives:

- first, contract definition helps to deploy synchronization points[1] ,

---

[1] Synchronization points are cooperative activities where partners synchronize their process exposed as process services.

B. Benatallah and M.-C. Shan (Eds.): TES 2003, LNCS 2819, pp. 78–90, 2003.
© Springer-Verlag Berlin Heidelberg 2003

- second, the contract definition allows partners to define process services[1] and partners needs and obligations,

To summarize, the three steps are: contract *definition*, contract *implementation* and contract *execution*. We are not interested in contract negotiation nor contract automatic writing. In fact, we suppose these steps are already done, and that every partner have already defined all the legal aspects of contracts. We are rather interested in the instantiation of the execution infrastructure.

Our contract model corresponds to the complex multiparty contracting situation. This is a composition of multiparty contracting and one-to-many contracting ([5]). It allows to describe the obligations of every partners in the context of a cooperative process. Thus, the contract becomes a support for the definition and activation of synchronization points and conversely, synchronization points guarantee the respect of the contract.

In order to couple the synchronization point model and the synchronization point manager, we use the contract model and translate contract clauses into ECA rules managed by synchronization points. Section 2 presents our contract lifecycle. The contract model is introduced in section 3, while section 4 details contract clauses to ECA rules translation. Section 5 introduces the implementation and section 6 concludes.

2   Contract Lifecycle

The first step of a contract definition is what we called the *intention* step. This step is splitted in two parts. In a first time, two (or more) organizations declare their intention to cooperate in order to achieve a common objective. To do so, they define a contract. In a contract, two organizations use artifacts that they have previously defined thanks to so-called *process services*. A process service provides details on the organization, its roles, available artifacts and available process fragments that can be used within the cooperative process. In a second time, organizations define a cooperative activity as a network of process services and synchronization points. They use a contract to define a set of clauses which is applied onto artifacts that will be share within the cooperative activity. This contract will be executed by a synchronization point.

The second step is devoted to the monitoring and the enforcement of the contract by synchronization points. A synchronization point takes inputs for some process services and provides outputs to the same or other process services in order to ensure that the cooperative activity executes as defined by the contract. Figure 1 details and summarizes the contract lifecycle. First, a contract describes the process services (1) that will be used for the cooperative activity and the synchronization points network (2). Then, the contract monitors and controls the cooperative activity, giving the ability to replan some of the activities since the synchronization point allows it (3). We will now describe precisely our contract model, and we will show how it applies on real world situations.

---

[1] A process service is an abstraction of an enterprise internal process. It is defined as a set of inputs, outputs and events to control its execution.

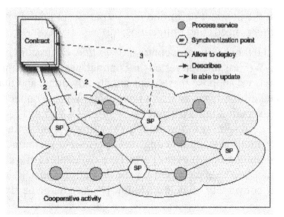

Fig. 1. Relation between contract and synchronization point.

3 The Contract Model

In order to create a synchronization points network as illustrated in figure 1, we propose the following contract model. Let us now introduce the synchronization point (SP) concept (see [11] for further details about the synchronization point model).

A SP relationship is the expression of a constraint between couple of objects (for instance, two processes, two roles, or two artifacts). A relationship, denoted *x rel y*, represents to some extent a contract between two objects and will be validated by one (or several) function called *Sat* functions. A *Sat* function takes in entry one or more objects or events. For example, one can have in entry either a document, or a date

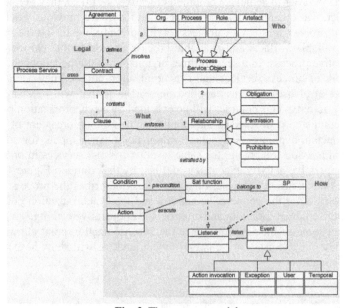

Fig. 2. The contract model

which will be used to establish if a deadline is respected or not. The result of a function is a boolean which determines whether the result of the function is correct or not, i.e. whether the SP relationship between artifact x and artifact y holds.

As depicted in figure 2, being given an intention to cooperate, we define a set of clauses that relate to relationships between partners. These relationships are satisfied by functions (the *Sat* functions) which belong to a synchronization point.

We now depict how the contract model is linked with the synchronization point model. From an abstract point of view, synchronization point information can be found in the four main components of a contract:

- the *Who* part defines the involved partners. A partner is involved within a contract thanks to the process services it has published and more precisely thanks to the objects these process services operate on. A partner is instantiated as a legal entity and it can be represented by a person or an organization. Then, an organization is involved with a given role that is defined later in the contract. This abstracts away from the activities which are defined for the corresponding roles.

- the *What* part contains the information about the contract subject, this means a set of clauses describing the core of the contract. This part defines the relationships to be satisfied. Relationships describe respectively obligations, permissions and prohibitions ([9]) of the involved partners. For instance, a relationship can express a QoS criteria such as cost. During the negotiation phase (which is not taken into account in our work), relationships are discussed and negotiated between partners. Then, satisfying the set of relationships is the goal of a SP that is created using contract definition. We use both these relationships and the *Sat* functions to define, deploy and execute synchronization activities.

- the *How* part describes the execution steps of a contract, i.e. the activities that have to be achieved. Contrary to the textual description of the relationships done in the What part, in this part, we define the relationships of a process services' objects and the way to satisfy them. It can be for instance the results (data or messages) to be delivered, deadlines, rules to apply in case of failure, access rights based on organizations, roles, persons, and so on. Relationships are used to generate synchronization point activities and in particular the ECA rules, the data transfers, the deadlines and the termination conditions of such cooperative activities.

- then, the fourth part of a contract, the *Legal* part, contains the textual clauses that address general agreements and conditions bound to a paper contract. It can be for instance references to existing applicable external contracts or legislation texts.

Taking a closer look, the contract model entities are as follows. An *organization* can take several different roles within a contract, depending on the process services it proposes. This allows for abstracting roles. Moreover, a person (not represented in the UML diagram) is bound to a role and contains information such as email, phone, address,... An organization can also describe a workflow management system, an application or any other end-point of a given activity. Every *relationship* is bound to a contract clause and defines an execution step. As said before, a relationship belongs to one of the three following classes: obligation, permission or prohibition and is related to objects published by process services. A *Sat* function belongs to a synchronization point, is associated to a relationship, is constrained by a *condition* and can execute an *action*. A condition is analyzed when an *event* is received by the synchronization point and by the *Sat* function. The different event types are temporal events (deadlines for instance), user events (deliver event for instance), action invocation event (raised by a *Sat* function for instance) and exception events (failure). Then, the *synchronization point* is in charge of the contract execution.

Our contract model is object-oriented and that makes possible to easily define actions that are linked to events. An action can also generate an event and this mechanism allows for chaining a set of actions, either in sequential or parallel mode. For instance, an object transfer will only be possible if and only if the object is *delivered* and if the associated *Sat* function is satisfied. To summarize, the contract execution goes through several steps that are:

- initially, a *contract template* is defined, that usually predefines the intention, means the "How" and the "Legal agreements" parts. Additionally, roles are defined and for each process service, a set of available objects. The template does not yet identify the exact obligations.

```
<contract id="#31459" name="contractName">
  <agreement>…</agreement>
  <cooperativeActivity>
    <processService name="renaultRE" ID="314"/>
    <processService name="peugeotRE ID="315""/>
  </cooperativeActivity>
  <relationships>
    <relationship>
      <obligation>
        <controlType>
          <event/>
          <condition/>
          <action/>
          <orderSet>
            <order source="" target=""/>
          </orderSet>
        </controlType>
        <dataType>
          <event/>
          <condition/>
          <action/>
        </dataType>
      </obligation>
      <permission>
        <event/>
        <condition/>
        <action/>
      </permission>
      <prohibition>
        <event/>
        <condition/>
        <filterType>roleFilter, processFilter</type>
        <references>r2filter.xsl</references>
      </prohibition>
    </relationship>
  </relationships>
</contract>
```

Fig. 3. A contract definition skeleton

- then, the "Who" and the "What" are defined. Partners are declared. This means that participants (resourceSet, resource, organizational unit, human or system) must be instantiated. In addition, the role of participants are defined. An activity has an owner (a person) that is a special participant that has the authority to declare the activity completed. A cooperative activity (i.e. a synchronization point) is set by a contract and includes a set of activities that can be declared as *process services*. A contract (see figure 3) defines then statements, including obligations, permissions or prohibitions. With regard to obligations, one distinguishes two cases: the satisfaction function relates to control (process service P completes, and the launching of the process service Q is dependent on the completion of process service P) and the data (the satisfaction function of a document must be checked). Permissions make it possible to specify the conditions the relationship objects must respect. Lastly, prohibitions make it possible to filter artifacts (documents more precisely) according to the rights of the synchronization point participants. With this information, we are able to create and deploy all the necessary synchronization points.

- afterwards, the contract is *executable*, i.e. in technical terms, it can be transferred to the synchronization point management system.

4   Contract Enforcement with a Synchronization Point

Let us first recall some of the concepts of the synchronization point (SP) model. The *synchronization point* uses an abstract view of organizations' internal processes, called process services. Then, a SP uses relationships in order to define the objects interactions that can arise within a cooperative activity, and it manages these relationships, giving the ability to check if a relationship is satisfied or not, to generate an action depending on the check result, or to replan the cooperative activity if necessary. We now briefly present these concepts and how a SP is using contract information to achieve its task.

```
<processService name="renaultRE" ID="#314">
  <organization>organization</organization>
  <service>
    <location>http://b2gether.loria.fr</location>
    <port>8083</port>
    <binding>wfms</binding>
  </service>
  <expires>date</expires>
  <coordinationMode>
    <isolation retriable="true"/> or
    <cooperative mode="compensatable" compensatableService="
  </coordinationMode>
  <participant>
    <resourceSet/>
    <resource/>
    <organizationalUnit/>
    <role/>
    <human/>
    <system/>
  </participant>
  <serviceOwner>
    participant that has the authority to declare the
    activity complete
  </serviceOwner>
  <inputContainer>
    <message/> or <data/>
  </inputContainer>
  <outputContainer>
    <message/> or <data/>
  </outputContainer>
</processService>
```

Fig. 4. Process service definition skeleton

4.1   Process Service

A *process service* is an abstract view of an existing process. A process service is defined by a location, a port and a binding. A *process service* also defines a coordination
mode that indicates the behavior of the internal activity with respect to its transactional properties. This mode could be either isolation or cooperative. If the mode is
isolation, a process service can be retriable. If the mode is cooperative, the process
service could be compensatable or pivot (this is compliant to the flexible transaction
model [10]). This means that this information helps us to compose process services
and to deal with exceptions or failures. Then, a process service lists its inputs (message or data) and the outcomes (message or data). The process service publishes a set
of objects that can be used by others and that can be involved within a cooperative
process. Objects can be an organization, process fragments, roles or artifacts (needed
or produced). The various possible roles are those internal to the organization but
restricted to those that the organization wishes to see appearing in the cooperation. It
can for example be the following roles: developer, task leader, task manager, writer...
A *process service* is connected to an application or a workflow management system
of an enterprise and its description is shown in figure 4.

4.2   From Contract Clauses to Relationships

A contract identifies what are the cooperative activities. For instance, a contract will
manage the following cooperative activity:

> « *CarBuilder1, CarBuilder2, EquipmentSupplier1 and EquipmentSupplier2
> collaborate to the design of a front automatic wiper system. This activity is
> collaborative and the result is a requirements document. The system uses the
> speed and the rain intensity to determine the swiping frequency.* »

- the activities of each partner,
- the participants and their roles,
- the deadlines, quality criteria,...
- a list of documents to be produced (both final and intermediate), and relationships that can exist between these documents,
- the documents available at the partners and associated access rights, obligations, permissions and prohibitions of each partner,
- what each participant is likely to offer.

An important part of a contract concerns who is involved within the cooperative
activity. Thus, activities, participants and roles are defined thanks to contract clauses.
A clause can take into account deadlines, documents to be produced, documents
available to partners, and obligations, permissions and prohibitions. We now refine
the description of the cooperative activity:

> « *EquipmentSupplier1 and EquipmentSupplier2 propose a joint requirements
> document that is enhanced or validated by CarBuilder1 and CarBuilder2.
> EquipmentSupplier1 and EquipmentSupplier2 are represented by two engi-*

*neers, while CarBuilder1 and CarBuilder2 are represented by a wiper system
project head. The validated document must be provided by the May 15, 2003.
Process service offered by partners is identified as "Requirement Edition".* »

Let us now present how we are transforming contract clauses into relationships. If
we consider the EquipmentSupplier1 organization, it will propose a requirements
document. This clause of the contract can be defined using the two following relationships. The first relationship expresses the fact that the process service $RE_{EquipmentSupplier1}$
is provided by EquipmentSupplier1, while the second says that the process service
$RE_{EquipmentSupplier1}$ is able to deliver the Requirements document. This is written:

rel1: organization(EquipmentSupplier1) *provides*
    organization(EquipmentSupplier1).processService($RE_{EquipmentSupplier1}$)

rel2: organization(EquipmentSupplier1).processService($RE_{EquipmentSupplier1}$) *delivers*
    organization(EquipmentSupplier1).processService($RE_{EquipmentSupplier1}$).artifact(Re-
    quirements)

rel3: organization(EquipmentSupplier2) *publishes*
    organization(EquipmentSupplier2).processService($RE_{EquipmentSupplier2}$)

rel4: organization(EquipmentSupplier2).processService($RE_{EquipmentSupplier2}$) *delivers*
    organization(EquipmentSupplier2).processService($RE_{EquipmentSupplier2}$).artifact(Re-
    quirements)

One of the objective of the cooperation between the two organizations is to obtain
a common version of the Requirements document. This criteria is described in our
model by a new relationship named *rel5*. In order to simplify the expressions, we omit
object naming. We write:

rel5: EquipmentSupplier1.$RE_{EquipmentSupplier1}$.Requirements *consistent with*
    EquipmentSupplier2.$RE_{EquipmentSupplier2}$.Requirements

Equipment suppliers propose solutions that meet their own internal developments.
In order to access available processes, we use the *process services* of the organizations. This means that both EquipmentSupplier1 and EquipmentSupplier2 provide a
process service that is in charge of an activity "Requirements edition". This activity is
an abstract activity that can be connected to an application, a workflow management
system or a human activity. In our example, the process service is bound to the corresponding activity of each equipment supplier, and the result of this process service is
the requirements document. A third process service common to the two organizations
is dedicated to the review of the two documents. Then, we define a new relationship
that stipulates that the document must be delivered before the May 15, 2003:

rel6: EquipmentSupplier1.$RE_{EquipmentSupplier1}$.Requirements *deadline* date(05/15/2003)

Once the relationships are defined, we associate the functions that are used to satisfy them. This can also be filters to manage access rights to documents. For instance,
we can express that when EquipmentSupplier1 publishes the requirements document,
this document is filtered according to the relationship *rel2*. Relationship *rel6* is associated to an obligation clause that must also be managed with a *Sat* function. Using
relationships, a contract becomes a set of ECA rules that are used within a synchronization point. Now, we detail how to translate clauses to ECA rules.

4.3   From Relationships to ECA Rules

Events

Events allow for specifying what are the changes that arrive within a *synchronization point*, and the reaction to undertake. For instance, a document that has not been delivered in time is an event. Another type of event is when a document is correctly delivered. A third type of event is the application of filters. When a MEP (Message Exchange Pattern, see [11]) is executed, several events are produced. A synchronization point can recover these events and execute a set of actions. For instance, there is several possible *Sat* functions that can be associated to a relationship. Possible events coming from the evaluation of *Sat* function are *trueEvent*, *falseEvent* and *NAEvent* (non available event). This allows the synchronization point to react to a given situation. The events are captured by the synchronization point thanks to the presence of *listeners* to which the synchronization point subscribes (see figure 2).

Let's suppose that we are May 16, 2003 and that the Requirements document was not delivered by EquipmentSupplier1. The *Sat* function associated to *rel6* cannot be satisfied by the system, so an exception is raised. The event is a temporal event, the condition is the fact that the document was not delivered, and an action is executed (either a corrective action or the replaning of the delivery date for instance). We can also generate other rules. For instance, rules can be preventive actions or corrective actions. Corrective actions are useful when replanification is not really necessary. Here is an example that allows for having a view of the situation before the deadline:

> **Event**: *user::check(SPrepository.requirements)*
> **Condition**: *delivered(SPrepository.requirements)*
> **Action**: *check(SPrepository.requirements)*

This rule works as follows: user wants to check the requirements documents within the SP repository. It fires an event by clicking on a button. The condition associated is that the document is ready to be checked, means that the document has been delivered. If the deliver has been done, the action to be executed is the effective consistency check (see *rel5*) in order to accept the document.

An other example is the following immediate corrective action:

> **Event**: *user::check(SPrepository.requirements)*
> **Condition**: *not available(SPrepository.requirements)*
> **Action**: *user::urgentRequest(SPrepository.requirements)*

With regards to permissions and prohibitions, one can model the access to the documents, such as for example: CarBuilder1 can access the Requirements document. The corresponding ECA rule can be written:

> **Event**: *user::read(SPrepository.requirements)*
> **Condition**: *hasRights(user)*
> **Action**: *download(SPrepository.requirements)*

A filter is a **transformation** applied to an object depending on the requester. For instance, the requester within the *synchronization point* context is either a role (this means a user) or a process service. This is the reason why we have two types of filters: *role filters* that are applied for a given role and *process filters* that are applied for a given process. We do not propose organization filters because they are subsumed by process filters, nor user filters because the role is an abstraction that alleviated from all the problems of directly managing users within the synchronization point. We can show a simple example of the filtering function. Let's say we have the following filters:

$$\text{filter f1: CarBuilder1.RE}_{\text{CarBuilder1}} \cdot x \rightarrow \text{CarBuilder2.RE}_{\text{CarBuilder2}}$$
$$\text{filter f2: CarBuilder1.RE}_{\text{CarBuilder1}} \cdot x \rightarrow \text{CarBuilder2.RE}_{\text{CarBuilder2}} \cdot \text{project manager}$$
$$\text{filter f3: CarBuilder1.RE}_{\text{CarBuilder1}} \cdot x \rightarrow \text{CarBuilder2.RE}_{\text{CarBuilder2}} \cdot \text{engineer}$$

The first filter applies when the process $\text{RE}_{\text{CarBuilder2}}$ belonging to CarBuilder2 desires to access the artifact x belonging the CarBuilder1Õs process $\text{RE}_{\text{CarBuilder1}}$. That is a *process filter*. The second filter applies when the user with role project manager in the process $\text{RE}_{\text{CarBuilder2}}$ belonging to CarBuilder2 desires to access the artifact x belonging to the CarBuilder1Õs process $\text{RE}_{\text{CarBuilder1}}$. That's a *role filter*, as the third filter.

Discussion

If we summarize the behavior of the synchronization point including ECA rules, we get the following scenario. Let us suppose a *synchronization point* (denoted $\text{RE}_{\text{EquipmentSupplier1}} \infty \text{RE}_{\text{EquipmentSupplier2}}$) coordinating two process services $\text{RE}_{\text{EquipmentSupplier1}}$ and $\text{RE}_{\text{EquipmentSupplier2}}$. These two process services respectively work on artifacts x and y. We can have the following relationships set R:

$$R = \{ \quad \textit{rel1}: \text{P has the rights to deliver the artifact } x$$
$$\textit{rel2}: \text{Q has the rights to deliver the artifact } y$$
$$\textit{rel3}: x \cap y \neq \varnothing$$
$$\textit{rel4}: \text{RE}_{\text{EquipmentSupplier1}} \infty \text{RE}_{\text{EquipmentSupplier2}} \cdot x \textit{ deadline } \text{date}(05/15/2003)$$
$$\textit{rel5}: \text{RE}_{\text{EquipmentSupplier1}} \infty \text{RE}_{\text{EquipmentSupplier2}} \cdot y \textit{ deadline } \text{date}(05/15/2003)$$
$$\textit{rel6}: \text{RE}_{\text{EquipmentSupplier1}} \infty \text{RE}_{\text{EquipmentSupplier2}} \cdot \text{rel3} \textit{ deadline } \text{date}(05/22/2003)$$
$$\}$$

In order to simplify the example, we only express a subset of the overall relationships set. The *synchronization point* will ensure that the relationships set R will be satisfied, or if not, it will help to replan or to adapt the cooperative context. *Sat* functions are translated as ECA rules, and the *synchronization point* will use these rules such as:

Event	Condition	Action
User:: $\text{RE}_{\text{EquipmentSupplier1}}.\text{deliver}(\chi)$	res = authorization($\text{RE}_{\text{EquipmentSupplier1}}.$ deliver$_\chi$)	Notification R1 = res
User:: $\text{RE}_{\text{EquipmentSupplier2}}.\text{deliver}(\gamma)$	res = authorization($\text{RE}_{\text{EquipmentSupplier2}}.$ deliver$_\gamma$)	Notification R2 = res
Action :: R1, R2	res = R1 $\wedge$ R2 $\wedge (\chi \cap \gamma \neq \emptyset)$	Notification R3 = res $\chi \cap \gamma \in \text{RE}_{\text{EquipmentSupplier1}} \infty$ üüü$\text{RE}_{\text{EquipmentSupplier2}}$
Temporal :: SP.date1	res = $\chi \in \text{RE}_{\text{EquipmentSupplier1}} \infty \text{RE}_{\text{EquipmentSupplier2}} \wedge$ (date1 $< 05/15/2003$)	Notification R4 = res
Temporal :: SP.date2	res = $\gamma \in \text{RE}_{\text{EquipmentSupplier1}} \infty \text{RE}_{\text{EquipmentSupplier2}} \wedge$ (date1 $< 05/15/2003$)	Notification R5 = res
Temporal :: SP.date3	res = (R3 == false) $\wedge$ (date3 $< 05/22/2003$)	Replan($\text{RE}_{\text{EquipmentSupplier1}} \infty \text{RE}_{\text{EquipmentSupplier2}}$)

As the previous table shows it, an action can generate an event. Then, this event can be treated in a new ECA rule. For instance, if the R4 rule is false, we can generate a new action which enforces the deliver of the object x. In the same way, the condition can be optional. Thus, we can have a new ECA rule:

Event	Condition	Action
Action :: R4	res = (not(R4))	UrgentRequest(RE$_{EquipmentSupplier2}$. ^{x})

We classify the events according to three categories: *temporal events* (e.g. a date), *user events* (e.g. the user initiates an event such as a deliver), and *action events* (e.g. events that are issued by an action such as a notification or a request). In our example, the User::processService.deliver(x) event is an event that pertains to the user class. On the other hand, the event Action::R1,R2 is an event that pertains to the action class. Finally, the event Temporal::SP.date3 is a temporal event.

5 Implementation Using RDF, RDFS, and RuleML

We implement our contract model within the *synchronization point* architecture. A contract is a XML document that is parsed and that instantiate a knowledge base designed with Protégé 2000. We get two files, a RDF document and a RDFS document. Then, we query the knowledge base thanks to RuleML rules and the OntoJava crosscompiler. The contract definition document includes all the information necessary to the execution of the *synchronization point*, such as the relationships and the *Sat* functions for instance. Given these relationships, we are able to associate the obligations, the permissions and the prohibitions.

```
<B2Gether_KB:PAL-QUERY rdf:about="B2GetherKB;B2GetherKB_00080"
 a:_pal_name="hasRight" rdfs:label="B2GetherKB_00080">
<a:_pal_description>
 Returns a Role_Mapping instance if it exists a given role name
 in a given organization with rights for doing a given action in
 the context of a given SP
</a:_pal_description>
<a:_pal_range>
 (defrange ?Role_Mapping :FRAME Role_Mapping)
 (defrange ?Right :FRAME Right)
 (defrange ?Org :FRAME Organization)
 (defrange ?SP :FRAME Synchronization_Point)
</a:_pal_range>
<a:_pal_statement>
 (findall ?Role_Mapping
   (and (Name ?Role_Mapping "Renault Project Manager")
     (exists ?Right
       (and  (SP_ROLE ?Right (SP_ROLE ?Role_Mapping))
         (Action ?Right "DELIVER")))
     (exists ?Org
       (and (Org ?Role_Mapping ?Org)
         (Name ?Org "Renault")))
     (exists ?SP
       (and (Roles ?SP ?Role_Mapping)
         (Name ?SP "SP1")))))
</a:_pal_statement>
</B2Gether_KB:PAL-QUERY>
```

Fig. 5. A PAL query.

Protégé is a tool that facilitates the construction of knowledge bases in a principle fashion from reusable components and the construction of domain ontologies. Protégé was used to create the ontology (RDFS and RDF format) and the RDFS and RDF files output by Protégé serve as the input of OntoJava. Ontojava is a cross compiler that automatically maps RDF facts, ontologies expressed in RDFS, rules and constraints represented in RuleML ([2]) into a Java object-oriented database. Here is an example (figure 5) of a RDF query that allows for testing if an organization pertains to a SP and have access rights to deliver a document within the SP repository. It is written in PAL (Protégé Axiom Language) language.

During its execution, the SP queries the knowledge base in order to guarantee that obligations, permissions and prohibitions related to a given relationship are ensured. The use of the knowledge base and RuleML enables us to manage ECA rules and temporal events. The overall architecture is described on figure 6.

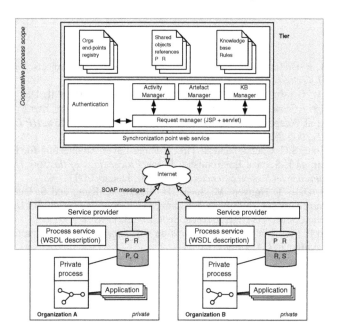

Fig. 6. Web services architecture of the contract model.

6   Conclusion

Contracts are a big issue in cross-organizational contexts. There are many papers on how to mediate a contract ([12] proposed a way to represent the contents of business contracts and contract negotiation based on event semantics) and how to support contract enactments with workflows. There are less works on how to use a contract to deploy an architecture and enforce a contract. CrossFlow ([8]) models virtual enterprises and proposes a contract model, but it does not support ECA rules based on cross-organizational events and just monitor workflow status. The COSMOS project ([7]) models combination of objects but it doesn't address contract enforcement issues. In eFlow ([3]), contract as a deployment tool and contract enforcement are not considered.

This paper has presented a model for contracts and how this model helps to instantiate an architecture for cross-organizational cooperative processes. We have shown how our contract model is able to describe cooperative activities and how it allows for enacting and enforcing the contract. The model, associated with the synchronization point model, makes it possible to derive from a set of relationships a set of ECA rules that are managed within a knowledge base. The use of standard technologies such as XML, SOAP, WebService, RDF and RuleML facilitates the interoperability and enhance the enforcement of a contract across organization boundaries.

References

1. S. Angelov, P. Grefen; B2B eContract Handling – A Survey of Projects, Papers and Standards. *CTIT Technical Report 01-21*, University of Twente, 2001.
2. H. Boley, B. Grosof, M. sintek, S. Tabet, and G. Wagner. RuleML DEsign, September 2002. http://www.dfki.uni-kl.de/ruleml/indesign.html
3. F. Casati, et al. Adaptive and Dynamic Service Composition in eFlow. *HP Lab's Technical Report HPL-2000-39*, March 2000.
4. D. K.W. Chiu, S.C. Cheung, and S. Till. A Three Layer Architecture for E-Contract Enforcement in an E-Service Environment. In the *Proceedings of the 36th Hawaii International Conference on System Sciences (HICSS-36)*, January 2003.
5. A. Dan, D. Dias, T. Nguyen, M. Sachs, H. Shaikh, R. King, and S. Duri. The Coyote Project: Framework for Multi-party E-Commerce, *Proceedings of the 7th Delos Workshop on Electronic Commerce*, Crete, Greece, Sept. 21–23, 1998.
6. A. Dan and F. Parr. Long running application models and cooperating monitors. In *HPTS workshop*, Asilomar, CA, 1999.
7. F. Griffel. Electronic Contracting with COSMOS Ð How to Establish, Negotiate and Execute Electronic Contracts on the Internet. *2nd Int. Enterprise Distributed Object Computing Workshop (EDOC '98)*, pp. 46–55, 1998.
8. Y. Hoffner, H. Ludwig, C. Gülcü, and P. Grefen, Architecture for Cross-Organisational Business Processes, Proceedings *2nd International Workshop on Advanced Issues of ECommerce and Web-Based Information Systems*, Milpitas, CA, USA, 2000, pp. 2–11.
9. O. Marjanovic, and Z. Milosevic. Towards formal modeling of e-Contracts, *Proceedings of 5th IEEE International Enterprise Distributed Object Computing Conference*, 2001.
10. S. Mehrotra, R. Rastogi, A. Silberschatz, and H.F. Korth. A Transaction Model for Multidatabase Systems. In *Proceedings of International Conference on Distributed Computing Systems – IDCDCS 92*, June 1992.
11. O.Perrin, F. Wynen, J. Bitcheva, and C. Godart. A Model to Support Collaborative Work in Virtual Enterprises. In *BPM 2003, International Conference on Business Process Management, On the Application of Formal Methods to "Process-Aware" Information Systems* (LNCS 2678). Eindhoven, The Netherlands. June 26–27, 2003.
12. Y.H. Tan, and W. Thoen. Using Event Semantics for Modeling Contracts. *Proceedings of the 35th Hawaii International Conference on System Sciences*, pp. 2198–2206, 2002.

A Reputation-Based Approach to Preserving Privacy in Web Services

Abdelmounaam Rezgui, Athman Bouguettaya, and Zaki Malik

E-Commerce & E-Government Research Lab
Department of Computer Science, Virginia Tech
7054 Haycock Road, Falls Church, VA 22043
{rezgui,athman,zaki}@vt.edu
http://www.nvc.cs.vt.edu/eceg

Abstract. The Web is an environment where users, Web services, and software agents exchange sensitive personal information. This calls for enforceable strategies to preserve people's privacy. In most solutions, users define their respective privacy requirements and must themselves make the decision about information disclosure. Personal judgments are usually made based on the *sensitivity* of the information and the *reputation* of the party to which the information is to be disclosed. The emerging semantic Web is expected to make the challenge more acute in the sense that it would provide a whole infrastructure for the automation of semantics in the Web. On the privacy front, this means that privacy invasion would net more quality and sensitive personal information. In this paper, we propose a reputation-based approach to automate privacy enforcement in a semantic Web environment. We propose a *reputation management system* that monitors Web services and *collects*, *evaluates*, *updates*, and *disseminates* information related to their reputation for the purpose of privacy protection.

1 Introduction

The Web has become an immense information repository with perpetual expansion and ubiquity as two of its intrinsic characteristics. With the recent flurry in Web technologies, the "data-store" Web is steadily evolving to a more "vibrant" environment where *passive* data sources coexist with *active* services that access these data sources and inter-operate with limited or no intervention from users. The Web has also brought a new *non-deterministic* paradigm in accessing information. In traditional, closed, deterministic multi-user systems (e.g., enterprise networks), data sources are accessible only by a few *known* users with a set of predefined privileges. On the contrary, the Web is an open environment where information is accessible (or potentially accessible) by far more numerous and a priori *unknown* users. The problem of access control in the open Web environment is not another "flavor" of the problem of access control that the security community has extensively studied in the context of closed systems. In fact, solutions resulting from that research are only of peripheral consequences to the

B. Benatallah and M.-C. Shan (Eds.): TES 2003, LNCS 2819, pp. 91–103, 2003.
© Springer-Verlag Berlin Heidelberg 2003

problem of protecting information in the Web context. For example, access control models (e.g., RBAC, TBAC, MAC, DAC [4]) that work for resources shared by a well-known, relatively small set of users are obviously of little help when the resources are information that may be accessed by millions of *random* Web clients. The problem of protecting Web-accessible information becomes more compelling when the information are *private*, i.e., related to *personal* aspects such as the health records of a hospital's patients, employment history of job seekers, etc. Accessing personal information through the Web clearly raises legitimate privacy concerns that call for effective, reliable, and scalable privacy preserving solutions.

Preserving privacy is a key requirement for the Web to reach its full potential. Recent studies and surveys show that Web users' concerns about their privacy are key factors behind their reluctance in using the Web to conduct transactions that require them to provide sensitive personal information. However, despite the recent growing interest in the problem of privacy, little progress appears to have been achieved. One reason is the excessive trend to assimilate privacy to the wide spectrum of security-related problems. Although not completely unrelated, the two problems of privacy and security are, essentially, different. Much of the research in securing shared resources views security as an "inward" concept where different users have different access rights to different shared objects. Contrarily to the concept of security, we see privacy as an "outward" concept in the sense that an information exposes a set of rules (i.e., privacy policies) to users. These rules determine if and how any arbitrary user may access that information. In contrast to typical shared information, private information is, generally, related to an individual who normally *owns* the information and has the authority to specify its associated *privacy policy*.

Solutions to the problem of preserving privacy in the Web may not be conceivable or even feasible if not developed for and using tomorrow's Web building blocks: Web services. These are, essentially, applications that expose interfaces through which they may be automatically invoked by Web clients. Many of the traditional problems of the Web have found elegant and effective solutions developed around Web services and a growing number of Web-based applications are being developed using Web services. Examples include health care systems, digital government, and B2B applications. In their pre-Web versions, these applications were based on an information flow where users divulge their private information only to known, trusted parties. The recent introduction of Web services as key components in building these applications has introduced new types of transactions where users frequently disclose sensitive information to Web-based entities (e.g., government agencies, businesses) that are unknown and/or whose trustworthiness may not be easily determined.

The privacy problem is likely to become more challenging with the envisioned *semantic Web* where machines become much better able to process and understand the data that they merely display at present [3]. To enable this vision, "intelligent" (mobile or fixed) software agents will carry out sophisticated tasks for their users. In that process, these agents will manipulate and exchange extensive amounts of personal information and replace human users in making decisions regarding their personal data. The challenge is then to develop agents that autonomously enforce the privacy of their respective users, i.e., autonomously determine, according to the current context, what information is private.

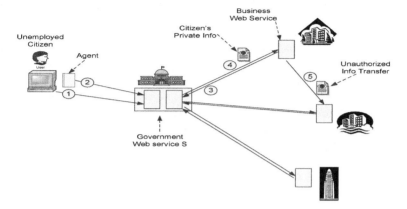

Fig. 1. A scenario of information exchange in the semantic Web.

Consider the example of a Digital Government (DG) infrastructure that offers a Web-based service S through which citizens access social and health plans (Figure 1). Part of the service's mission is to assist unemployed citizens in job placement and to deliver other related social and educational benefits. An unemployed citizen subscribes to the service S and delegates to his semantic Web agent the task of permanently interacting with the service S to look for potential job opportunities and any other government-sponsored benefits destined to jobless citizens. As part of this interaction, the citizen's agent must submit personal information to the service S (e. g., employment history, family and health information). For the job placement plan to be effective, the government may offer incentives to businesses that commit to hire 20% of their employees from citizens subscribed in the government plan. Businesses interested in these incentives deploy Web services that a government semantic Web agent Ag periodically invokes to learn about any new job opportunities. This agent exploits these job opportunities on behalf of the citizens who qualify for the plan. In this process, it may be necessary for the agent Ag to transfer personal data to some of these external services. In some cases, these services are unknown to Ag, i.e., Ag does not have any history of prior interactions with these services. This obviously raises the problem of *trust* in an environment where semantic Web agents and Web services interact with no or limited interaction history. The challenge is to, automatically, determine which information may be disclosed to which services.

The previous example highlights the need for a solution that enables a privacy preserving interaction amongst semantic Web agents and Web services. We believe that the linchpin of such a solution is a reliable *reputation* management mechanism that provides an *objective* evaluation of the *trust* that may be put in any given Web service. This mechanism must have functionalities to *collect, evaluate, update*, and *disseminate* information related to the reputation of Web services. Moreover, this mechanism must meet two requirements:

Verifiability. Web services may expose *arbitrary* privacy policies to their users. Currently, users are left with no means to verify whether or not Web services actually abide by the terms of their privacy policies. Ideally, a privacy preserving infrastructure must provide a practical means to check whether advertised privacy policies are actually enforced.

Automatic Enforcement. In the envisioned semantic Web, software agents will have to make *judgments* about whether or not to release their users' private data to other agents and Web services. Thus, a privacy preserving solution must not require an extensive involvement of users.

In this paper, we propose a reputation-based solution to the problem of preserving privacy in the semantic Web. The solution is based on two principles. First, the reputation of Web services is quantified such that high reputation is attributed to services that are not the source of any "leakage" of private information. Second, the traditional invocation scheme of Web services (discovery-selection-invocation) is extended into a reputation-based invocation scheme where the reputation of a service is also a parameter in the discovery-selection processes.

The paper is organized as follows. Section 2 introduces the key concepts used throughout the paper. In Section 3, we present a general model for reputation management in a semantic Web environment. In Section 4, we describe an architecture for deploying the proposed general model. In Section 5, we report on some research work that has addressed various aspects of trust and reputation in the Web. Section 6 concludes the paper.

2   Services, Agents, and Attribute Ontology

In this section, we set the framework for our discussion. We first clearly define the terms of *Web services* and *Web agents*. We then introduce the two concepts of *attribute ontology* and *information flow difference* on which is built our reputation management model described in Section 3.

2.1   Services and Agents

In the envisioned semantic Web, two types of entities interact: Web services and Web agents. The former are applications that may be invoked through the Web. For instance, in our DG example, a business may deploy a service that provides the list of current job opportunities. Services may have access to private information. Upon invocation, they may also *deliver* private information. In the dynamic Web environment, the number of Web agents and services may not be known *a priori*. In this paper, we consider a dynamic set S of Web services that interact with a potential exchange of private information. Web agents are "intelligent" software modules that are responsible of some specific tasks (e. g., search for an appropriate job for a given unemployed citizen in the previous DG example).

2.2   Attribute Ontology

An operation of a Web service may be viewed as a "processing" unit that consumes input parameters and generates output parameters. The invocation of a given operation may potentially result in privacy violation when one or more of the output parameters correspond to private attributes (e. g., Last Name, Address, Phone Number). A requirement for *automating* privacy preservation is to formally capture any possible leakage of sensitive information that may result from service invocation. Our approach is based on a concept called *Information Flow Difference* that provides an estimate of services' potential to release private information. The definition of this concept is based on a *scaled attribute ontology* that captures two important characteristics of attributes, namely, *synonymy* and *privacy significance order.*

Synonymy. Consider two operations that both expect as their input a person's home phone number and return the same person's family name. The description of the first operation names the parameters: PhoneNumber and FamilyName while the description of the second operation names these parameters: PhoneNumber and LastName. Clearly, from a privacy perspective, these two operations are *equivalent.* This is due to the *semantic* equivalence of FamilyName and LastName. To capture this equivalence amongst attributes, the proposed attribute ontology defines sets of *synonymous* attributes. The following are examples of sets of synonymous attributes:

$T_1 = \{$ FamilyName, LastName, Surname, Name $\}$
$T_2 = \{$ PhoneNumber, HomePhoneNmuber, ContactNumber, Telephone, Phone $\}$
$T_3 = \{$ Address, HomeAddress, Location $\}$

Privacy Significance Order. Private attributes do not have the same sensitivity. For example, most people consider their social security number as being more sensitive than their phone number. To capture the difference in attributes' sensitivity, we define the *Privacy Significance Level* as a function defined over the set of attributes and that, given an attribute a, associates a number $PSL(a) \in \mathbb{N}$ that reflects attribute a's significance from a privacy perspective. For any two given attributes a and b, a is said to be of higher privacy significance if its privacy significance level, $PSL(a)$, is greater than b's privacy significance level, $PSL(b)$. This establishes a *privacy significance order* between any pair of attributes. Of course, this order may not be universally valid. For example, two different persons may rank two attributes in different orders. Our approach assumes that, statistically, any two attributes are ranked consistently by a majority of individuals. However, the solution may readily be extended to employ *user-defined* attribute ontologies where *users* specify the sensitivity of the different attributes.

2.3   Information Flow Difference

Let s_i be a Web service in the set S and Op_j an operation of the service s_i that has p *input* attributes and q *output* attributes. Let $Input(Op_j)$ denote the set of input attributes for operation Op_j, and $Output(Op_j)$ denote the set of output attributes for operation Op_j.

Definition 1: The *Information Flow Difference IFD* of operation Op_j is defined by:

$$IFD(Op_j) = \sum_{a \in Input(Op_j)} PSL(a) - \sum_{a \in Output(Op_j)} PSL(a)$$

Example 1: Assume that Op_j has as its input the attribute SSN and as its output the attribute PhoneNumber. The values of the function PSL for attributes SSN and PhoneNumber are respectively 6 and 4. In this example, $IFD(Op_j) = 2$. The meaning of this (positive) value is that an invocation of operation Op_j must provide information (SSN) that is *more* sensitive than the returned information (PhoneNumber). Intuitively, the *Information Flow Difference* captures the degree of "permeability" of a given operation, i.e., the difference (in the privacy significance level) between what it gets (i.e., input attributes) and what it discloses (i.e., output attributes).*Box*

In general, positive values for the function IFD do not necessarily indicate that invocations of the corresponding operation actually preserve privacy. In the previous example, a service invoking Op_j may still be unauthorized to access the phone number although it already knows a more sensitive information (i.e., the social security number). However, invocations of operations with negative values of the function IFD necessarily disclose information that is *more* sensitive than their input attributes. They must, therefore, be considered as cases of privacy violation.

Definition 2: A service $s \in S$ is said to have an information flow that violates privacy if and only if it has an operation Op such that: $IFD(Op) < 0$.

Definition 3: The *Information Flow Difference* of a Web service s is the sum of the IFD's of all of its operations.

3   General Model for Reputation Management

In the previous section, we introduced the concepts of *attribute ontology* and *information flow difference*. We also showed how these concepts are used to capture the sensitivity of the private information flowing to and from Web services. The incentive behind introducing these concepts is to develop mechanisms that *automatically* quantify services' reputation. In this section, we present a general model for a semantic Web environment where interactions are based on reputation. The objective of the proposed model is to enable Web services and agents to interact in an environment where the decision to disclose private sensitive information becomes an *automatic, reputation-driven* process that does not require the intervention of human users. Our approach mimics the real life business and social environments where (good) *reputation* is a prerequisite (or, sometimes, the reason) for any transactions. The basic idea is to deploy a *reputation management system* that continuously monitors Web services, assesses their reputation and disseminates information about services' reputation to (other) services and agents. To each Web service, we associate a *reputation* that reflects a *common* perception of other Web services towards that service. In practice, different criteria may be important in determining the reputation of a Web service. For example, the reputation of a service that searches for "best" airline fares clearly depends on whether or not it actually delivers the best fares. In this paper, services' reputation depends only on the effectiveness of their enforcement of the privacy of their users. To simplify our discussion, we will use "services" instead of "services and agents" in any context where "services" is an *active* entity (e. g., "service" s invokes operation Op). We propose five criteria that are the basis in the process of reputation assessment.

3.1   Criteria for Reputation Assessment

To automate the assessment of services' reputation, we identified a set of criteria that: (i) reflect the "conduct" of services with regard to how they protect private information that they collect from users, and (ii) may be automatically and *objectively* assessed.

Degree of Permeability. We previously introduced the function IFD that determines services' *Degree of Permeability* (DoP), i.e., their proneness to the disclosure of sensitive information. We also use this function to rank Web services according to their DoP. For example, let s_1 and s_2 be two Web services. If $IFD(s_1) < IFD(s_2) < 0$, then s_2 is said to be less permeable than service s_1.

Authentication-Based Disclosure of Information. Web services use different approaches to authenticate the senders of the received requests. The reputation of a service clearly depends on the strength of the mechanism used to authenticate clients. For example, the reputation-based infrastructure may adopt the rule that services using Kerberos-based authentication schemes have better reputation than services that use schemes based on user/password authentication.

Across-User Information Disclosure. In some situations, a Web service may properly authenticate its users but has the potential of across-user information disclosure. This characteristic corresponds to the situation where the service discloses private information about *any* valid user to *any* valid user. This flaw in the behavior of Web services must be considered in the process of evaluating services' reputation.

Use of Encryption Mechanisms. This criterion captures the efficiency of the encryption mechanisms used by Web services. For example, a service whose messages are encrypted using a 128-bit encryption scheme may be ranked better than another service whose messages are encrypted using a 64-bit encryption scheme.

Seniority. This criterion reflects the simple "fact" that, similarly to businesses in the real world, trust in Web services increases with the length of their "lifetime".

If the *dates of deployment*, d_1 and d_2, of two services s_1 and s_2, are known, then the reputation of s_1 may be considered better than that of s_2 if d_1 precedes d_2.

3.2   A Weighted Definition of Reputation

We now present a formal definition of the reputation of Web services. Let $\mathcal{R}$ be the set of m criteria used in the process of reputation assessment ($m = 5$ in the proposed list of criteria) and c_i^j the value of criterion c^j for service s_i. The values of these m criteria are normalized such that:

$$\forall s_i \in \mathcal{S}, \forall c^j \in \mathcal{R}, 0 \leq c_i^j \leq 1$$

In practice, the criteria used in reputation assessment are not equally important or relevant to privacy enforcement. For example, the *seniority* criterion is clearly less important than the *degree of permeability*. To each criterion $c^j \in \mathcal{R}$, we associate a weight w_j that is proportional to its relative importance as compared to the other criteria in $\mathcal{R}$. A Web service's reputation may then be defined as follows:

Definition 4: For a given service $s_i \in \mathcal{S}$, the reputation function is defined by:

$$Reputation(s_i) = \sum_{k=1}^{m} w_k . c_i^k \qquad (1)$$

The intuitive meaning of formula (1) is that the reputation of service s_i is the weighted sum of its performances along each of the considered reputation criteria.

4   The Architecture

We now describe the architecture (Figure 2) supporting the proposed reputation model. The proposed architecture has three main components: the *Reputation Manager*, the *Probing Agents*, and *Service Wrappers*.

4.1   Reputation Manager

The *Reputation Manager* (RM) is the core of the reputation system. It is a *unanimously trusted* party responsible of (i) collecting, (ii) evaluating, (iii) updating, and (iv) disseminating reputation information. To understand the operation of the *Reputation Manager*, consider the following typical scenario enabled by this architecture. A Web service s_i (or an agent) is about to send a message M containing private information to a Web service s_j. Before sending M to s_j, the service s_i submits to the *Reputation Manager* a request asking for the reputation of service s_j. If a value of $Reputation(s_j)$ is available and accurate (i.e., reasonably recent), the RM answers s_i's request with a message containing that value. Based on the value of the received reputation and its local policy, the

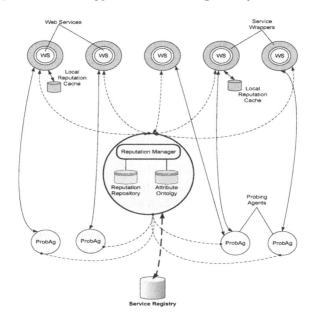

Fig. 2. Architecture of the reputation management system.

service s_i may or may not decide to send the message M to s_j. If the reputation of s_j is outdated or not available (i.e., has not been previously assessed), the *Reputation Manager* initiates a *reputation assessment process* that involves one of a set of *Probing Agents*. To assess the reputation of a Web service s_i, the RM collects information that are necessary to evaluate the given criteria for reputation assessment (discussed in Section 3). The evaluation of most of these criteria is based on the (syntactic) description of the service s_j. For example, to evaluate the *degree of permeability* of s_j, the RM reads s_j's description (by accessing the appropriate service registry), computes $IFD(s_j)$ (s_j's *Information Flow Difference*), and maps that value to the corresponding *degree of permeability*. The RM maintains an *attribute ontology* that is used in computing the degree of permeability of the different Web services. Once the DoP of service s_j is evaluated, it is stored in the local *Reputation Repository*. The other criteria may be obtained using similar processes. Once all the criteria are evaluated, the RM computes s_j's reputation (as described in Section 3), stores the obtained value in the *Reputation Repository*, and sends it to the service s_i.

4.2   Anonymous Probing Agents

Services' reputations are not static values. Different types of updates may affect a service's reputation. The *Reputation Manager* must permanently maintain an accurate perception of services' reputations. Two alternatives are possible for a *continuous monitoring* of Web services. In the first, the *Reputation Manager* permanently retrieves services' descriptions and issues requests to services to collect the information necessary to evaluate the different criteria of reputation assessment. This approach is clearly inadequate. First, it leads to a huge traffic at the RM. Second, *malicious* Web services may easily identify requests originating at the RM and reply with messages that do not reflect their actual behavior. To overcome these drawbacks, our solution deploys a set of η *probing agents* (or, *probers*) that collect information necessary to the process of reputation assessment and share it with the *Reputation Manager*. These agents are responsible of permanently monitoring the services and reporting the collected information to the *Reputation Manager*. These agents are not co-located with the RM and are, *a priori*, anonymous to the Web services being monitored, i.e., services may not distinguish probing requests from ordinary requests.

Services with *low* reputation present a greater potential for unauthorized information disclosure. Therefore, the process of monitoring Web services must be distributed such that services with *low* reputation get probed more aggressively and more frequently. To meet this requirement, services are partitioned into δ ($\delta \in \mathbb{N}$) clusters $C_0, C_1, .., C_{\delta-1}$ such that services in the same cluster have "comparable" reputations. δ is called the *clustering factor*. Formally,

$$\forall C_j, s_i \in C_j \implies \frac{j}{\delta} < Reputation(s_i) \leq \frac{j+1}{\delta} \tag{2}$$

To enable a variable probing policy, we associated η_i *probing agents* to each cluster C_i ($\delta \leq \eta = \sum_{k=0}^{\delta-1} \eta_k$). A reasonable distribution of the η probers on the δ clusters is one in which:

$$\forall i, 0 \leq i < \delta, \overline{\mathcal{R}}_i.\eta_i = \alpha$$

where: α is a constant and $\overline{\mathcal{R}}_i$ is the average reputation of services in cluster C_i, i.e.,

$$\overline{\mathcal{R}}_i = \frac{\sum_{s_k \in C_i} Reputation(s_k)}{\delta_i}$$

where δ_i is the size of cluster C_i. Probing agents associated with cluster C_i continuously and randomly invoke services in C_i to determine the values of the different criteria in the set $\mathcal{R}$. In the monitoring process, they may also have to access service registries and retrieve service descriptions.

An advantage of this clusters-based monitoring approach is that it is flexible and may be easily "tuned" to accommodate *loose* and *strict* privacy enforcement. For example, the parameter α may be set higher (for all clusters) to achieve stricter privacy control. Also, if a specific cluster or set of clusters (e. g., corresponding to businesses with low reputation) turn out to be more prone to information disclosure than others, only their probing agents may be instructed to switch to a more aggressive monitoring mode.

4.3   Service Wrappers

A significant challenge in deploying the proposed approach is to, *a posteriori*, introduce a privacy preserving mechanism to existing Web services that are already built without a mechanism for privacy enforcement. The solution clearly requires to modify the service invocation scheme to accommodate the added mechanism. Moreover, the solution must not induce a high upgrading cost on "legacy" services. To achieve this transition to *privacy preserving services*, we introduce components called *service wrappers*. A *service wrapper* associated with a service s_i is a software module that is co-located with s_i and that handles all messages received or sent by the service s_i. To send a privacy sensitive message M to a service s_j, the service s_i first submits the message to its wrapper. If necessary, the wrapper sends a request to the *Reputation Manager* to inquire about s_j's reputation. Based on the answer received from the RM, s_i's wrapper may then forward the message M to s_j or decide to cancel sending M to s_j. To avoid an excessive traffic at the *Reputation Manager*, the wrapper may locally maintain a *Reputation Cache* that contains information about the reputation of the most frequently invoked services.

5   Related Work

Among all Web applications, E-commerce is the one where the concept of reputation was the most extensively studied. Online businesses have deployed reputation systems that improve customers' trust and, consequently, stimulate sales [7]. Examples include: *Ebay*, *Bizrate*, *Amazon*, and *Epinions*. Several studies have investigated and, generally, confirmed the potential positive impact of reputation systems on online shoppers' decisions to engage in business transactions (e. g., the study reported in [5] that targeted *Ebay*'s reputation system).

Current reputation systems are based on the simple idea of evaluating the reputation of a service or a product using feedbacks collected from customers that, in the past, have purchased similar or comparable services or products. Customers may then make "informed shopping" in light of past experiences. Different variations derived from this general model have been proposed. For example, in [9], the authors presented two models based on the *global* and *personalized* notions of reputation. The global model, *Sporas*, is similar to the reputation model used at *Ebay* while the personalized model, *Histos*, takes the identity of the inquirer and the environment in which the inquiry is carried out into account.

In most E-commerce systems, a typical transaction involves two parties (e. g., a seller and a buyer). In some cases, one of the parties (the seller) is also the provider of the reputation service (i.e., assesses and/or disseminates the reputation). These reputation systems inherently lack the *objectivity* that generally characterizes systems based on a *neutral* third party. An example of such a system was proposed in [2]. It is based on a trust model that uses *intermediaries* to bolster the buyer's and seller's confidence in online transactions. An intermediary agent, known as a *trust service provider* (TSP), is responsible for making sure that the end-parties (buyer and seller) behave as expected (e. g., the buyer pays and the seller delivers). The whole process is invisible to the transacting parties as the TSP carries out the transaction in an automatic fashion. Another approach to introduce more objectivity in reputation systems was proposed in

[1]. It treats trust as a non-transitive concept and takes into account the credibility of the source providing a recommendation. The proposed approach assumes that the recommender may lie or state contradictory recommendations.

Other solutions have also been proposed for other types of Web applications. In a previous work [8,6], we addressed the problem in the context of Digital Government applications. The solution was developed to enforce privacy in Web-accessible (government) databases. Its principle was to combine *data filters* and *mobile privacy preserving agents*. The former were used to protect privacy at the server side (i.e., the databases) and the latter were used to preserve privacy at the client side (i.e., Web clients requesting private information).

The reputation system proposed in this paper differs from the previously mentioned (and other) systems in three aspects: First, contrarily to most existing systems that target Web *sites* or Web *databases*, our system targets a semantic Web environment hosting Web services and software agents. Second, reputation in our system is not directly based on business criteria (e. g., quality of a service or a product) but, rather, it reflects the "quality of conduct" of Web services with regard to the preservation of the privacy of (personal) information that they exchange with other services and agents. Finally, reputation management in our system is fully automated and does not use (or necessitate) potentially subjective human recommendations or feedbacks.

6   Conclusion

In this paper, we presented a reputation management system for Web services. The proposed system aims at automating the process of privacy enforcement in a semantic Web environment. The solution is based on a general model for assessing reputation where a reputation manager permanently probes Web services to evaluate their reputation. Currently, we are investigating three alternatives to the proposed centralized model. These are a distributed, registry-based and peer-to-peer reputation models. The objective of investigating these four models is to extricate the components and features of an ideal reputation management system for Web services.

Acknowledgment. This research is supported by the National Science Foundation under grant 9983249-EIA and by a grant from the Commonwealth Information Security Center (CISC). The authors would also like to thank Mourad Ouzzani for his valuable comments on earlier drafts of this paper.

References

1. A. Abdulrahman and S. Hailes. Supporting Trust in Virtual Communities. In *Proceedings of the 33rd Annual Hawaii International Conference on System Sciences*, 2000.
2. Yacine Atif. Building Trust in E-Commerce. *IEEE Internet Computing*, 6(1):18–24, January–February 2002.
3. T. Berners-Lee, J. Hendler, and O. Lassila. The Semantic Web. *Scientific American*, May 2001.

4. J. Joshi, A. Ghafoor, W. G. Aref, and E. H. Spafford. Digital Government Security Infrastructure Design Challenges. *Computer*, 34(2):66–72, February 2001.
5. D. Lucking-Reily, D. Bryan, N. Prasad, and D. Reeves. Pennies From eBay: The Determinants of Price in Online Auctions. In: *www.vanderbilt.edu/econ/reiley/papers/PenniesFromEBay.pdf*, January 2000.
6. B. Medjahed, A. Rezgui, A. Bouguettaya, and M. Ouzzani. Infrastructure for E-Government Web Services. *IEEE Internet Computing*, 7(1), January/February 2003.
7. P. Resnick, R. Zeckhauser, E. Friedman, and K. Kuwabara. Reputation Systems. *Communications of the ACM*, 43(12):45–48, December 2000.
8. A. Rezgui, M. Ouzzani, A. Bouguettaya, and B. Medjahed. Preserving Privacy in Web Services. In *Proc. of the 4th ACM Workshop on Information and Data Management (WIDM'02)*, pages 56–62, McLean, VA, November 2002.
9. G. Zacharia, A. Moukas, and P. Maes. Collaborative Reputation Mechanisms in Electronic Marketplaces. In *Proceedings of the 32nd Annual Hawaii International Conference on System Sciences*, 1999.

Reliable Web Service Execution and Deployment in Dynamic Environments*

Markus Keidl, Stefan Seltzsam, and Alfons Kemper

Universität Passau, 94030 Passau, Germany
{keidl,seltzsam,kemper}@db.fmi.uni-passau.de

Abstract. In this work, we present novel techniques for flexible and reliable execution and deployment of Web services which can be integrated into existing service platforms. The first technique, dynamic service selection, provides a layer of abstraction for service invocation offering Web services the possibility of selecting and invoking Web services at runtime based on a technical specification of the desired service. The selection can be influenced by using different types of constraints. The second technique, a generic dispatcher service capable of automatic service replication, augments Web services with load balancing and high availability features, without having to consider these features at the services' development. We implemented these techniques within the ServiceGlobe system, an open Web service platform.

1 Introduction

Web services are a new technology for the development of distributed applications on the Internet. By a Web service (also called service or e-service), we understand an autonomous software component that is uniquely identified by a URI and that can be accessed by using standard Internet protocols like XML, SOAP, or HTTP [18]. Due to its potential of changing the Internet to a platform of application collaboration and integration, Web service technology gains more and more attention in research and industry; initiatives like HP Web Services Platform, Microsoft .NET, or Sun ONE show this development. All these frameworks share the opinion that services are important for easy application collaboration and integration and they try to provide appropriate tools and a complete infrastructure for implementing and executing Web services.

Our objective in this work is to present new techniques for Web service execution and deployment in dynamic environments. The first technique we present is dynamic service selection. It offers the possibility of selecting and invoking services at runtime based on a technical specification of the desired service. Therewith, it provides a layer of abstraction from the actual services. Constraints enable Web services to influence dynamic service selection, e.g., services can be selected based on the metadata available about them.

We address load balancing and high availability by providing a generic, modular dispatcher service for augmenting services with these features, without having to consider them during the services' development. The dispatcher is a software-based layer-7

---

* This research is done in cooperation with the Advanced Infrastructure Program (AIP) group of SAP.

B. Benatallah and M.-C. Shan (Eds.): TES 2003, LNCS 2819, pp. 104–118, 2003.

switch with the known advantages: it forwards requests to different service instances and therefore reduces the risk of a service being unavailable and speeds up request processing because of load balancing respectively load sharing. Our dispatcher implements a new feature called automatic service replication. Using this feature, new (individually configured) services can be installed on idle hosts on behalf of the dispatcher to leverage available computing power. Additional advantages are that the dispatcher is integrated into the service platform and is completely transparent to the callers of a service.

We implemented both techniques, dynamic service selection and the dispatcher, within the ServiceGlobe system [11] which is described in the next section. The techniques can also be integrated into existing service platforms without major modifications. A demo of ServiceGlobe was given at VLDB'02 [12]. As part of SAP's adaptive computing infrastructure, the ServiceGlobe system is installed on a blade server with 160 processors overall (with 2 and 4 processors per server blade, respectively), which is operated by the Advanced Infrastructure Program group of SAP. Several performance evaluations with high-volume business applications are conducted using this system. The presented technologies are currently integrated into the SAP NetWeaver platform to supplement its service virtualization capabilities. A demonstration was shown at the Sapphire 2003 [1], SAP's user conference.

The remainder of this paper is structured as follows: Section 2 introduces the ServiceGlobe system. Sections 3 and 4 present dynamic service selection and the generic dispatcher capable of automatic service replication, respectively. Finally, Section 5 gives some related work and Section 6 concludes this paper.

2   Architecture of ServiceGlobe

The ServiceGlobe system is a lightweight, distributed, and extensible service platform. It is fully implemented in Java Release 2 and based on standards like XML, SOAP, UDDI, and WSDL. Additionally, the system supports mobile code, i.e., services can be distributed and instantiated during runtime on demand at arbitrary Internet servers participating in the ServiceGlobe federation. Of course, ServiceGlobe offers all the standard functionality of a service platform like a transaction system and a security system [19]. These areas are well covered by existing technologies and are, therefore, not the focus of this work. We will now explain the ServiceGlobe infrastructure. First of all, we distinguish between external and internal services.

External Services are services currently deployed on the Internet, which are not provided by ServiceGlobe itself. Such services are stationary, i.e., running only on a dedicated host, are realized on arbitrary systems on the Internet, and have arbitrary interfaces for their invocation. If they do not provide an appropriate SOAP interface, we use *adaptors* to transpose internal requests to the external interface and vice versa, to be able to integrate these services independent of their actual invocation interface, e.g., RPC. This way, we are also able to access arbitrary applications, e.g., ERP applications. Thus external services can be used like internal services.

Internal Services are native ServiceGlobe services implemented in Java using the service API provided by the ServiceGlobe system. ServiceGlobe services use SOAP to communicate with other services. There are two kinds of internal services, namely

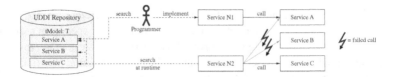

Fig. 1. An Example of Dynamic Service Selection

dynamic services and *static* services. Static services are location-*dependent*, i.e., they cannot be executed dynamically on arbitrary ServiceGlobe servers, because, e.g., they require access to certain local resources like a DBMS. In contrast, dynamic services are location-*independent*. They are state-less, i.e., the internal state of such a service is discarded after a request was processed, and do not require special resources or permissions. Therefore, they can be executed on arbitrary ServiceGlobe servers.

Internal services are executed on *service hosts*, i.e., hosts connected to the Internet which are running the ServiceGlobe runtime engine. ServiceGlobe's internal services are mobile code, therefore their executables can be loaded on demand from *code repositories* into a service host's runtime engine (this feature is called *runtime service loading*). A UDDI server is used to find an appropriate code repository storing a certain service. Thus, the set of available services is not fixed and can be extended at runtime by everyone participating in the ServiceGlobe federation. If internal services have the appropriate permissions, they can also use resources of service hosts, e.g., databases. These permissions are part of the security system of ServiceGlobe which is based on [19] and they are managed autonomously by the administrators of the service hosts. This security system also deals with the security issues of mobile code introduced by runtime service loading. Thus, service hosts are protected against malicious services.

Runtime service loading allows *service distribution* of dynamic services to arbitrary service hosts, opening optimization potential: Several instances of a dynamic service can be executed on different hosts for load balancing and parallelization purposes. Dynamic services can be instantiated on service hosts having the optimal execution environment, e.g., a fast processor, large memory, or a high-speed network connection to other services. Of course, this feature also contributes to reliable service execution because unavailable service hosts can be replaced dynamically by available service hosts. Together with runtime service loading this provides the flexibility needed for load balancing or optimization issues.

3   Dynamic Service Selection

In UDDI, every service is assigned to a tModel[1] which provides a semantic classification of a service's functionality and a formal description of its interfaces. So, a service can be called an *implementation* or an *instance* of its tModel. With dynamic service selection (DSS), instead of explicitly stating an actual access point in a service, it is also possible

---

[1] In fact, a service in UDDI can be assigned to several tModels. DSS could be adjusted to allow calling services which implement several tModels. As there is no essential difference to calling a single tModel, this will not be considered in the following.

to reference or "call" a tModel. Thus, one defines the functionality of the service that should be called rather than its actual implementation. Without DSS, the selection of services from UDDI based on a search criteria like a tModel has to be done manually by a programmer when implementing a Web service. Furthermore, the search criteria available in UDDI are less general and there are no criteria for influencing service invocation or for filtering service replies.

As example for DSS, see Figure 1: Three services are assigned to tModel T: Service A, B, and C. Assume, that a programmer wants to implement a new Web service which should invoke a service assigned to tModel T. Without DSS, the programmer would search UDDI for an appropriate service, e.g., Service A, and use its access point in the new Service N1. With DSS, the programmer will instead develop Service N2. This service does not contain any hard-coded access point, instead it contains a call to the tModel T. At runtime, the service will query UDDI for an appropriate Web service and invoke it. If an invocation fails, alternative services are tried until an invocation succeeds (as depicted in Figure 1) or no more alternative services are available.

As already mentioned, DSS is implemented within ServiceGlobe. The ServiceGlobe API provides methods for Web services to invoke tModels and to optionally specify constraints and/or use constraints contained in the service's context.

3.1 Constraints

Constraints are used to influence DSS. They can be passed to a service platform within a service's context or by specifying them directly when calling a tModel. The term context refers to information about the consumer of a Web service which is used by the service to adjust its execution and output to provide a customized and personalized version of itself. In the ServiceGlobe system, context is transmitted in the header of the SOAP messages that services send and receive. The integration of constraints into context information enables not only the invoked services to take advantage of them, but also further services invoked by these services, as the context information of a service is (automatically) included into SOAP messages sent by it.

Constraints can be differentiated into *preferences* and *conditions*.[2] Conditions must be fulfilled, whereas preferences should be fulfilled. When considering preferences in DSS, a service platform at first invokes services that fulfill these preferences. If there is an insufficient number of such services, additional services are invoked which do not fulfill all preferences (but, of course, they must fulfill all conditions). Orthogonally, there are five different types of constraints: metadata, location, mode, reply, and result constraints. For each type, there are preferences and conditions; though, for mode and result constraints, preferences are useless.

Metadata Constraints. Prior to the invocation of services, when the service platform requests all services assigned to a tModel, metadata constraints are applied as filter on all services returned by UDDI. Metadata constraints are basically XPath [6] queries that are applied to the metadata of a service. Metadata about a service includes primarily its UDDI data. Also, additional metadata which is stored in other metadata repositories [10] and that

---

[2] A similar classification of conditions of SQL statements in hard and soft constraints is described in [13].

cannot be found in UDDI may be contained. The following example shows a metadata preference that favors services assigned to a businessEntity with name Company:

```
<metadataPreference>
  /businessEntity/name="Company"
</metadataPreference>
```

Location Constraints. Location constraints are used to specify the place of execution of a Web service, i.e., the service host. For static services, this allows their selection based on their location. For dynamic services, this ensures that they are instantiated and executed preferably (preference) or strictly (condition) at the given location. The information about the location of services and service hosts is retrieved from the UDDI repository. The location can be specified by, e. g., a host's network address or geographically based on GPS coordinates or ISO 3166 codes.

Mode Constraints. DSS is not limited to invoke only one instance of a given tModel; it is also possible to invoke several instances. With a mode constraint the number of services that should be invoked can be specified. There are three modes available:[3] Using the *one mode*, only one instance out of all tModel instances is called. In case of a failure, e.g., unavailability of a service, an alternative service is tried. Using the *some mode*, a subset of all services returned by UDDI is called in parallel.[4] The number of services is specified as an absolute value or as a percentage. Services which fail are replaced with alternative services. Using the *all mode*, all returned tModel instances are called. Obviously, no alternative services can be called if failures occur. The following example shows a mode constraint that specifies that five percent of the available services should be invoked:

```
<modeCondition modeType="Some" number="5%" />
```

Reply Constraints. Reply constraints are evaluated after a reply of an invoked service was received. Every reply not fulfilling all relevant reply constraints is discarded. There are two kinds of reply constraints. *Selection constraints* are XPath queries which are applied to the reply of a service, including its SOAP parts. With *property constraints*, replies can be selected based on a set of properties of the reply. Properties must be provided either by the service platform or by the invoked service. A service accomplishes this by including corresponding XML elements in its reply. ServiceGlobe itself supports properties for encryption, signature, and age of data. Using the first two properties, it is possible to verify if a reply is encrypted or signed, respectively, and by whom it is signed. The third property can be used to check the age of the returned data.

Result Constraints. Result constraints refer to all replies received so far. There are two kinds of result constraints. With a *timeout constraint*, a maximal waiting time for replies of invoked services can be set. After its expiry, all pending services are aborted and all replies received so far are returned to the calling service. The following constraint is an example of a timeout constraint:

```
<timeoutCondition value="100" valueUnit="Seconds"/>
```

With *first-n constraints*, the call to a tModel can be ended after a predetermined number of replies was received. The calling service gets only these replies as result of its call. Services that have not responded until this moment are aborted.

---

[3] These modes are similar to unicast, multicast, and broadcast communication on networks.

[4] It should be noted that one and all mode are obviously special cases of the some mode.

```
<orGroup>
  <metadataCondition>
    /businessEntity/name="Company"
  </metadataCondition>
  <timeoutCondition value="100" valueUnit="Seconds"/>
</orGroup>
```

Fig. 2. Combination of Constraints

3.2   Combination of Constraints

Constraints can be combined using the operators AND and OR. By the combination of constraints, conflicts can be created which may prevent fulfilling all given constraints. As a consequence, only a subset of the given constraints may be fulfillable, as the example in Figure 2 shows (orGroup represents the OR operator).

Initially, the service platform has two choices: On the one hand, it can invoke *only services of the company* Company and wait for their replies (therewith fulfilling only the first constraint). On the other hand, it can invoke *all services* assigned to the tModel. But if a timeout occurs, the service platform faces the situation that it either must return all replies received so far immediately (therewith fulfilling only the second constraint) or that it must ignore the timeout and wait at least for all replies (therewith fulfilling only the first constraint). In the latter case, though, it invoked too many services initially. So, in general, the service platform is unable to fulfill both constraints at the same time.

3.3   Evaluation of Constraints

This section explains how a tModel call is actually executed and how constraints are evaluated in this process. At first, constraints from all different sources are combined conjunctively into one single combined constraint, called *main constraint*, using the AND operator. This constraint is passed as input to the tModel call. Its evaluation consists of two phases: First, it is transformed into disjunctive normal form (DNF) and conflicts are resolved. Second, UDDI is queried for services assigned to the given tModel and the services are invoked considering the main constraint.

Preprocessing of Constraints. First, the main constraint is transformed into DNF. Note, that the same constraint can now be present multiple times in the transformed constraint. Afterwards, all constraints of an *AND term*, i.e., a term only containing AND operators, are sorted according to their time of evaluation. The order is: metadata, location, mode, reply, and result constraints.

Then, the main constraint is checked for conflicts. Only conflicts within a single AND term are resolved in this phase, conflicts between different AND terms are resolved later, during the invocation phase. Within an AND term, a conflict occurs if it either contains more than one mode constraint or more than one result constraint. For mode constraints, this is obvious. For result constraints, there are some rare situations where several result constraints would make sense. But, as we see no real benefit, two or more result constraints per AND term are prohibited.[5] Of course, conflicts between metadata,

---

[5] The implementation would be straightforward, although requiring many, even though simple case discriminations.

location, or reply constraints are possible in principle, e.g., an AND term that contains metadata constraints with contradictory XPath queries. Detecting this type of conflict would require a detailed investigation of the XPath queries.

Conflicts are resolved by keeping only the constraint with the maximum priority and removing all other conflicting constraints. Priorities range from 0 (minimum) to ∞ (maximum) and they can be assigned to a term by its creator, e.g., the consumer or a Web service. An additional, implicit prioritization is given by the sequence of the terms in their XML representation. The later a term is defined there the less its priority is. If two terms have the same explicit priority, their implicit priority decides which one has the higher priority.

At last, identical mode and result constraints which are contained in several AND terms because of the transformation into DNF are merged.[6] The resulting terms are called *merged AND terms*. Without merging, a service platform would evaluate identical mode and result constraints multiple times which would result in a different result. Only mode and result constraints are considered for merging because, unlike the other constraint types, they are restrictions on sets of services respectively replies, not on single services or replies. Therefore, the result of the main constraint is only modified by duplicating them when transforming the main constraint into DNF.

Invocation of Web Services. After the main constraint has been preprocessed, UDDI is queried for all information about services assigned to the given tModel. These services as well as their metadata are stored in a *services list*. Initially, there is one such services list for every merged AND term. In the following, services which do not fulfill a condition are removed from a services list. Preferences are used to sort this list.

Now, metadata constraints are applied to the services list of their merged AND term, followed by location constraints. For the evaluation of location constraints for dynamic services, all available service hosts are retrieved from UDDI first. Then, the location constraints are used to filter and sort this list of service hosts (similar to services lists). For each merged AND term, the corresponding service hosts list is assigned to all dynamic services of this term.

Next, all mode constraints of the main constraint are evaluated in parallel, i.e., Web services are invoked as specified by the mode constraints considering all relevant services lists. As a consequence of the merging of identical mode constraints, services lists from more than one merged AND term may have to be considered. For each invocation of Web services based on a single mode constraint, the corresponding services list is processed sequentially, starting with the service at the top (which has the highest priority). Thereby static services are invoked only once, dynamic services can be invoked as often as there are service hosts in their service hosts list (service host are chosen according to their priority).

Every time the reply of a Web service is received, all relevant reply constraints are applied to it. Note, that the Web service may be contained in several services lists, so there can be more than one merged AND term with relevant reply constraints. The service platform must also check whether the invocation phase must be ended. This is the case if the result constraint with the highest priority is fulfilled. After the invocation phase

---

[6] Basically, merging means factoring out identical mode and result constraints.

ended, all outstanding requests are aborted and all replies are returned to the calling Web service.

4   Load Balancing and Service Replication

For large-scale, mission-critical applications, such as an enterprise resource planning system like SAP with thousands of users working concurrently, a single service host is not sufficient to provide low response times. Even worse, if there are any problems with the service or the service host, the service will be completely unavailable. Such downtime can generate high costs, even if a service host is only down for some minutes. Therefore, it is necessary to run several instances of a service on multiple service hosts for fault tolerance reasons and a load balancing component to avoid load skew. A server blade architecture is very beneficial for this purpose, because scale-out of computing power can be done on demand by adding additional server blades. Of course, a traditional cluster of service hosts connected by a LAN can be used as well but with higher total cost of ownership and normally slower network connections.

Since it is very expensive and error-prone to integrate the functionality for the co-operation of the service instances directly into every new service, we propose a generic solution to this problem: a modular *dispatcher service* which can act as a proxy for arbitrary services. Using this dispatcher service, it is possible to enhance many existing services or develop new services with load balancing and high availability features without having to consider these features during their development. All kinds of services are supported as long as concurrency control mechanisms are used, e.g., by using a database as back-end (as many real-world services do). The concurrency control mechanisms ensure a consistent view and consistent modifications of the data shared between all service instances. Of course, if there is no data sharing between different instances of a service, the dispatcher can be used as well. An additional feature of our dispatcher is called *automatic service replication* and enables the dispatcher to install new instances of static services on demand.

4.1   Architecture of the Dispatcher

Our dispatcher is a software-based layer-7 switch[7]. Such switches perform load balancing (or load sharing) using several servers on the back-end with identically mirrored content and a dispatching strategy like round robin or more complex strategies using load information about the back-end servers. Our solution is a pure software solution and – in contrast to existing layer-7 switches – is realized as a regular service. Thus, our dispatcher is more flexible, extensible, and seamlessly integrated into the platform.

Figure 3 shows our dispatcher monitoring three service hosts running two instances of Service S (both connected to the same DBMS). The database server is monitored as well using a stand-alone monitoring application. Using information from monitoring services and monitoring applications, the dispatcher generates the dispatcher's local view of the load situation of the service hosts. Upon receiving a message (in this case

---

[7] This kind of switch is also used in the context of Web servers [4].

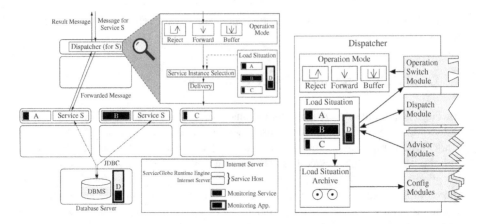

Fig. 3. Survey of the Load Balancing System   **Fig. 4.** Dispatcher's Architecture

for Service S), the dispatcher looks for the service instance running on the least loaded service host and forwards the message to it. As already mentioned, our dispatcher is modular, as shown in Figure 4. There are four types of modules:

Operation Switch Module. This module controls the operation mode of the dispatcher on a per-service level. In our implementation, the standard operation mode is *forward*, other modes are *buffer* or *reject*. The latter two modes are set to prevent the more expensive execution of the dispatch module when there are no suitable service hosts.

Dispatch Module. This module implements the actual dispatching strategy. It can access the load situation of service hosts and of other resources for the assignment of requests to service instances. Possible results of a dispatch strategy are an assignment of a request to a service instance, a command to initiate a service replication (see below), a reject command, or a buffer command. We implemented a strategy which assigns requests to the service instance on the least loaded service host based on the CPU load. We additionally implemented a more sophisticated strategy which handles the load of CPU and main memory on different types of resources (e.g., service hosts and database management systems) needed for the execution of a service. This strategy prevents overload situations not only on service hosts but also on other resources like DBMSs. Currently, we are working on performance experiments for these strategies.

Advisor Modules. Advisor modules are used to collect data for the dispatcher's view of the load situation of all relevant resources. We implemented advisor modules to measure the average CPU and memory load on service hosts (using the monitoring services) and on hosts running database management systems (using the monitoring applications). There are lots of reasonable different advisor modules. The simplest kind of advisor module only knows two conditions of a resource: available or unavailable. For service hosts, this could be done by a simple *ping* on the host running the ServiceGlobe system. More complex advisors can provide more detailed information like CPU or main memory load of a service host, or the load of a database management system depending on CPU, memory, disc I/O, and others.

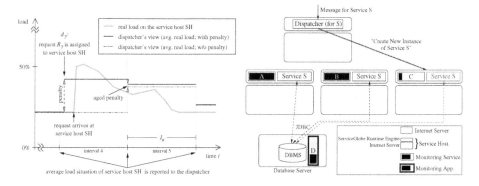

Fig. 5. Different Views of the Load Situation   **Fig. 6.** Automatic Replication of Service S

Config Modules. The configuration modules are used to generate the configuration for new service instances. The modules can access the load situation archive which stores aggregated load information to find, e.g., the database host which was least loaded in the last few days. This is very beneficial if there are, e.g., several instances of a database system working on replicated data. Using historic load information, a new service instance can be advised to connect to the instance of the DBMS which had the lowest average load in the past.

To turn an existing service into a highly available and load balanced service, a properly configured dispatcher service must be started. Additionally, some new UDDI data has to be registered and some existing data has to be modified so that all service instances and all service hosts can be found by the dispatcher. After that, the service instances are no longer contacted directly, but via the dispatcher service controlling the forwarding of the messages. A cluster of service hosts can be easily supplemented with new service hosts. The administrators of these service hosts only have to install the ServiceGlobe system and register them at the UDDI repository using the appropriate tModel, e.g., ServiceHostClusterZ, indicating that these service hosts are members of cluster Z. The dispatcher will automatically use these service hosts as soon as it notices the changes to the UDDI repository.

4.2   Load Measurement

The dispatcher's view of the load situation is updated at intervals of several seconds to prevent overloading the network. Thus, this view is constant between two updates. Therefore, a service host SH will still be considered having low load, even if several requests have been assigned to it after the last load update. Without precautions, the dispatcher might overload SH for this reason. To avoid these overload situations, the dispatcher adds "penalties" to its view of the load once a request is assigned. Figure 5 illustrates the load of SH, the load reported to the dispatcher (load without penalties), and the load with penalties.

The grey, thick line represents the load $L_{\mathrm{SH}}(t)$ of the service host SH. The dashed line represents the dispatcher's view $D'_{\mathrm{SH}}(t)$ of the load of SH which is the average load of SH over the last update interval of length I_u. This average load is calculated by SH and sent to the dispatcher at regular intervals. The function $int(t)$ calculates the number of the interval containing a given time t:

$$int(t) := \lfloor t / I_u \rfloor$$

The dispatcher's view can now be written as follows:

$$D'_{\text{SH}}(t) := \text{avg}\left\{L_{\text{SH}}(t') \mid int(t') = int(t) - 1\right\}$$

The black, solid line shown in Figure 5 represents the dispatcher's view including penalties $D_{\text{SH}}(t)$. The initial (maximum) value of a penalty (represented by $P^m_{\text{SH,S}}$ in the equations) depends on the service S and the performance of the service host SH and is configurable. This way, every assignment of a request R_i, i.e., every dispatch operation (represented by d_i, $i \in \mathbb{N}$; d_7 in the figure), has an effect on the dispatcher's view of the load situation, immediately. If there is a load update from SH shortly after an assignment of a request R_i, but before SH started to process R_i, the associated penalty would be lost if the dispatcher would replace its view with the reported load, because this load would not include load caused by R_i. Thus, the load reported by the load monitors and the dispatcher's view of the load situation are remerged using aging penalties: the penalties are decreasing over time and added to further load values reported by the service host until the penalties are zero. The time I_p until a penalty is zero is configurable and normally shorter than shown in the picture, e.g., twice the time a request R_i needs to arrive at SH plus the time SH needs to start processing R_i. After I_p, we assume that a request R_i arrived at SH and that the load caused by R_i is already included in the reported load, so that the dispatcher needs not to further add any penalties for R_i. Using our notation and defining $time(d_i)$ to indicate the time of the assignment d_i, $host(d_i)$ to indicate the destination host of the assignment d_i, and $service(d_i)$ to indicate the destination service of the assignment d_i, the view with penalties $D_{\text{SH}}(t)$ can be calculated as follows: The penalty P_{d_i} for the assignment d_i is zero before the assignment. After I_p, it is zero again. In between this interval the penalty is calculated using a linear function $f_{d_i}(t)$ with the following constraints: $f_{d_i}(0) = P^m_{host(d_i),service(d_i)}$ and $f_{d_i}(I_p) = 0$.

$$P_{d_i}(t) := \begin{cases} 0 & \text{if} \quad t < time(d_i) \vee t > time(d_i) + I_p \\ f_{d_i}(t - time(d_i)) & \text{else} \end{cases}$$

When receiving load updates from the service host SH, i.e., $t = x * I_u$ for $x \in \mathbb{N}$, the load including penalties is calculated by adding all aged penalties of assignments to this SH to the reported value:

$$Ass_{\text{SH}} := \left\{a \in \mathbb{N} \mid host(d_a) = \text{SH}\right\}$$

$$D_{\text{SH}}(t) := D'_{\text{SH}}(t) + \sum_{i \in Ass_{\text{SH}}} P_{d_i}(t) \quad \text{if} \quad \exists x \in \mathbb{N} : t = x * I_u$$

Within an update interval, penalties of new assignments to SH, i.e., assignments done within the current update interval, are added to this load as soon as they occur:

$$\text{NewAss}_{\text{SH}}(t) := \big\{ a \in \text{Ass}_{\text{SH}} \mid int(\text{time}(d_a)) = int(t) \wedge t > \text{time}(d_a) \big\}$$

$$D_{\text{SH}}(t) := D_{\text{SH}}\left(int(t) * I_u \right) + \sum_{i \in NewAss_{\text{SH}}(t)} P^m_{\text{SH}, service(d_i)} \quad \text{if} \quad \forall x \in \mathbb{N} : t \neq x * I_u$$

4.3   Automatic Service Replication

If all available service instances of a static service[8] are running on heavily loaded service hosts and there are service hosts available having a low workload, the dispatcher
can decide to generate a new service instance using a feature called automatic service
replication. Figure 6 demonstrates this feature: service hosts A and B are heavily loaded
and host C currently has no instance of Service S running. Thus, the dispatcher sends a
message to service host C to create a new instance of Service S. The configuration of
the new Service S is generated using the appropriate configuration module. If no service
hosts having low workload are available, the dispatcher can buffer incoming messages
(until the buffer is full) or reject them depending on the configuration of the dispatcher
instance and the modules.

4.4   High Availability / Single Point of Failure

Using several instances of a service greatly increases its availability and decreases the
average response time. Just to get an impression about the high level of availability,
we want to sketch this very simple analytical investigation. Assuming that the server
running the dispatcher itself and the database server (in our example the database server
is needed for service S) are highly available, the availability of the entire system depends
only on the availability $\alpha_{ServiceHost} = \alpha$ of the service hosts. The availability of a pool
of service hosts can be calculated as follows:

$$\alpha = \frac{\text{MTBF}}{\text{MTBF} + \text{MTTR}} \quad (1) \qquad \alpha_{pool} = \sum_{i=1}^{N} \alpha^i (1 - \alpha)^{(N-i)} = 1 - (1 - \alpha)^N \quad (2)$$

Equation 1 calculates the availability of a single service host based on its MTBF
(mean time between failures) and MTTR (mean time to repair). The availability of a pool
of N service hosts can be calculated using Equation 2. Even assuming very unreliable
service hosts with MTBF = 48h and MTTR = 12h a pool with 8 members will only be
unavailable about 1.5 minutes a year.

Because database management systems are very often mission critical for compa-
nies, there are different approved solutions for highly available database management
systems [3,9]. Thus, the remaining single point of failure is the dispatcher service. There
are several possibilities to reduce the risk of a failure of the dispatcher. A pure software
solution is to run two identical dispatcher services on two different hosts. Only one of
these dispatchers is registered at the UDDI server. The second dispatcher is the spare
dispatcher and it monitors the other one ("watchdog mechanism"). If the first dispatcher
fails, the spare dispatcher modifies the UDDI repository to point to the spare dispatcher.

---

[8] Dynamic services can be executed on arbitrary service hosts and need not be installed anyway.

If the clients of the dispatcher call services according to the UDDI service invocation pattern, any failed service invocation will lead to a check for service relocation. Thus, failures of the first dispatcher will lead to an additional UDDI query and an additional SOAP message to the second dispatcher. Of course, there are many other possible solutions which are adaptable for a highly available dispatcher service known from the fields of database systems [3,9] and Web servers [4] including solutions based on redundant hardware, but this is out of the scope of this paper.

5   Related Work

The success of Web services results in a large number of commercial service platforms and products, e.g., the Sun ONE framework which is based on J2EE, Microsoft .NET, and HP Web Services Platform. Furthermore, there are research platforms like Service-Globe [12,11] and SELV-SERV [2] which focus on certain aspects in the Web service area. In SELV-SERV, services with equal interfaces are grouped together into service communities, but no strategies for selecting services out of these service communities are presented. The project focuses rather on composing Web services using state charts. The eFlow system [5] models composite services as business processes, specified in eFlow's own composition language, and provides techniques similar to DSS. With dynamic service discovery, a composite service searches for services based on available metadata, its own internal state, and a rating function. Multiservice nodes allow to invoke several services in parallel, similar to DSS mode and result constraints, though with different termination criteria. In contrast to eFlow, DSS allows the combination of all these different constraints in a flexible way. In addition, eFlow does not utilize standards like UDDI or WSDL for its adaptive techniques.

In [15] and [17], agent-based architectures are presented which provide service selection based on a rating system for Web services. In Jini [20], clients utilize a lookup service to discover services based on the Java interfaces they implement and service attributes. The lookup service's attribute search is limited to searching only for exact matches [16]. Extensions have been proposed to support, e.g., attributes providing context information about services [14] or more sophisticated match types [16]. Based on WSDL, WSIF [21] allows a Web service to select a specific port of a service it wants to invoke, i.e., its actual access point and the communication protocol and message format to use, at runtime. The selection is limited to the information provided by WSDL documents, as no service repositories like UDDI are considered.

A lot of work has been done in the area of load balancing, e.g., load balancing for Web servers [4] and load balancing in the context of Grid computing [8]. Grid computing is focused on distributed computing in wide area networks involving large amounts of data and/or computing power, using computers managed by multiple organizations. Our dispatcher is focused on distributing load between hosts inside a LAN. In contrast to dispatchers for Web servers [4], dispatchers for service platforms cannot assume that all requests to services produce the same amount of load, because the computational demands of different services might be very different. There are also commercial products available, e.g., DataSynapse [7] which offers a self-managing distributed computing solution. One of the key differences of this system is, that it works pull-based, i.e., hosts are requesting work, instead of using a dispatcher pushing work to the hosts. Additionally, DataSynapse requires an individual integration of every application, which is not necessarily an easy task for arbitrary applications.

6   Conclusion

In this work, we presented novel techniques for flexible and reliable Web service execution and deployment in dynamic environments. We introduced dynamic service selection which offers Web services the possibility to select and invoke services at runtime based on a technical specification of the desired service. We showed how constraints can be used to influence dynamic service selection. We also addressed load balancing and high availability issues by providing a generic, modular, and transparent dispatcher for load balancing including automatic service replication. We implemented these techniques within ServiceGlobe, an open Web service platform. For the future, we plan to work on caching of SOAP messages and to investigate context for Web services.

Acknowledgments. We would like to thank Wolfgang Becker und Thorsten Dräger of SAP's Advanced Infrastructure Program group for their cooperation.

References

1. SAP Keynote: Turning Vision into Reality: Customer Roadmaps to Lower TCO. http://www.sap.com/community/events/2003 orlando/keynotes.asp, 2003. SAPPHIRE '03.
2. B. Benatallah, M. Dumas, Q. Z. Sheng, and A. H. H. Ngu. Declarative Composition and Peer-to-Peer Provisioning of Dynamic Web Services. In: *Proc. of the 18th Intl. Conference on Data Engineering (ICDE)*, pages 297–308, 2002.
3. R. Breton. Replication Strategies for High Availability and Disaster Recovery. *Data Engineering Bulletin*, 21(4): 38–43, 1998.
4. V. Cardellini and E. Casalicchio. The State of the Art in Locally Distributed Web-Server Systems. *ACM Computing Surveys*, 34(2): 263–311, 2002.
5. F. Casati and M.-C. Shan. Dynamic and adaptive composition of e-services. *Information Systems*, 26(3):143-163, 2001.
6. J. Clark and S. DeRose. XML Path Language (XPath). http://www.w3.org/TR/ xpath, 1999. W3C Recommendation.
7. DataSynapse Homepage. http://www.datasynapse.com/, 2003. DataSynapse, Inc.
8. Globus Project Homepage. http://www.globus.org/, 2003. Globus Project.
9. H. Hsiao and D. J. DeWitt. A Performance Study of Three High Availability Data Replication Strategies. In: *Proc. of the Intl. Conf. on Parallel and Distributed Information Systems (PDIS)*, pages 18–28, 1991.
10. M. Keidl, A. Kreutz, A. Kemper, and D. Kossmann. A Publish & Subscribe Architecture for Distributed Metadata Management. In:*Proc. of the 18th Intl. Conference on Data Engineering (ICDE)*, pages 309–320, 2002.
11. M. Keidl, S. Seltzsam, and A. Kemper. Flexible and Reliable Web Service Execution. In: *Proc. of the 1st Workshop on Entwicklung von Anwendungen auf der Basis der XML Web-Service Technologie*, pages 17–30, 2002.

12. M. Keidl, S. Seltzsam, K. Stocker, and A. Kemper. ServiceGlobe: Distributing E-Services across the Internet (Demonstration). In: *Proc. of the Conf. on Very Large Data Bases (VLDB)*, pages 1047–1050, 2002.

13. W. Kieling. Foundations of Preferences in Database Systems. In: *Proc. of the Conf. on Very Large Data Bases (VLDB)*, pages 311–322, 2002.

14. C. Lee and S. Helal. Context Attributes: An Approach to Enable Context-awareness for Service Discovery. In:*2003 Symposium on Applications and the Internet (SAINT)*, pages 22–30. IEEE Computer Society, 2003.

15. E. M. Maximilien and M. P. Singh. Agent-based Architecture for Autonomic Web Service Selection. In: *Workshop on Web-services and Agent-based Engineering (WSABE)*, 2003.

16. M. B. Møller and B. N. Jørgensen. Enhancing Jini's Lookup Service Using XML-Based Service Templates. In: *13th IEEE International Conference on Tools with Artificial Intelligence (ICTAI)*, pages 19–31. IEEE Computer Society, 2003.

17. S. K. Mostéfaoui and G. K. Mostéfaoui. Towards A Contextualisation of Service Discovery and Composition for Pervasive Environments. In:*Workshop on Web-services and Agentbased Engineering (WSABE)*, 2003.

18. E. Rahm and G. Vossen, editors. *Web & Datenbanken: Konzepte, Architekturen, Anwendungen.* dpunkt-Verlag, 2002.

19. S. Seltzsam, S. Börzsönyi, and A. Kemper. Security for Distributed E-Service Composition. In:*Proc. of the 2nd Intl. Workshop on Technologies for E-Services (TES)*, volume 2193 of *Lecture Notes in Computer Science (LNCS)*, pages 147–162, 2001.

20. J. Waldo. The Jini Architecture for Network-centric Computing.*Communications of the ACM*, 42(7): 76-82, 1999.

21. Web Services Invocation Framework (WSIF). `http://ws.apache.org/wsif/`, 2003. The Apache Software Foundation.

Reliable Execution Planning and Exception Handling for Business Process

Liangzhao Zeng, Jun-Jan Jeng, Santhosh Kumaran, and Jayant Kalagnanam

IBM Research Division
T.J. Watson Research Center
Yorktown Heights, NY 10598
{lzeng,jjjeng,sbk,jayant}@us.ibm.com

Abstract. Business process integration and management have become the key success factors of transforming a company into an adaptive enterprise. Experiences show the fact that most of expenses for automating business processes attribute to the activities of both detecting business exceptions and repairing the emerging problems, due to highly dynamic business environments. In this paper, we describe our ongoing project of active business process. The finest granular management unit in this framework is a BPBot that manifests behaviors of both business services and resources by enabling them with autonomic features. A business process is executed by a collection of BPBots that dynamically form a hierarchical community. We formulate the execution of business process as a discrete-time system and adopt integer programming to generate optimal and reliable execution plan. The QoS exception handling is enabled at runtime by optimization algorithms. The optimization algorithms aim for resolving the exceptions locally and optimally.

1 Introduction

A *business process* consists of a set of activities (also called tasks), control flows, data flows and transactional dependence. A system that is used to manage business processes is called *Business Process Management System* (BPMS). Today, BPMSs are widely used by different organizations to integrate and automate their business processes. However, with ever developing international markets, today's business organizations have to operate their businesses in a global economy. The reasons cited for adopting dynamic and adaptive business processes into modern enterprise include increasing customer satisfaction, improving QoS of business operations, reducing cost, and facing new business challenges, and meeting ever changing business goals.

In this paper, we propose an autonomic framework of realizing adaptive business process management system. The cornerstone of this framework is the component named BPBot (**B**usiness **P**rocess ro**Bot**). We adopt a hierarchical control-based framework to develop BPBots. In our framework, a business process is executed by a collection of BPBots that are dynamically organized as a hierarchical structure. BPBots are different from the components in conventional BPMSs. Not only does the BPBots enable business process automation, but also handle ad-hoc and unexpected changes in business process lifecycle in an autonomic fashion both systematically and optimally. The major contributions of this paper are: (i) Based on a novel task execution model and user's preference, integer programming is used to generate optimal and reliable execution plans. (ii)

B. Benatallah and M.-C. Shan (Eds.): TES 2003, LNCS 2819, pp. 119–130, 2003.
© Springer-Verlag Berlin Heidelberg 2003

During the runtime, the QoS exception handling is enabled by optimization algorithms. The solution of exception handling aims for resolving the exceptions both locally and optimally.

The remainder of this paper is organized as follows: Section 2 overviews our solution. Section 3 discusses the proposed techniques that enable reliable execution planning for business processes. Section 4 presents the details about QoS driven exception handling. Section 5 illustrates some aspects of the implementation. Finally, we discuss some related work in Section 6 and conclude paper in Section 7.

2   Autonomic Business Process Management Framework

In this section, we first introduce the conceptual structure of a BPBot, then we present the business process execution model. Finally, we use a scenario to illustrate the execution procedure of a business process.

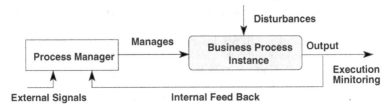

Fig. 1. BPBot's Control Structure

2.1   BPBot's Conceptual Structure

The conceptual control structure of a BPBot is depicted in Figure 1, where the process manager senses the signals emitted from both the business environment and the target business process instances, detects the business exceptions, and responds to the exceptions via the orchestration of management actions rendered to the target business process instances. The outputs of business process instances (e.g., execution status, QoS of task execution result, etc.) are considered as internal feedbacks for the BPBot, while business changes (e.g., changing business goals, changing business schemas, etc) are considered as external signals for the BPBot. Note that disturbances can be introduced into the target process instances while they are being executed. An example of such disturbance can be an occurrence of a QoS exception. In a nutshell, the BPBot imposes autonomic control behaviors on the managed business processes.

2.2   Hierarchical Business Process

In this framework, we adopt Statecharts [6] to represent process schemas. The choice of using Statecharts to specify process schemas is motivated by three main reasons: (i) Statecharts have a well-defined semantics; (ii) Statecharts offers the basic flow constructs found in contemporary process modeling languages (i.e., sequence, conditional branching, structured loops, concurrent threads, and inter-thread synchronization); and

(iii) Statecharts provide a formalism for describing hierarchical business processes. In our framework, a business process can be decomposed into sub-processes which can be decomposed further into lower-level processes until those sub-processes are atomic "activities". Therefore, business processes tend to be constructed as a hierarchical structure. Figure 2 gives an example of using Statecharts to define business process in a hierarchical manner. In this example, the Statechart diagram presents the first level business process, which is a business process of creating a new sedan car by replacing the old `petrol engine` with the new `electric engine`. It should be noted that each state in the diagram can be decomposed as to a next level's business process.

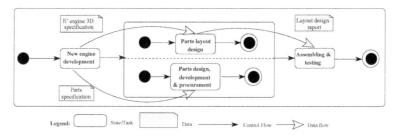

Fig. 2. Top Level Process Schema for Replacing Engine

2.3   Executing Business Process by BPBots

We adopt the service-oriented infrastructure[3] to build our framework. The infrastructure consists of three roles: service providers, service requestors and service brokers. A BPBot can be considered as a service provider, or a service requester, or both. In this paper, we do not discuss issues about service brokers. We assume that with the help of service brokers, a BPBot can locate other BPBots that can offer requested service and satisfy QoS requirements.

In our framework, a business process can be executed by constructing BPBot hierarchical community dynamically and incrementally. Figure 3 shows a snapshot of a BPBot hierarchical community, in which each BPBot manages a business process instance and its child BPBots manage the sub-processes of the managed process. At level

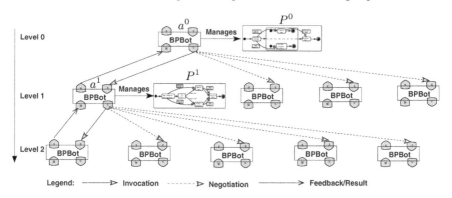

Fig. 3. Incremental Constructing BPBot Hierarchical Community

0, a BPBot a^0 is used to manage a business process instance P^0. It starts the business process execution by initiating the first task, where a BPBot a^1 at level 1 is selected to execute the task. Since BPBots adopt late binding strategy, the BPBot a^0 will communicate with other BPBots that can be used to execute the tasks in P^0. It will assign a task to a BPBot when the task's previous task is completed and its pre-condition is satisfied. When the BPBot a^1 starts the task execution, it will initiate and execute a sub-process by invoking the BPBots at level 2. Note that each BPBot either possesses a state machine (represented in Statecharts) that manifests the behavior of the target business process or provides elementary service to execute a task. A managing manager, which is also a BPBot, is able to monitor the business events that are generated by the state machine of the target business process. Business events that carry metrics and important data allow BPBots to detect the execution exceptions and to take appropriate actions against them. Considering exception handling for the business processes, each BPBot actually monitors and manages specifically the exceptions occurring in its target business process. It will attempt to resolve the exception occurring from the target business process through the reasoning capabilities. Should the exception not be resolved in a timely manner, it will be thrown to the parent BPBot (through sensor) for further processing.

3 Reliable Business Process Planning

In this section, we model a business processexecution as a *discrete-time dynamic system* and present reliable execution planning by integer programming.

3.1 Problem Formulation

We start by modeling the process execution as a discrete-time dynamic system. We make the following assumptions: (i) a business process P^l is executed at level l by a BPBot; (ii) the Statechart (i.e., process schema) can be converted into a Directed Acyclic Graph (DAG). Details about converting Statecharts into DAGs can be found in [11]. P^l consists of a set of sub-processes (i.e., task) P_i^{l+1}, denoted as $P^l = \{P_1^{l+1}, P_2^{l+1}, ..., P_n^{l+1}\}$. It should be noted that P_i^{l+1} itself is a business process at level $l + 1$, which is managed by a BPBot. Assuming x_k is the snapshot of execution status at time k (e.g., at time k, there is a BPBot a_{kj} completes task execution), the execution of a business process (i.e., Statechart) can be considered as a discrete-time system of the form

$$x_{k+1} = f_k(x_k, u_k, w_k), k = 1, ..., n \tag{1}$$

where w_k is an event that incurs at time t. The event can be the completion of a task P_i^{l+1} execution , or the delay of a task completion by a BPBot, etc. u_k is the response to the event occurred in time t by the BPBot that executes the business process P_i^l, in that the reaction can be assigning a BPBot to execute the task P_i^{l+1}, renegotiating with a BPBot on SLA (Service Level Agreement) for task P_i^{l+1}, etc. n is the horizon or the number of times a control is applied, and f_k is a function that describes how the business process execution status x_k transitions to x_{k+1}.

Assuming that once BPBots are selected to execute tasks, they are able to complete the tasks successfully and conform to their SLA properties. For a business process instance, the expected status can be $x_1, x_2, ..., x_n$, here n is the number of the tasks in process. The cost function $g_k(x_k)$ indicates the cost incurred at time k (i.e., the cost of executing task P_k^{l+1}). Here the cost of task execution is based on a predefined set of quality criteria (e.g., non-functional properties, for example, execution price, or domain specific key performance indicators). We assume m quality criteria to be used to evaluate the cost of executing task: $q = \{q_1, q_2, \ldots, q_m\}$. Assuming that task P_k^{l+1} is executed by a_k, then $g_k(x_k)$ can be denoted as:

$$g_k(x_k) = \begin{pmatrix} q_1(a_k) \\ q_2(a_k) \\ \vdots \\ q_m(a_k) \end{pmatrix} \tag{2}$$

So, the total cost of executing business process P^l is

$$C(P^l) = \coprod \left(g_1(x_1), g_2(x_2), ..., g_n(x_n) \right) \tag{3}$$

where $\coprod()$ is an aggregation function to compute the total cost of executing business process P^l. We therefore can optimize the execution of the business process P^l by minimizing the *expected cost* C_e

$$C_e(P^l) = min \left(E \left(\coprod \left(g_1(x_1), g_2(x_2), ..., g_n(x_n) \right) \right) \right) \tag{4}$$

where $E()$ is the utility function that represents a user preference on QoS of business process P^l.

3.2   Integer Programming Solution

In our previous work [11], we adopted Multiple Criteria Decision Marking [8] techniques and used the integer programming (IP) approach to generate optimal execution plans. Our work is summarized as follows.

In order to solve process execution optimization problem using IP, three inputs are needed:-

Objective Function. We use $\mathbb{Q}_i(P^l)$ to represent the score on criteria q_i for the whole business process P^l, which aggregates quality criteria score for each task. For simplicity, we assume that the value of each $\mathbb{Q}_i(P^l)$ has been scaled to $[0, 1]$ and the higher the value, the lower the quality. Considering equation 4, by applying the aggregation function and MCDM technique, we can have the objective function as follows:

$$C_e(P^l) = min \left(E \left(\mathbb{Q}_1(P^l), \mathbb{Q}_2(P^l), ..., \mathbb{Q}_m(P^l) \right) \right) = min \left(\sum_{k=1}^{m} (\mathbb{Q}_k(P^l) * W_k) \right) \tag{5}$$

where $W_j \in [0, 1]$ and $\sum_{j=1}^{m} W_l = 1$. W_j represents the weight of each criterion.

Integer Variable. For each task P_i^{l+1} in P^l, there is a set of candidate service providers A_j, where $A_j = \{a_{j1}, a_{j2}, \ldots, a_{jm_j}\}$. We use integer variables y_{ij} to represent the selection of BPBots. A variable y_{ij} can only take values either 1 or 0, where the value 1 indicates BPBot a_{ij} has been selected for task P_j^{l+1} and 0 otherwise. Therefore, we have the property as $\sum_{i=1}^{\|A_j\|} y_{ij} = 1$.

Constraints. For each quality criteria q_k, if the aggregation function $\mathbb{Q}_k(P^l)$ is a linear function, then we can have constraints such as $a <= \mathbb{Q}_k(P^l) <= b$, where a and b will typically be provided by a user to reduce search space. For example, q_{rep} (i.e., service reputation) is a service quality criterion. Since the aggregation function $\mathbb{Q}_{rep}$ ($\mathbb{Q}_{rep}(P^l) = \frac{1}{n} \sum_{j=1}^{n} (\sum_{i=1}^{\|A_j\|} q_{rep}(a_{ij}) y_{ij})$) is a linear function, we can have a constraint such as $\mathbb{Q}_{rep}(P^l) >= 0.9$ if the user decides that only execution plans with 0.9 reputation or above should be selected. Similarly, the user can impose constraints on execution duration, price, etc.

On the other hand, if the $\mathbb{Q}_k(p)$ is a nonlinear function, then we need to convert it into a linear function $\mathbb{Q}'_k(p)$ first. After substituting the $\mathbb{Q}_k(p)$ with $\mathbb{Q}'_k(p)$ in the objective function, we can give constraints on $\mathbb{Q}'_k(p)$. For example, q_{rel} (i.e., service reliability) is a service quality criterion. The aggregation function $\mathbb{Q}_{rel}(\mathbb{Q}_{rel}(p) = \Pi_{i=1}^{n}(e^{\sum_{i=1}^{\|A_j\|} q_{rel}(a_{ij})z_{ij}}))$ is a non-linear function (z_{ij} indicate whether service provider a_{ij} is a critical service or not). By applying the logarithm function ln on $\mathbb{Q}_{rel}(p)$, we obtain:

$$ln(\mathbb{Q}_{rel}(p)) = \sum_{j=1}^{n} ln\left(e^{\sum_{i=1}^{\|A_j\|} q_{rel}(a_{ij})z_{ij}}\right) = \sum_{j=1}^{n}\left(\sum_{i=1}^{\|A_j\|} q_{rel}(a_{ij})z_{ij}\right) \qquad (6)$$

Let $\mathbb{Q}'_k(p) = ln(\mathbb{Q}_k(p))$, where $\mathbb{Q}'_k(p)$ is a linear function. After replacing the $\mathbb{Q}_k(p)$ with $\mathbb{Q}'_k(p)$ in the objective function, we can have a constraint on reliability such as $\mathbb{Q}'_k(p) \geq ln(0.7)$ if the user decides that only execution plans with 70% reputation or above should be selected.

Therefore, assuming that all the constraints are feasible, the output of integer programming indicates selection of appropriate BPBots to execute task P_i^{l+1} in P^l, the selection result can be denoted as an execution plan (see Definition 1).

Definition 1 (*Execution Plan*). A set of pairs $p = \{< P_1^{l+1}, a_1 >, < P_2^{l+1}, a_2 >, \ldots, < P_n^{l+1}, a_n >\}$ is an execution plan of a business process P^l iff:

- $\{P_1^{l+1}, P_2^{l+1}, \ldots, P_n^{l+1}\}$ is the set of tasks in P^l.
- For each 2-tuple $< P_i^{l+1}, a_i >$ in p, BPBot a_i is assigned the execution of task P_i^{l+1}. □

3.3   Reliable Execution Planning

In previous subsection, when executing business processes, we assume that all the BPBots are able to complete the execution. Therefore, for each task, we only select one service provider. There are two problems in this assumption. First, the system may select a service provider that offers high score on all the quality criteria but reliability. It could be very costly to recover from the task execution failure. Second, when some task execution fails, the execution plan becomes unexecutable, then the execution has to be suspended until the replanning is completed. In order to overcome the above shortcomings, we propose a novel task execution model. We assume that for task k, it needs to retry r times of service binding before completing the task execution (see Figure 4). Accordingly, the execution status is x_k^1, x_k^2, ..., x_k^r. So, instead of one service provider being selected, r service providers are selected as ordered candidate service providers to execute the target task. In this task execution model, for BPBot a_{k1}, the possibility of task execution failure is ρ_1 and the possibility of task completion is $\rho_1^{k,k+1}$, where $\rho_1 + \rho_1^{k,k+1} = 1$. For BPBot a_{ki}, when it reports an execution failure, in average, it spends cost of $g^f(a_{k,i})$ for service invocation. If task execution is completed, then task x_{k+1} will be triggered, otherwise, another BPBot $a_{k,i+1}$ will be used to execute the task P_k^{l+1} again. According to this execution model, there are r potential successful execution paths

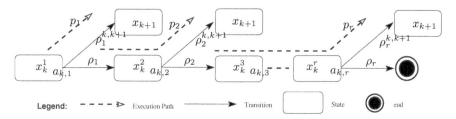

Fig. 4. Task Execution Model

$p_1, p_2, ...p_r$, where the execution path denoted as, for example, $p_1 = < x_k^1 \longrightarrow x_{k+1} >$, $p_2 = < x_k^1 \longrightarrow x_k^2 \longrightarrow x_{k+1} >$, $p_m = < x_k^1 \longrightarrow x_k^2, ..., x_k^m \longrightarrow x_{k+1} >$. If the actual execution path follows $< x_k^1 \longrightarrow x_{k+1} >$, then the expected cost of state x_k is $C_{p_1}(x_k)$: $C_{p_1}(x_{k+1}) = g_k(a_{k1})$. It should be noted that the possibility of actual execution that follows path $< x_k^1 \longrightarrow x_{k+1} >$ is $\rho_1^{k,k+1}$. To be more general, for execution path p_r, the expected state x_k is $C_{p_r}(x_k)$:

$$C_{p_r}(x_k) = \coprod \left(\begin{pmatrix} q_1(a_{k,r}) \\ q_2(a_{k,r}) \\ \vdots \\ q_m(a_{k,r}) \end{pmatrix}, \begin{pmatrix} q_1^f(a_{k,1}) \\ q_2^f(a_{k,1}) \\ \vdots \\ q_m^f(a_{k,1}) \end{pmatrix}, ..., \begin{pmatrix} q_1^f(a_{k,r-1}) \\ q_2^f(a_{k,r-1}) \\ \vdots \\ q_m^f(a_{k,r-1}) \end{pmatrix} \right) \quad (7)$$

So, the average cost of state x_k is $C_a(x_k)$:

$$C_a(x_k) = \sum_{i=1}^{r} ((\prod_{j=1}^{i} \rho_j) * \rho_j^{k,k+1} * C_{p_i}(x_k)) \quad (8)$$

It should be noted that the provider of the business process P^l needs r (i.e., times to retry the execution) for each task P_i^{l+1} in P^l. By replacing the $g_k(x_k)$ with $C_a(x_k)$, now the optimization problem becomes selecting r independent BPBots for each task and sort them in proper sequence. The details about replacing $g_k(x_k)$ with $C_a(x_k)$ in IP are outside the scope of this paper for space reasons. Now the output of IP is a reliable execution plan that can be defined as follows:

Definition 2 (*Reliable Execution Plan*). A set of pairs $p = \{< P_1^{l+1}, A_{i1} >, < P_2^{l+1}, A_{i2} >, ..., < P_n^{l+1}, A_{in} >\}$ is an execution plan of an execution path P^l iff:

- $\{P_1^{l+1}, P_2^{l+1}, ..., P_n^{l+1}\}$ is the set of tasks in P^l.
- A_{ij} is a sequence BPBots, and $\|A_{ij}\| = r_i$.
- For each 2-tuple $< P_j^{l+1}, A_{ij} >$ in p, every BPBot a in can be A_{ij} assigned the execution of task P_j^{l+1}. $\qquad\qquad\qquad\qquad\qquad\qquad\qquad\qquad\qquad\square$

4   Quality Driven Exception Handling

We assume that at level l, the business processes P^l is executed by a BPBot a^l and each task in P^l is assigned a BPBot at level $l + 1$. For business process at level $l - 1$, the BPBot a^l promises a SLA s^l according to service quality criteria, where s^l is denoted as:

$$s^l = \begin{pmatrix} q_1^l \\ q_2^l \\ \vdots \\ q_m^l \end{pmatrix} \qquad\qquad (9)$$

The BPBot a^l tries to conform the SLA s^l by enforcing constraints $0 <= \mathbb{Q}_j(P^l) <= q_j^l, j = 1, 2, ..., m$ when planning the execution. After it generates the optimal execution plan, the BPBot a^l will start the execution based on the plan. As we discussed earlier, the selected BPBots at level $l + 1$ can not always complete tasks and conform to their SLA. The execution exceptions can be either (1) execution is failure. (2) QoS violates SLA, which may include QoS improvement, e.g., completes task earlier than it promised in SLA, or QoS downgrade, e.g., spend more time then it promised in SLA. In the following, we will present the details on handling these two kinds of exceptions.

4.1   Handling Execution Failure

We discuss the handling the execution failure first. Based on the execution statuses of tasks, P^l can be partitioned into three regions. The first region (denoted as R_α^{l+1}) contains tasks that have been completed by service providers. The second region (denoted as R_β^{l+1}) contains tasks that are currently being executed. The third region (denoted as R_γ^{l+1}) contains tasks that are not yet assigned to any service providers. An example of partitioning a business process can be found in Figure 5 a. When a BPBot at level $l + 1$ fails to complete the execution of task P_f^{l+1}, it will report to the BPBot a^l at level l. In this case, the BPBot a^l will first try the next candidate BPBot in the current execution plan to re-execute the task, if the current execution plan can satisfy the SLA constraints. Otherwise, it needs to regenerate a new execution plan for task P_f^{l+1} and tasks in R_γ^{l+1}.

As we discussed in Section 3.2. there are three inputs in IP: *variables*, an *objective function* and *constraints* on the variables. When we replan the execution of business process in runtime, the failure task execution is considered as a completed task in region R_α. An example can be found in Figure 5 b. In addition to the constraints we have in pre-execution time, we add some constraints that represent the current execution status. More precisely, each task's execution results in region R_α^{l+1} and each task's assignment results

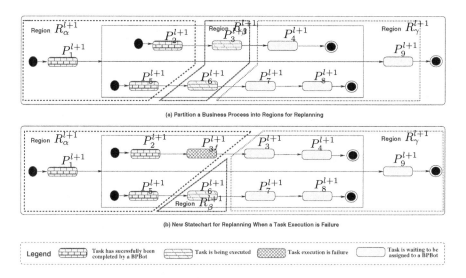

(a) Partition a Business Process into Regions for Replanning

(b) New Statechart for Replanning When a Task Execution is Failure

Legend Task has successfully been completed by a BPBot   Task is being executed   Task execution is failure   Task is waiting to be assigned to a BPBot

Fig. 5. Business Process Regions for Replanning

in region R_β^{l+1} are used to generate the constraints for the IP. For example, assuming that the task t_1 is completed by the BPBot a_{14}, the actual task execution duration is 20 seconds and the execution cost is ·10 dollars, then the following constraints can be generated:

$$y_{14} = 1, \tag{10}$$

$$q_{du}(a_{14}) = 20, q_{price}(a_{14}) = 10 \tag{11}$$

Constraint 10 indicates that the BPBot a_{14} is selected to execute the task. Constraint 11 indicates that IP uses the actual execution duration and execution price of the task P_1^{l+1} to select the optimal execution plan. For another example, assume that the task P_3^{l+1} is currently being executed by the BPBot a_{39}, then a constraint $y_{39} = 1$ can be generated. It should be noted that if the predefined number of execution attempts for task P_f^{l+1} is r_f, then $r_f - 1$ should be used when conducting the replanning.

With the above constraints, the output of IP will give an optimal execution plan for tasks in region R_γ^{l+1} and task P_f^{l+1}, if all the QoS constraints are still able to be enforced. In some cases, the task execution failure cannot be handled by replanning, since extra costs have been spent on executing task P_f^{l+1} because of the failure execution. This means some constraints (e.g., execution duration) on the whole business process may become infeasible. In such case, the BPBot a^l is going to violate its SLA, therefore it needs to report the estimated SLA to the BPBot a^{l-1}. The estimation can be done by relaxing these infeasible constraints.

When the BPBot a^{l-1} receives the estimated SLA violation, it will first try to handle it by replanning the execution of P^{l-1} in region R_γ^{l-1}, without replacing the BPBot that reports SLA violation with another BPBot. If the replanning is successful, then the estimated SLA violation is handled without validating a^{l-1}'s SLA. However, if the replanning fails (i.e., some constraints are not feasible), it can try to replan the execution by replacing the BPBot that reports SLA violation with another BPBot. If the replanning

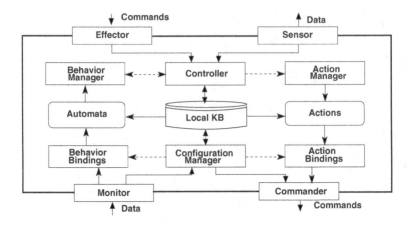

Fig. 6. BPBot Internal Structure.

is still unsuccessful, then it has to propagate the SLA violation to the upper level. The SLA validation may be propagated to level 0 and need to be handled by the user of business process P^0. Service replacement is done by process migrations, detail discussion on process migration is outside the scope of this paper.

4.2 Handling SLA Violation

The BPBot at level l also needs to handle SLA violations that occur at level $l+1$, despite the fact that the task execution is completed. In some cases, QoS property downgrade is unacceptable. For example, some safety requirements on production can not be downgraded, such SLA violations can be considered as task execution failures, which need to be re-executed as we discussed in previous section. In other cases, the BPBot a^l needs to replan the task execution in region R_γ^{l+1}. It either handles the SLA violations by replanning, or needs to propagate the SLA violations to the upper level.

5 Implementation Aspects

Figure 6 shows the internal physical structure of a BPBot. The behavior of the target business process is defined by the state machine represented in Statecharts, and monitored by the Behavior Manager. The Controller orchestrates the autonomic behavior of the BPBot as a whole including detecting business exceptions, performing analysis and enforcing actions. Action managers contain the set of available actions for the current BPBot where they are residing. Note that actions are logical entities in BPBot, hence it is desirable to realize the bindings between the intended actions and the lower-level BPBots before the actual rendering of target actions. Similarly, the bindings between monitoring data and state machines are also required since a datum needs to be transformed into understandable format before it can be processed by the state machine. The action manger is responsible for selecting and maintaining such binding information for the BPBot. Change of bindings from existing ones may result from the unsatisfied quality of services of the target business process, or from exceptions occurring during the execution of business process. The main focus of this paper is to enable the selection of the optimal bindings and the generation of new execution plan in response to the emerging specifications. There are four communication ports in an BPBot: (1) an *effector* that receives commands from the parent BPBot; (2) a *sensor* that transmits data from current BPBot to its parent BPBot; (3) a *monitor* that senses the data from child BPBots; and (4) a *commander* that renders actions to the child BPBots. A BPBot exposes management interfaces to the external manager for changing its own configuration. For example, the associated state machine can be migrated into different one if the business rules require it to do so. The rules of action bindings that are stored in the local knowledge base can also be modified if more suitable rules are chosen for different business situations. The Configuration Manager carries the execution of BPBot's configuration. The operations of the configuration can be triggered via two ways: (1) the parent BPBot issues a configuration command through the Effector; or (2) the Action Manager renders a configuration action directly to the Configuration Manager. The latter operation actually realizes the functionality of self-configuration.

6   Related Work

Previous work has investigated dynamic service selection based on given user requirements. Related projects include Market-based workflow [10], CMI [4] and eFlow [2]. They tend to focus on optimizing service selection at a single task level. Our approach, on the other hand, focuses on optimizing service selection at the level of a business process instances level. We have proposed a novel service selection approach that uses integer programming techniques to generate reliable execution based on given task execution models.

   Exception handling in workflows and business processes is widely discussed in literatures [1,5,7,9]. In [1], ECA rules are used to handle expected exceptions. A rich *exception-specification language* is proposed. It also provides patterns to facilitate the designing of execution handling rules. In [9], justified ECA rules are used to handle the expected exceptions. Furthermore, a case-based reasoning (CBR) mechanism with integrated human involvement is used to improve the exception handling capabilities. This involves collecting cases to capture experiences in handling exceptions, retrieving similar prior exception handling cases, and reusing the exception handling experiences captured in those cases in new situations. In [7], it provides an approach to facilitate users in proposing solutions for resolving a given exceptions. It scans through the previous records in handling exceptions, looking for those that are close to the current exception. The ways in which those exceptions were handled serve as useful information in determining how to handle the current one. The work described in [5] tries to solve the problem in another way: it aims at analyzing exceptions to understand why they occur, and predicting and preventing their occurrence, rather than handling them. Different from above approaches, our work actually focuses on handling QoS exception in an autonomic fashion. We adopt the integer programming to generate optimal and reliable execution plans. The QoS exception handling is enabled at runtime by optimization algorithms. The optimization algorithms are used for resolving the exceptions both locally and optimally.

7   Conclusion

The next generation of enterprise solutions will be characterized by their ability to adapt to changing business conditions with ease and flexibility. Business process management systems in conjunction with optimization technologies and autonomic computing, which are described in this paper, will provide a firm foundation of creating adaptive infrastructure for modern enterprise. This paper presents our early work towards realizing such technological foundation.

References

1. F. Casati, S. Ceri, S. Paraboschi, and G. Pozzi. Specification and Implementation of Exceptions in Workflow Management Systems. *TODS*, 24(3): 405–451, 1999.
2. F. Casati and M.-C. Shan. Dynamic and Adaptive Composition of E-Services. *Information Systems*, 26(3): 143–162, May 2001.
3. F. C. et al. Unraveling the Web Services: an Introduction to SOAP, WSDL, and UDDI. *IEEE Internet Computing*, Mar/Apr issue 2002.
4. D. Georgakopoulos, H. Schuster, A. Cichocki, and D. Baker. Managing Process and Service Fusion In Virtual Enterprises. *Information System, Special Issue on Information System Support for Electronic Commerce*, 24(6): 429–456, 199.
5. D. Grigori, F. Casati, U. Dayal, and M.-C. Shan. Improving Business Process Quality through Exception Understanding, Prediction, and Prevention. In *Proceedings of 27th International Conference on Very Large Data Bases*, pages 159–168, Roma, Italy, 2001.
6. D. Harel and A. Naamad. The STATEMATE Semantics of Statecharts. *ACM Transactions on Software Engineering and Methodology*, 5(4): 293–333, 1996.
7. S.-Y. Hwang, S.-F. Ho, and J. Tang. Mining Exception Instances to Facilitate Workflow Exception Handling. In *Proceedings of the Sixth International Conference on Database Systems for Advanced Applications (DASFAA), April 19-21, Hsinchu, Taiwan*, pages 45–52. IEEE Computer Society, 1999.
8. M. Köksalan and S. Zionts, editors. *Multiple Criteria Decision Making in the New Millennium*. Springer-Verlag, 2001.
9. Z. Luo, A. P. Sheth, K. Kochut, and J. A. Miller. Exception Handling in Workflow Systems. *Applied Intelligence*, 13(2): 125–147, 2000.
10. C. Stricker, S. Riboni, M. Kradolfer, and J. Taylor. Market-Based Workflow Management for Supply Chains of Services. *Proceedings of the 33rd Hawaii International Conference on System Sciences*, 1998.
11. L. Zeng, B. Benatallah, M. Dumas, J. Kalagnanam, and Q. Z. Sheng. Quality Driven Web Services Composition. In *Proceedings of the 12th international conference on World Wide Web (WWW), Budapest, Hungary*. ACM Press, May 2003.

L-ToPSS – Push-Oriented Location-Based Services*

Ioana Burcea and Hans-Arno Jacobsen

Department of Electrical Engineering and
Department of Computer Science
University of Toronto
{ioana,jacobsen}@eecg.toronto.edu

Abstract. The advance in wireless networks and in positioning systems has led to a new class of mobile applications: *location-based services* (LBS). LBS offer highly personalized services to mobile users based on their locations, user profiles and static and dynamic content information. The publish/subscribe paradigm is an information dissemination model appropriate for the implementation of LBS. However, existing publish/subscribe systems do not include location information in their models. In this paper we present an extension for the publish/subscribe paradigm that can effectively support push-oriented LBS.

1 Introduction

The proliferation of mobile devices and the significant increase of data on the Internet has led to the development of a new generation of mobile applications that offer highly personalized services to mobile users. One of the most powerful ways to personalize mobile services is based on the location of the mobile client. Knowing the geographic position of the mobile user at any given time adds a new dimension to the types of offered services. Thus, *location-based services* (hereafter referred to as LBS) represent information services that exploit the location information of mobile terminals to offer highly customized information content to mobile users. Examples of LBS include: requesting the nearest business or service (e.g., the nearest restaurant or ATM), receiving proximity-based reports (e.g., traffic/weather/news reports) or proximity-based notifications (e.g., e-coupons, advertisements), payment based on proximity, tracking resources or assets, and location-based games.

Based on the information delivery method, we identify two types of LBS: push and pull-based services. Pull-based services rely on the traditional request/response paradigm, where the client browses the available services and sends a specific request to the server. The server locates the user and answers to his request considering the specific location information. In push-based applications, the infrastructure autonomously pushes information to mobile terminals based on user profiles/subscriptions and their current location.

* This research is partially funded by IBM Toronto Lab, Center for Advanced Studies, Canada

B. Benatallah and M.-C. Shan (Eds.): TES 2003, LNCS 2819, pp. 131–142, 2003.
© Springer-Verlag Berlin Heidelberg 2003

In pull-based LBS, clients have to poll the server for any information updates, which may lead to server resource contention and network overload. Furthermore, mobile systems like cell phones, PDAs and wearable computers are less suitable for browsing and query-based information retrieval due to their limited input device capabilities. The current trend toward even smaller devices will amplify this problem. Moreover, energy represents a scarce resource for mobile devices, therefore, they are better suited as passive listeners than as active tools for searching information.

The limitations presented above may be effectively addressed by a push-oriented LBS model. Push-oriented LBS offer highly personalized information to their users notifying them about events that match both their profiles / subscriptions and their current location. For example, a user can be interested in receiving information about his favorite books. He can subscribe to a targeted advertising LBS specifying his interests. While walking through the city, he can receive on his mobile device an advertisement that says his favorite book is on sale at the next corner bookstore. This kind of services would be widely accepted and used only if the information is highly relevant to the user. We believe that profile and subscription-based techniques represent effective means to achieve this goal.

The research challenges implied by this kind of applications refer to information processing. The middleware platform supporting such applications must filter information for potentially millions of users [8], given their continuously changing location information, their profiles/subscriptions and, moreover, dynamic and static content information. We argue that this kind of services can be supported extremely well by an architecture based on the publish/subscribe paradigm. The paradigm has recently gained a significant interest in the database community as support for information dissemination applications [1,4,6] for which other models turned out to be inadequate.

In publish/subscribe systems, clients are autonomous components that exchange information by publishing events and by subscribing to events of interest. In these systems, publishers act as information producers, while subscribers act as information consumers. A publisher usually generates a message when it wants the external world to know that a certain event has occurred. All subscribers that have previously expressed their interest in receiving such an event will be notified about it. The central component of this architecture is the event broker. This component records all subscriptions in the system. When a certain event is published, the event broker matches it against all subscriptions in the system. When the incoming event verifies a subscription, the event broker notifies the corresponding subscriber.

Due to the scalability of publish/subscribe systems in terms of number of supported clients and number of processed events per second [6], we believe that this is an extremely promising approach for push-oriented LBS.

L-ToPSS (Location-aware Toronto Publish/Subscribe System) is our research prototype that provides LBS in a push-oriented style, correlating content provider data, user profiles and continuously changing location information. In our system, content provider data is modeled as publications, while user profiles represent subscriptions. More formally, the problem that we address in this paper can be expressed as follows: given a set of mobile or stationary publishers P and their publications, a set of mobile or stationary subscribers S and their subscriptions, and continuously changing location information L about mobile entities in the system, the notifications about the matching publications are sent to the subscribers only when they are close by the corresponding publishers.

This paper is organized as follows. In the next section we briefly present some examples of LBS applications from which we derive an LBS taxonomy used to classify the problem space. Section 3 discusses the L-ToPSS research prototype and its architecture. In Section 4 we describe our experimental platform. Section 5 presents the related work. Section 6 concludes with the experience gained during the design of our model.

2   LBS – From Applications to Taxonomy

Generally speaking, LBS provide and deliver information to its users in a highly selective manner exploiting mobile terminal location information. Examples of applications comprise route planning applications (e.g., finding the shortest path between two locations), enhanced directory assistance (e.g., finding the nearest restaurant or ATM), location-aware advertisement (e.g., ads are targeted to consumer within a certain radius of one of the retailer's locations), safety services (e.g., tracking the location of mobile 911 callers), resource management (e.g., tracking and dispatching mobile resources) and so on. In this section we briefly describe some LBS applications that can benefit from the push-oriented style of the service.

Location-Aware Mobile Commerce allows clients to purchase goods or services from retailers that are close to their current location. Thus, a location-based coupon service can send special offers to clients according to their profiles or preferences. Thus, clients do not have to periodically check the offers, as they are notified about them when they pass within a certain distance of the retailer's location. In this cases, the information provider has a fixed, known location, while the information requester is mobile. Moreover, the retailer's offer can be valid for an extended period of time or only at its release time.

Proximity-Based Alerts inform users about certain events of interest to them. For example, a user can be informed about an accident that has occurred on the highway 2 miles ahead. Based on this information, the user can request an alternative route to his destination. This kind of information is characterized by its momentary validity.

Common Profile Matching services allow users to be notified when a person with a compatible profile is in the area. Similarly, a buddy finder applications can notify users when a member of the family or a friend is nearby. In these scenarios, both users are mobile.

Inferring from the applications presented above, we classify the LBS based on two dimensions: the mobility scenario of the information provider (publisher) and information requester (subscriber) and the type of the publication.

Table 1. Mobility scenarios and application examples.

Publisher	Subscriber	Application
Stationary	Mobile	Targeted advertising
Mobile	Stationary	Airport automatic check-in
Mobile	Mobile	Friend finder

Based on entities mobility, we distinguish three categories of scenarios that are presented in Table 1, where *stationary* means that the entity has a fixed, known location, while *mobile* refers to an entity that changes its location. Note that the case where both the publisher and the subscriber are stationary is not interesting from the LBS point of view. This case is addressed in traditional publish/subscribe systems.

According to the life-time of the publication in the system, there are two different cases: *instantaneous* publications - the publication is valid only at its publication time, it is matched against the existing subscriptions, then discarded [1] - and *long-lived* publications - the publication inserted into the system is persistent until a corresponding delete command is performed by the publisher such that subscriptions submitted at a later point are matched against this publication. Table 2 presents examples of applications for each category.

Table 2. Publication types and application examples.

Publication type	Application
Instantaneous	Location-based games
Long-lived	Targeted Advertisement

3   L-ToPSS – System Model and Architecture

L-ToPSS (Location-aware Toronto Publish/Subscribe System) is our research prototype. The issue of obtaining location updates of mobile clients is independent of the system behavior and it is beyond the scope of our research [16]. We assume that the system can periodically receive location information about its users as *(latitude, longitude, altitude)* coordinates. With the advances in positioning technologies, we believe that getting location updates does not represent an issue anymore.

3.1   System Model

The main component of the system is the filtering engine that matches the publications against the subscriptions in the system. In the model we propose, the publications describe real life objects, such as books that, for example, can be characterized by title, author, and edition. This type of information can be represented by semi-structured data used in traditional publish/subscribe systems. In our system, the publication is expressed as a list of attribute-value pairs. The

---

[1] In current publish/subscribe systems, the publications are always instantaneous.

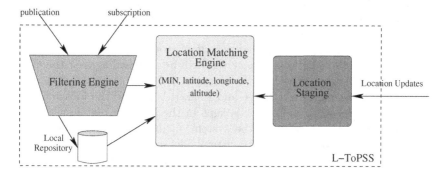

Fig. 1. L-ToPSS System Architecture

formal representation of a publication is given by the following expression: $\{(a_1,$ $val_1),\ (a_2,\ val_2),\ ...,\ (a_n,\ val_n)\}$. For the book example presented above, the publication can be expressed as:

$\{(title, "Location-based\ service"),\ (author,\ "H\text{-}A.Jacobsen"),\ (edition,\ 2003)\}$.

The subscriptions describe user interests or user profiles. In our system, subscriptions are represented as conjunctions of simple predicates. Each predicate expresses a value constraint for an attribute name. For example, the predicate $(edition > 2000)$ restricts the value of the attribute *"edition"* to a value greater than 2000. In a formal description, a simple predicate is represented as *(attribute_name relational_operator value)*. A predicate *(a rel_op val)* is matched by an attribute-value pair *(a', val')* if and only if the attribute names are identical *(a = a')* and the *(a rel_op val)* boolean relation is true. In our system, a subscription s is matched by a publication p if and only if all its predicates are matched by some pair in p.

If either the publisher or the subscriber is stationary, we assume that the publication or the subscription, respectively, is associated with the fixed location of the corresponding entity. The location information is expressed as *(latitude, longitude, altitude)* coordinates. Similarly, when an entity is mobile, the information it produces contains the *Mobile Identification Number* (MIN) - a unique identifier of the mobile device.

3.2   System Architecture

The system architecture is depicted in Figure 1. First, we explain how the system works for the stationary publisher-mobile subscriber case. Then, we argue that the mobile publisher-stationary subscriber scenario can be treated symmetrically. Finally, we present the mobile publisher-mobile subscriber case.

Both subscriptions and publications are sent to the filtering engine. When a subscription is matched by a publication, a *location constraint* that contains the *MIN* of the subscriber and the *(latitude, longitude, altitude)* coordinates of the publisher is sent to the location matching engine. This component stores the location constraints, as well as the associations with the subscriptions and the publications that have generated them.

If the publication is a long-lived one, it is stored in a local repository. In this way, subscriptions entering the system will be matched against the existing publications in the repository. For each match, a location constraint is created in the same way as explained above and then, it is sent to the location matching engine. The location constraint is kept in the location matching engine as long as the publication exists in the system. Conversely, if the publication is instantaneous, it is not stored in the system. The instantaneous publication and the location constraints that it produces are discarded after a period of time equal to the duration of a cycle of location updates (i.e., the time needed for receiving and processing the location updates for all connected clients). This means that in order to receive notifications about instantaneous publications, interested subscribers have to be in the area of the publisher at the moment when the publication is issued.

The system periodically receives updates of users' location. This information is processed in the location staging component. Each location information is represented as a *(user_MIN, current_latitude, current_longitude, current_altitude)* tuple. This tuple is forwarded to the location matching engine that matches it against the location constraints in the system. A tuple *(user_MIN, current_latitude, current_longitude, current_altitude)* matches a location constraint *(MIN, latitude, longitude, altitude)* if and only if $MIN = user\_MIN$ and the distance[2] between the two points determined by *(current_latitude, current_longitude, current_altitude)* and *(latitude, longitude, altitude)* does not exceed a certain value. If a location constraint is matched, this means that the corresponding subscriber is close to a point of interest for him. Therefore, the system will send a notification to the user about the publication associated with the location constraint. The notification is sent to the mobile device identified by the *MIN*. After the notification is sent, the location constraint is deleted. In this way, the user will be notified at most once about a publication, avoiding sending the user the same piece of information over again.

The mobile publisher-stationary subscriber case can be modeled symmetrically. In this case, the static location is associated with the subscription, while the *MIN* is contained in the publication. The system processes the information in the same way as in the previous case. In this scenario, the stationary subscriber will be notified when the publisher comes nearby.

For the mobile publisher-mobile subscriber case, each entity has associated a MIN: MIN_{pub} and MIN_{sub}. In this case, the location constraint contains only the (MIN_{pub}, MIN_{sub}) tuple and it is associated with the corresponding publication and subscription. For each MIN that appears in the location constraints, the system stores the last location update and the timestamp when it was received. The location matching proceeds as follows. When a location update $(MIN_1, latitude, longitude, altitude)$ enters the system, the corresponding location information and the timestamp are updated. Moreover, for all the loca-

---

[2] The distance can be expressed as a function defined by the subscriber

tion constraints (MIN_1, MIN_2), the system checks if the last location received for MIN_2 is close to that of MIN_1 and also if the timestamps are close in time. If this is the case, the appropriate subscriber is notified about the publication associated with the location constraint.

Both the publisher and the subscriber can retrieve their publication or subscription, respectively. When a publication or a subscription is deleted, all the corresponding location constraints have to be deleted.

3.3   Information Processing

In this subsection we present the sequence of operations that correspond to information processing in the system, i.e., subscriptions, publications, location updates. The operations are considered in the stationary publisher - mobile subscriber case.

Insert Publication: insert a long-lived publication in the system
Input: publication P, location of the stationary publisher $(lat_p, long_p, alt_p)$

- store the publication P in the local repository
- match the publication P against the subscriptions in the system and retrieve the set of all matching subscriptions $\{(MIN_{k_1}, S_{k_1}), (MIN_{k_2}, S_{k_2}), \ldots, (MIN_{k_m}, S_{k_m})\}$
- create the corresponding location constraints $\{(MIN_{k_1}, S_{k_1}, P, lat_p, long_p, alt_p), (MIN_{k_2}, S_{k_2}, P, lat_p, long_p. alt_p), \ldots, (MIN_{k_m}, S_{k_m}, P, lat_p, long_p, alt_p)\}$ and send them to the location matching engine

Delete Publication: delete a publication from the system
Input: publication P

- delete P from the local repository
- delete all location constraints that are associated with P from the location matching engine

Match Publication: send an instantaneous publication to the system
Input: publication P, location of the stationary publisher $(lat_p, long_p, alt_p)$

- match the publication P against the subscriptions in the system and retrieve the set of all matching subscriptions $\{(MIN_{k_1}, S_{k_1}), (MIN_{k_2}, S_{k_2}), \ldots, (MIN_{k_m}, S_{k_m})\}$
- create the corresponding location constraints $\{(MIN_{k_1}, S_{k_1}, P, lat_p, long_p, alt_p), (MIN_{k_2}, S_{k_2}, P, lat_p, long_p, alt_p), \ldots, (MIN_{k_m}, S_{k_m}, P, lat_p, long_p, alt_p)\}$ and send them to the location matching engine specifying that the publication is instantaneous

Insert Subscription: insert a subscription in the system
Input: subscription S, mobile identification number MIN

- store the subscription in the filtering engine

- query the local repository and retrieve the set of all matching publications $\{(P_{l_1}, lat_{l_1}, long_{l_1}, alt_{l_1}), (P_{l_2}, lat_{l_2}, long_{l_2}, alt_{l_2}), \ldots, (P_{l_n}, lat_{l_n}, long_{l_n}, alt_{l_n})\}$
- create the corresponding set of location constraints $\{$(MIN, S, P_{l_1}, lat_{l_1}, $long_{l_1}$, alt_{l_1}), (MIN, S, P_{l_2}, lat_{l_2}, $long_{l_2}$, alt_{l_2}), $\ldots$, (MIN, S, P_{l_n}, lat_{l_n}, $long_{l_n}$, alt_{l_n})$\}$ and send the location constraints to the location matching engine

Delete Subscription: delete a subscription from the system
Input: subscription S

- delete the subscription S from the filtering engine
- delete all location constraints that are associated with S

Match Location Update: match a location update against the location constraints in the system
Input: mobile identification number MIN and the corresponding location information $(lat_{MIN}, long_{MIN}, alt_{MIN})$

- retrieve all location constraints that contain MIN: $\{$(MIN, S_{k_1}, P_{l_1}, lat_{l_1}, $long_{l_1}$, alt_{l_1}), (MIN, S_{k_2}, P_{l_2}, P_{lat_2}, $long_{l_2}$, alt_{l_2}), $\ldots$, (MIN, S_{k_r}, P_{l_r}, lat_{l_r}, $long_{l_r}$, alt_{l_r})$\}$
- for i := 1 to r do
  - if the distance between $(lat_{MIN}, long_{MIN}, alt_{MIN})$ and $(lat_{l_i}, long_{l_i}, alt_{l_i})$ is within a certain value, send P_{l_i} to the mobile device identified by MIN and delete the location constraint (MIN, S_{k_i}, P_{l_i}, lat_{l_i}, $long_{l_i}$, alt_{l_i})
  - else if P_{l_i} is instantaneous, then delete the location constraint (MIN, S_{k_i}, P_{l_i}, lat_{l_i}, $long_{l_i}$, alt_{l_i})

3.4   Modeling Applications with L-ToPSS

In this subsection we present three examples of applications and show how they can be modeled with our system: the targeted advertising application we referred to earlier in the paper, an application for automatic airport check-in and a friend finder application.

Targeted Advertising Application
This scenario demonstrates the deployment of an LBS application that informs its users about objects of interests that are close to their current position. The objects of interest are matched according to user profiles. Thus, users are notified about discounts or sale for items that correspond to their interests and are available in their proximity. In this type of application, mobile clients act as subscribers in our model, while content providers represent stationary publishers. User profiles represent subscriptions, while information made available by the content providers is inserted as publications in the system. Thus, when a mobile user submit its profile to the system, the method *insert subscription*

is called with the appropriate parameters: the MIN of the client and the profile expressed as a subscription (see Section 3.1, for details). Similarly, the information made available by the content provider is inserted into the system using the method *insert publication* or *match publication* depending on whether the publication is instantaneous or a long-lived one. The location updates of the mobile client will be sent to the system by the *match location update* method.

Automatic Airport Check-In
This application addresses the following scenario. A client buys a plane ticket. When he arrives at the airport, the check-in system detects his presence at the airport and performs automatic check-in for the client. This application can be supported in our system using the mobile publisher-stationary subscriber approach. The mobile client acts as a publisher. When he buys the plane ticket, the ID of the flight and the MIN of the user's mobile device are inserted into the system as a publication, using the *insert publication* method. The airport check-in system acts as a subscriber: when the check-in procedure for a certain flight has to start, it subscribes to the ID of that particular flight, using the method *insert subscription*. This subscription will match all publications that contain that particular flight ID. In this way, a set of location constraints are created and sent to the location matching engine. When the client arrives at the airport, the corresponding location update will match the location constraint of that client; thus, the check-in system (i.e., the subscriber) is notified and it can perform automatic check-in for the client.

Friend Finder Application
This service allows mobile users to specify a member of the family or a fried about whom they would like to be notified when he is in the same area. This application follows the mobile publisher-mobile subscriber scenario. Practically, this scenario coordinates the positions of the two mobile users. Each mobile user has associated a MIN of the mobile device. When one user subscribes to the service for receiving notifications when his buddy is nearby, the corresponding location constraint is created (i.e., (MIN_1, MIN_2)). The location constraint will be matched only when the two mobile users are in the same area and the appropriate notification is sent to the subscriber.

These three applications presented above cover all mobility scenarios described in Section 2. All other applications that follows a particular scenario can be modeled in a similar way.

4   L-ToPSS – Experimental Platform

Our experimental platform is depicted in Figure 2. In order to experiment with our system, we use two IBM tools designed to facilitate LBS testing: City Simulator [11] and Location Transponder [14] . The City Simulator tool produces trace-files that simulate the motion of up to 1 million people. The trace-files contain timestamped data records representing coordinate positions of mobile objects (e.g., cell phone users). The Location Transponder takes as input the

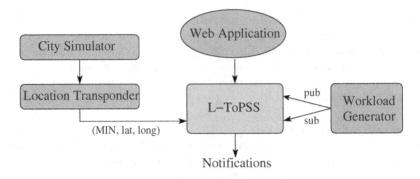

Fig. 2. L-ToPSS Experimental Platform

Table 3. ToPSS matching engine: matching performance for one event and different number of subscriptions.

# subs	matching time (ms)	# subs	matching time (ms)
1000	0.10	100000	8.10
5000	0.27	500000	79.00
10000	0.63	1000000	190.70
50000	3.85	5000000	1056.00

trace-files produced by the City Simulator and transmits the data to a receiving LBS application/server using HTTP requests, SOAP calls, UDP datagrams or a user-provided custom method. Thus, the Location Transponder will provide the location information updates to our system.

To experiment with the applications presented above, we develop a web application for client registration/profile input as well as for specifying publications. In order to simulate the activity of a real-life system, we use a workload generator which sends subscriptions and publications randomly into the system. The location matching engine and the repository used for storing publications are implemented using fastDB [7]

We believe that the main bottleneck in this architecture is the filtering engine. Our filtering engine is based on the ToPSS high-throughput matching kernel. The kernel implements a variety of counting algorithms [3]. We have evaluated its performance on a dual-CPU Pentium II workstation with an i686 CPU at 900MHz and 1.5GB RAM operating under Linux RedHat 7.2. Table 3 summarizes the experimental results for matching an event against different number of subscriptions. As the matching of location updates and the matching of subscriptions represent queries against tables, they are not interesting from an experimental point of view. Therefore, we do not include results about them.

5   Related Work

The work in this paper is part of the Toronto Publish/Subscribe System (ToPSS) project of the Middleware Systems Research Group (MSRG). Other recent and ongoing projects in the MSRG include Approximate ToPSS [13], Semantic ToPSS [15], and Subject Spaces [12].

A lot of research has been devoted to developing publish/subscribe systems [1,2,4,6]. Only recently, some research addresses location information in publish/subscribe systems. Chen et al [5] present an architecture for filtering spatial events (i.e., location updates). However, they do not support in their model the correlation of user profiles, content provider data and location information. [9] presents a multidimensional model for representing the information in LBS. Other topics of research related to our work are querying location dependent data, spatial databases and moving objects [10,17]. These topics address issues related to data management, data indexing and representation. Publish/subscribe systems solve a problem inverse to the database query processing: subscriptions represent queries, while publications represent data items; usually, publish/subscribe systems filter data items against queries. [10] contains an approach similar to the publish/subscribe model: in contrast with traditional approach of building indexes on moving objects, they introduce query indexing (queries remain active for a long period of time, while moving objects change their position continuously). In industry, content and location providers have implemented different aspects of LBS, but they focus on pull-oriented services.

6   Conclusions

In this paper we present an extended model for a publish/subscribe system that is location-aware. While the results presented in the paper are only preliminary, we consider that the model introduced can effectively support location based services in a push-oriented style. During the design of the model, we learned that there are cases when the publications need to be persistent in the system. Moreover, the location information can be processed independently from the matching between publications and subscriptions. In this way, we avoid updating subscriptions with each location change of the subscriber.

References

1. Marcos Kawazoe Aguilera, Robert E. Strom, Daniel C. Sturman, Mark Astley, and Tushar Deepak Chandra. Matching events in a content-based subscription system. In *Symposium on Principles of Distributed Computing*, pages 53–61, 1999.
2. Mehmet Altinel and Michael J. Franklin. Efficient filtering of xml documents for selective dissemination of information. In *Proceedings of the 26th VLDB Conference*, 2000.
3. Ghazaleh Ashayer, Hubert Ka Yau Leung, and H.-Arno Jacobsen. Predicate matching and subscription matching in publish/subscribe systems. In *Workshop on Distributed Event-based Systems*, Vienna, Austria, 2–5 July 2002.
4. Antonio Carzaniga, David S. Rosenblum, and Alexander L Wolf. Design and evaluation of a wide-area event notification service. *ACM Transactions on Computer Systems*, 19(3): 332–383, August 2001.

5. Xiaoyan Chen, Ying Chen, and Fangyan Rao. An efficient spatial publish/subscribe system for intelligent location-based services. In *Workshop on Distributed Event-based Systems*, San Diego, California, 8 June 2003.

6. Francoise Fabret, H.-Arno Jacobesen, Francois Llirbat, Joao Pereira, Kenneth Ross, and Dennis Shasha. Filtering algorithms and implementation for very fast publish/subscribe systems. In *SIGMOD Conference*, 2001.

7. Fastdb. http://www.ispras.ru/~knizhnik/fastdb.html.

8. H.-Arno Jacobsen. Middleware services for selective and location-based information dissemination in mobile wireless networks. In *Workshop on Middleware for Mobile Computing, Middleware 2001*, Heidelberg, Germany, 12–16 November 2001.

9. Christian S. Jensen, Augustas Kligys, Torben Bach Pedersen, and Igor Timko. Multidimensional data modeling for location-based services. In *The tenth ACM international symposium on Advances in geographic information systems*, Virginia, Germany, 2002.

10. Dmitri V. Kalashnikov, Sunil Prabhakar, Susanne Hambrusch, and Walid Aref. Efficient evaluation of continuous range queries on moving objects. In *DEXA 2002, Proc. of the 13th International Conference and Workshop on Database and Expert Systems Applications*, Aix en Provence, France, September 2–6 2002.

11. James Kaufman, Jussi Myllymaki, and Jared Jackson. City simulator. November 2001. IBM alphaWorks emerging technologies toolkit, http://www.alphaworks.ibm.com/tech/citysimulator.

12. Hubert Leung and H.-Arno Jacobsen. Subject spaces: A state-persistent model for publish/subscribe systems. In *Computer Science Research Group Technical Report CRSG-459*, University of Toronto, September 2002.

13. Haifeng Liu and H.-Arno Jacobsen. A-topss – a publish/subscribe system supporting approximate matching. In *Very Large Databases (VLDB'02)*, University of Toronto, August 2002.

14. Jussi Myllymaki and James Kaufman. Location transponder. April 2002. IBM alphaWorks emerging technologies toolkit, http://www.alphaworks.ibm.com/tech/transponder.

15. Milenko Petrovic, Ioana Burcea, and H.-Arno Jacobsen. S-topss – a semantic publish/subscribe system. In *Very Large Databases (VLDB'03)*, Berlin, Germany, September 2003.

16. Y.Zhao. Standardization of mobile phone positioning for 3g systems. IEEE Communcantions Magazine, July 2002.

17. Jun Zhang, Manli Zhu, Dimitris Papadias, Yufei Tao, and Dik Lun Lee. Location-based spatial queries. In *SIGMOD Conference, to appear*, 2003.

A Process and a Tool for Creating Service Descriptions Based on DAML-S[*]

Michael Klein and Birgitta König-Ries

Institute for Program Structures and Data Organization
Universität Karlsruhe
D-76128 Karlsruhe, Germany
{kleinm,koenig}@ipd.uni-karlsruhe.de
http://www.ipd.uni-karlsruhe.de/DIANE/en

Abstract. In distributed environments, collaboration is often achieved with the help of services. To enable automatic service trading, semantically expressive, automatically comparable, flexible, and editable service descriptions are needed. Our analysis shows that only ontology-based service descriptions like DAML-S offer the necessary expressiveness and flexibility. Unfortunately, up to now, DAML-S offers just a generic framework and lacks support for creating and editing appropriate service descriptions for specific classes of services. Therefore, in this paper, we present an approach to improving the usability of DAML-S. The two main building blocks of our approach are a process and a tool. The process guides through the steps necessary to create adequate service descriptions by introducing a layered ontology of services. The graphical tool, DINST, implements these ideas, thus offering a comfortable way to edit service descriptions.

1   Introduction

In the last few years, services have become the major basis for collaboration in distributed environments. In such environments, on the one hand, the members provide their resources as services and on the other hand, use the functionalities offered by other members to complement their applications. In many service oriented systems, the components are loosely coupled. Examples are the internet-based web services or services in networks with higher dynamics like peer-to-peer or ad hoc networks. In these cases, like on a marketplace, service offers have to be explicitly described and published, whereas service requests need to be paraphrased and compared with the offer descriptions. For this reason, what is needed, is a dedicated service description language.

Obviously, service descriptions can be done in various levels of detail. They range from simple keyword-based to highly complex ontology-based approaches and many different languages have been proposed in the last years. However, for

[*] This work is partially funded by the Deutsche Forschungsgemeinschaft (DFG) within SPP 1140 [1].

B. Benatallah and M.-C. Shan (Eds.): TES 2003, LNCS 2819, pp. 143–154, 2003.

a good service description language, several requirements have to be fulfilled, which are partially competitive:

Semantically Expressive. In general, the service description has to be expressive enough so that other applications can understand the functionality of the service without human help. Therefore, it is crucial to include the functional semantics of the service into the description. It describes, how the service transforms inputs into outputs and which side effects it produces. Moreover, with an increasingly complex service description it becomes less and less likely that a service request and a service description match exactly. Therefore, the language has to be able to describe services on various levels of abstraction, which allows to find similar services. To enhance the expressiveness when searching for services, it should be possible to add complex conditions to a request description.

Automatically Comparable. Service description should enable an automatic comparison, which can be done without the help of an additional human analysis. Thus, service descriptions need to have a certain structure.

Flexible. Contradictory to a structured language, flexibility is another requirement. Generally, the service description language should not be a fixed template for the following reasons: (1) The functionality of the described services (i.e. the inputs and outputs, their relationship as well as the side effects) are too diverse to be adequately expressed with one unique and common template. (2) Services operate on data from various domains. To express them appropriately, the description template should not be fixed, but yield the possibility to be adapted to different fields of knowledge by configuration. (3) When describing a service offer or request, the user is frequently confronted with elements she does not know in advance, whereas additional elements cannot be inserted into the template reasonably. A flexible description language would help to solve these problems.

Editable. The service description must have the ability to be created, read and edited by human users. As services are especially interesting in mobile environments, this needs to be easy enough to be done on mobile devices with limited display and input facilities.

In the following, we will analyze existing service description languages in terms of these requirements (Section 2). It turns out that ontology-based description languages like DAML-S [2] are well suited for these demands. However, DAML-S only offers a very generic framework which cannot be used directly without further work. Therefore, in this paper, we enhance the usability of DAML-S by presenting a process for creating a service description and DINST, a graphical Java-based tool that implements the presented process. Both were developed in our research project DIANE [3], which aims at enabling semantic service trading in ad-hoc-networks. Section 3 contains the description of the process and illustrates it using the example of information services, a typical and important service category, while Section 4 describes DINST.

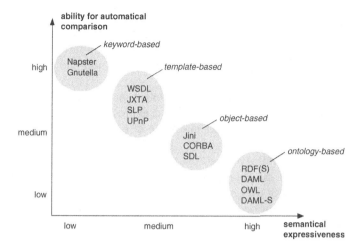

Fig. 1. Categorization of service description approaches by semantical expressiveness and ability for automatic comparison.

2   Existing Approaches

In this section, we examine existing approaches for service description languages and categorize them along the first two requirements: semantical expressiveness and the ability for automatic comparison. As a result, we can distinguish four clusters of description languages: keyword-based, template-based, object-based and ontology-based descriptions (see Figure 1).

The simplest form of service description is a *keyword-based approach* that tries to approximate the semantics of a service by providing some open keywords or a human-readable text. A typical example for this can be found in file-sharing networks like Gnutella [4] or Napster [5], where each participant offers its files as several "file downloading services", which are described by one or a few keywords only – namely the filename of the offered document. In general, these techniques suffer from a low semantic expressiveness (resulting in low values for precision and recall), which often requires the human user to manually examine the numerous results in order to find the desired files. However, the comparison of two service descriptions is very easy and can be performed automatically and efficiently.

More sophisticated approaches as used in WSDL [6], ebXML [7], JXTA-Search [8], SLP [9] or UPnP [10] rely on a *template-based description*. They enhance the expressiveness by dividing the description into several properties that can be filled with concrete keywords or values. Very similar to that are *object-based* descriptions, which additionally allow to use object references to link objects in a service description. Typical representatives are the description languages used in Sun's Jini [11] and CORBA [12]. In both, often only the non-functional aspects as well as the inputs and outputs of the service can be described. The functional semantics, i.e. what the service does, must be derived from name, textual description and parameters. In general, precision and recall are increased, but humans are still necessary to analyze the found results. Therefore, in most cases, an automatic computer-to-computer interaction is not possible. Nonetheless, comparison is still easy to medium and can be performed quickly in most cases.

Ontology-based service descriptions promise far higher values for precision and recall. This results from their increased expressiveness stemming from the introduction of rich ontologies that make use of many different property types. Besides generic ontology languages like RDF [13], DAML [14] and OWL [15], the most prominent ontology-based description language especially for services is DAML-S [2]. DAML-S achieves a large expressiveness by providing an upper ontology for all types of services. This ontology proposes a rough structure for a general service description by defining common properties for non-functional as well as functional attributes (like input, output, precondition, and effect). Unfortunately, DAML-S is extremely generic as most of its attributes' types are left open, which leads to difficulties when comparing two descriptions.

When examining our requirements from the previous section, we come to the conclusion that only ontology-based description languages provide enough expressiveness for an automatic service trading. However, up to now, much has to be done to fulfill the other requirements:

- *Comparison* of two ontology-based descriptions is very difficult, as their structure is constrained just for the first one or two levels. This results from the fact that most of the parameters can be built up arbitrarily because no type constraints prescribe their structure.
- Although the extreme generality enables a high *flexibility*, a usage of such a description is only reasonable, if there are standardizations to structure the relationships between the parameters as well as the use of different categories and domains.
- *Editing* such service descriptions is very tedious as the files have to match some given flexible service ontology. It is possible to use an ordinary text or XML editor, but they are not designed for the language's specialities and offer no directed support for it.

As a result, in this paper, we will take DAML-S as a starting point for a service description, but enhance its use by presenting a process and a tool, which help to fulfill the requirements from the previous section.

3 A Process for Creating a Service Description Based on DAML-S

In this section, we present a process for creating DAML-S 0.9 based service descriptions. It consists of four steps (see Figure 2): (1) acquiring the upper service ontology, (2) defining the service category, (3) inserting domain ontologies, and (4) instantiating the description. In the first three steps, a layered service ontology is constructed, which is taken as a template in the last step. Although

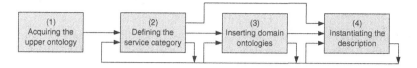

Fig. 2. A process for creating an ontology-based service description.

this process seems strictly sequential, in most cases, the steps will be traversed iteratively, e.g. parts of the service description could already be instantiated before additional domain ontologies are included. In the following subsections, the steps are explained in more detail. We will exemplify them by constructing a concrete example description for a printing service.

3.1 Acquiring the Upper Service Ontology: DAML-S

When describing a service, we start with the upper service ontology DAML-S (see Figure 4a). Generally, this upper ontology defines the basic structure of a service description, i.e. services have to be presented in three aspects: the description of the functionality in a black-box view as Profile, the operating sequence in a glass-box view as Model, and the technical access path to the service as Grounding (see Figure 3). As we are interested in a description for service trading, in the following, we will concentrate on the service profile. Its properties can be divided into two main groups: functional and non-functional parameters. Non-functional properties provide meta-information about the service, i.e. its name, its offerer, quality parameters and so on. The functional properties try to capture what the service does (i.e. its functional semantics). In DAML-S, this is achieved by the four attributes input and output (describing control data entering and leaving the correctly working service) as well as precondition and effect (describing the state of the affected part of the world before and after successful service execution). To gain high usability and flexibility, the range type of these functional parameters is ParameterDescription, which is very generic as it is not restricted any further.

Notice that besides DAML-S other upper service ontologies could have been used. However, it is important that this ontology is unique and commonly accepted in the community that wants to trade services. Furthermore, such an ontology usually is rather small and generic.

For describing our example printing service, we just have to acquire the upper ontology in this step. No further action is needed.

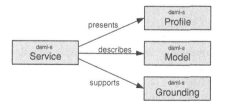

Fig. 3. Basic structure of a service description as proposed in DAML-S v0.9

3.2   Defining the Service Category

The middle layer of our service ontology describes different service categories (Figure 4b). This layer is needed because the classes of functionalities offered by services span an incredibly wide range. A service can be anything from the possibility to download a document, to the selling of shoes, to a complex computation. Obviously, the service descriptions for these services will need to address widely varying parameters and will thus be very different from one another.

The service category layer of the ontology is our approach to group the space of services into different classes. Each service category is characterized by possible types of the function parameters input, output, precondition, and effect. Moreover, these types are not simple data or enumeration types, but in most cases complex graphs of classes. Therefore, as a guideline, these types should be defined by class hierarchies or by aspect separation, which helps to reduce their complexity and enhance their readability. In short, a service category ontology consists of two parts: (1) type restrictions for the functional parameters as well as (2) hierarchical, aspect separating ontologies for these types.

Notice that the service categories themselves can build a hierarchy. This results from the possibility to vary the generality of the types that are used to specify the functional parameters of each category. However, we expect the existence of only a few different top level service categories, and at most a few dozen specialized service categories.

For our example printing service, we need one very important service category: the category of information services. We define an information service as a service that changes the state of a piece of information, i.e. a document. Typical

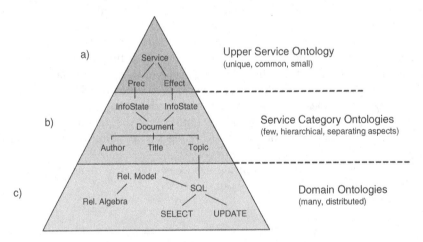

Fig. 4. Layered service ontology. On top, one unique, small, and commonly accepted upper service ontology can be found describing the general structure of a service description. It is specialized by one of a few service categories, which mainly defines and fans out the types of the functional parameters. At the bottom, one or more ontologies (taken from a large distributed pool) set up the domain specific vocabulary of the description.

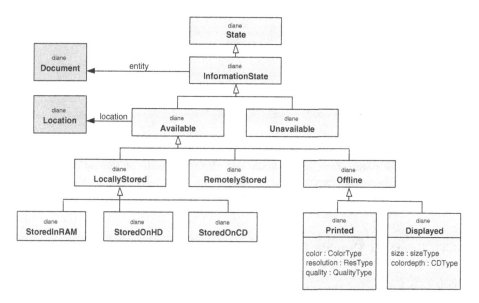

Fig. 5. Example ontology for states of documents. Instances of it are used to describe the precondition and effect (=postcondition) of an information service.

states for documents are depicted in the hierarchical state ontology of Figure 5. Generally, a document can be available (which means that the user can access the document) or not. We distinguish three degrees of availability: the document is locally stored on the user's device (e.g. in the RAM, on hard disk, or on CD), the document is remotely stored in the network, but its location is known and accessible to the user, or the document is not stored electronically, but available in an offline manner (e.g. printed or simply displayed on a screen). The description of a document itself can be structured in an aspect separating manner as described in [16].

As information services change the state of documents, typical information services are our printing service, which transforms the state from LocallyAvailable to Printed, a downloading service, which transforms the state from Unavailable to StoredOnHD, or a scanning service, which transforms the state from Printed to LocallyAvailable. To generalize, the typical structure of an information service can be found in Figure 6. Input and output are used for controlling information only, not for the documents itself (i.e. our printing service does not *output* the printed document, but possibly the time when the printing will be finished). Precondition and effect denote the state of the information before and after successful service execution. Note that this structure is not conform to DAML-S directly as preconditions and effects have to point to ParameterDescriptions. One possibility to solve this problem could be the declaration of the topmost class State as subclass of ParameterDescription resulting in a syntactically correct but semantically problematic solution. Therefore, we propose to substitute the range of precondition and effect to some sort of State which would help to more clearly describe the "change of the world" resulting from the service.

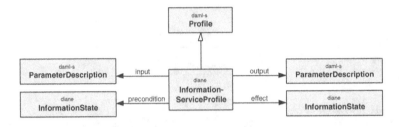

Fig. 6. Profile for an information service. Input and output are describing controlling information as parameters, precondition and effect the state of the (affected) world before and after service execution. Note that this is not conform to DAML-S 0.9 as it demands the range of precondition and effect to be ParameterDescription, too.

3.3   Inserting Domain Ontologies

The lowest layer of the ontology describes different application domains (see Figure 4c). Consider, for instance, a service offering access to documents on relational database systems and a user looking for information on SQL. Quite probably, the service would be able to provide the user with the desired information. However, for a computer to be able to determine that this is the case, it needs the information that SQL is a subtopic of relational database systems. Such information can be formalized by domain specific ontologies. Typically, such ontologies consist of three parts: (a) a general part (or TBox in description logics) describing types and possible relationships (like Topic and isSubtopicOf) and (b) a concrete world description (or ABox) by listing concrete instances and their relationship (e.g., SQL is a subtopic of RelationalModel), and (c) a domain specific comparison function.

There exists a potentially large number of these domain specific ontologies, ranging from databases, to pediatrics, to locations. It is not expected that everybody knows all these ontologies. Rather, whenever a service is offered or searched for, the appropriate ontology needs to be acquired. This could be achieved by special expert services offering access to these domain ontologies. Information about which ontology was used is part of the service description. Notice that in general, instances of domain ontologies can only be usefully compared with the appropriate domain specific matching functions.

To describe at which location the printout of our example service will be available, we use the domain ontology describing locations on an university campus from Figure 7. Its general part (a) differentiates Locations into Buildings and Rooms and allows a isNeighboredTo and a within relation. With that, the situation of the real world is described in the second part (b). The domain specific comparison function (not shown) could for example use the isNeighboredTo and within relation to calculate a "hop" distance between arbitrary Locations.

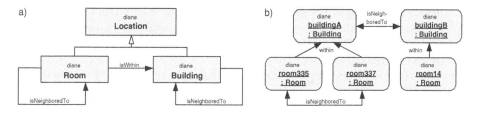

Fig. 7. Example domain ontology for locations.

3.4   Instantiating the Layered Service Ontology

To obtain the concrete service description, the layered service ontology created in the first three steps has to be instantiated. Therefore, appropriate (mostly rather specific) classes are chosen from the ontology, transformed to instances and connected to other instances with valid property instances. Moreover, XML schema datatypes like `xsd:string` or `xsd:integer` are filled with concrete values, whereas enumeration types are instantiated by picking one predefined instance from a set.

An example of a printing service instance is depicted in Figure 8. The service changes the state of an arbitrary pdf document from LocallyAvailable to Printed in room 335 with the parameters black/white, high quality and 600 dpi. Two characteristics of the description have to be mentioned in detail:

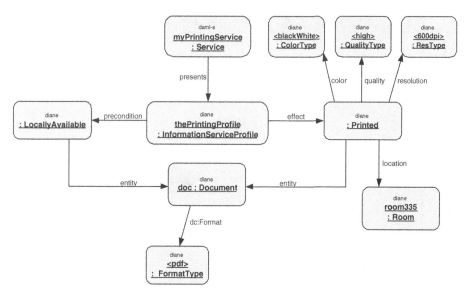

Fig. 8. Typical description of a printing service. Basically, it transforms the state of a document from LocallyAvailable to Printed. Note that precondition and effect are not independent, but connected through the Document of interest. Moreover, all parameter values are instantiations of enumeration types to enhance the expressiveness.

— Precondition and effect are not independent, but connected via the entity-property of their states pointing to the same document instance. In more complex service descriptions, the effect and the output may also be dependent from the input.

— All values for describing the characteristics of the printout and the document are instances of predefined enumeration types like ColorType or FormatType. The chosen instance is denoted within angle brackets like <600dpi>. Avoiding instances of generic data types from XML schema (like xsd:string or xsd:decimal), we increase the expressiveness and comparability of the description as the properties are restricted to values that uniquely correspond to characteristics from the real world.

3.5   Evaluation

In this section, we analyze whether the proposed process helps DAML-S to fulfill the requirements identified in Section 2. Generally, descriptions that are complying with the process are well *comparable*: the overall structure of the description is fixedly given by the upper ontology whereas the category ontology structures the details of the functional parameters. Moreover, although the used domain vocabularies are more or less unstructured, they can be compared with the domain specific matchers that come with each ontology. On the other hand, *flexibility* is not restricted too much, as arbitrary (but standardized) categories

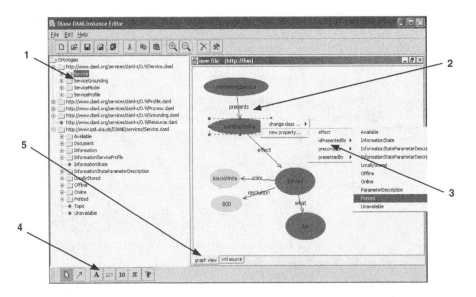

Fig. 9. Screenshot of DINST - a tool for instantiating DAML-S based service descriptions: (1) Area for loading ontologies, (2) graphical representation of the description, (3) context sensitive operations to extend and modify the description, (4) buttons to add datatype instances, (5) switch to change between graphical and XML view.

and domains can be used. Furthermore, elements can be added and omitted optionally which is possible thanks to the RDF basis. However, this can lead to penalties when matching. In the next section, we will introduce a graphical tool that eases *editing*.

4 A Tool for DAML-S Instantiation: DINST

Manually writing DAML-S based service descriptions in the style of the presented process is a tedious task. Thus, we have developed the tool that supports the process from Section 3 in a purely graphical manner. A screenshot of DINST is depicted in Figure 9. In Area 1, different DAML ontologies can be loaded. Typically, the editor starts with the DAML-S ontology and the user loads own category and domain ontologies. Ontologies are represented as folders that contain the classes of the ontology when opened. Classes themselves are folders containing possible properties for this class. To create an instance of a class, it is possible to drag and drop a class from Area 1 to Area 2. By right-clicking on an instance, the user can choose from two options (Area 3): (1) changing the class of the instance to a subclass from a list, which is often necessary when a class has to be specialized because of an ontology that has been loaded afterwards (e.g., a general instance of State is refined to a special state like Printed after the information service category has been loaded.) (2) enlarging the instance graph by adding a property and a correct typed range instance to the current node selectable from a list (e.g. right-clicking on an information service profile instance yields the possibility to add a property instance of effect and an instance of a state like Printed.). For reasons of flexibility, it is also possible to add property and datatype instances that are not represented in the ontology by using the tools from Area 4. Finally, Area 5 provides a switch for changing between graphical and XML view, which helps to get an idea of the final result. To summarize, DINST offers the functionality to edit a layered service description in a purely graphical manner. In principle, it can also be used to edit the other parts of the description, namely the ServiceModel and the ServiceGrouding.

5 Conclusion and Future Work

In this paper, we have presented a process for creating a DAML-S based service description. This process sets up a layered service ontology consisting of an upper service ontology, an ontology for the service category, and several domain ontologies, which is instantiated to a concrete service description at the same time. A typical service category for information services and an example of an appropriate service instance have been presented. To describe the functional semantics of information services, we introduced a state ontology dealing with states of documents and proposed to change the range of ServiceProfile's precondition and effect properties in DAML-S from ParameterDescription to some sort of state. Finally, we presented DINST, a Java-based tool that supports the user when creating service descriptions by offering a graphical interface which leads him through the layering and instantiating process.

Currently, we are in the process of developing ontologies for further service categories beyond information services. We are also implementing and describing a number of example services. With that, we hope to gain more insights into possible dependencies between inputs, outputs, preconditions and effects.

Acknowledgement. We would like to thank Ting Zheng for the implementation of DINST.

References

1. Deutsche Forschungsgesellschaft (DFG): Schwerpunktprogramm 1140: "Basissoftware für selbstorganisierende Infrastrukturen für vernetzte mobile Geräte". http://www.tm.uka.de/forschung/SPP1140/
2. Defense Advanced Research Projects Agency: DARPA agents markup language - services (DAML-S). http://www.daml.org/services/
3. Institute for Program Structures and Data Organization, Universität Karlsruhe: DIANE project. http://www.ipd.uni-karlsruhe.de/DIANE/en
4. Gnutelliums: Gnutella. http://gnutella.wego.com
5. Napster: Protocol specification. http://opennap.sourceforge.net/napster.txt
6. World Wide Web Consortium: Web service description language (WSDL). http://www.w3.org/TR/wsdl
7. OASIS, UN/CEFACT: ebXML. http://www.ebxml.org/
8. Waterhouse, S.: JXTA search: Distributed search for distributed networks. Sun Microsystems Whitepaper – http://search.jxta.org/JXTAsearch.pdf (2001)
9. Network Working Group: Service location protocol – RFC 2165. http://www.ietf.org/rfc/rfc2165.txt (1997)
10. Microsoft Corp.: Universal plug and play. http://www.upnp.org
11. Sun Microsystems: Jini. http://www.jini.org/
12. CORBA: Trading object service specification. http://cgi.omg.org/docs/formal/00-06-27.pdf
13. World Wide Web Consortium: Resource description framework (RDF). http://www.w3.org/RDF/
14. Defense Advanced Research Projects Agency (DARPA): DARPA agent markup language (DAML). http://www.daml.org/
15. World Wide Web Consortium: Web ontology language (OWL). http://www.w3.org/TR/owl-ref/
16. König-Ries, B., Klein, M.: Information services to support e-learning in ad-hoc networks. In: First International Workshop on Wireless Information Systems (WIS2002). (2002) 13–24

Mathematical Web Services: A Case Study

Yannis Chicha and Marc Gaëtano

I3S/Université de Nice-Sophia Antipolis
ESSI, 930 route des Colles, BP 145
06903 Sophia Antipolis Cedex, France
tel. : +33 (0)492 965 157
fax.: +33 (0)492 965 055
{chicha,gaetano@}essi.fr

Abstract. This paper presents a attempt to use the semantic web technologies to deploy and interact with a mathematical package called Bernina. This work is carried out within a European Union funded project called MONET aiming at demonstrating the application of the latest ideas for creating a semantic web to the world of mathematical software. While many of these ideas address the general problem of delivering online web services, they need to be tailored to suit mathematical services. After a brief overview of Bernina we focus on the problem of mathematical services discovery and describe the broker, a key component in the MONET framework. In order to register to a broker, a mathematical service should be able to describe the problem it is intended to solve. We discuss the ontology and taxonomy aspects of the project and show on a small example how it could be used to describe Bernina functions. Before some concluding remarks, we present our prototype implementation of Bernina as a mathematical web service.

1 Introduction

The number of mathematical packages has increased dramatically during the last decade. Whether general purpose or specialized, these computer assistants for mathematical problem solving have become essential in many areas such as engineering, research or education. In order to increase the accessibility of these packages it seemed reasonable to apply the latest ideas and technologies of the semantic web to the world of mathematical software. This paper reports on the development and deployment of a mathematical web service called Bernina. This work has been carried out within MONET, a European Union funded project aiming to demonstrate the applicability of the latest ideas for creating a semantic web to mathematical software, in particular using sophisticated algorithms to match the characteristics of a problem to the advertised capabilities of available services and then invoking the chosen services through a standard mechanism.

1.1 Mathematical Packages

Mathematical packages range from general purpose commercial systems like Maple or Mathematica to experimental and specialized software like Bernina.

B. Benatallah and M.-C. Shan (Eds.): TES 2003, LNCS 2819, pp. 155–167, 2003.
© Springer-Verlag Berlin Heidelberg 2003

Although there are many mechanisms for connecting software components together, no common, standard architecture has yet emerged in the area of mathematical software. The development of standards such as OpenMath or MathML only gives a common format for expressing both the rendering and the semantics of the underlying mathematical data objects.

The challenge is to develop a framework in which such services can describe their capabilities in as much detail as is necessary to allow a sophisticated software agent to select a suitable service based on an analysis of the characteristics of a user's problem. This challenge appears to be a special case of the overall challenges of the semantic web.

Mathematical software can be used to solve a broad variety of problems whose applications cover various domains such as engineering, medicine, finance, management, education or even art. Unfortunately, most of these mathematical packages remain unknown from a significant part of their potential users: too difficult to use for non-specialists, not available on the user's platform or environment, or simply not advertised enough, mathematical packages rarely evolve beyond the stage of prototypes. Turning them into commercial products by adding a GUI, documentation, technical support would be too costly compared to the relatively small community of users. Web services appear to be a suitable solution, providing direct access to the computational core of the package. In this context, it would also be possible for an academic institute to charge for the services offered to support high-quality and up-to-date software.

1.2   Bernina: A Case Study

Bernina is an interactive interface to the `Sum it` [1] library that provides efficient computations involving operators in $Q[x, d/dx]$ or $Q(x)[d/dx]$. Currently Bernina can be used interactively through a limited CGI-based interface available on the Web. Bernina and the underlying library `Sum it` are written in Aldor [2], a programming language dedicated to the efficient implementation of mathematical algorithms. Aldor was originally developed to provide an improved extension language for the AXIOM computer algebra system.

The work described in this paper consisted of replacing the current web-based interface of Bernina by a web service accessible through a web page. In this context, we use the MONET framework to create the Bernina service and access it as a client. The advantages are obvious since one could not only access Bernina through a web page but also from any piece of software (e.g. Maple) that would provide access to the MONET libraries.

2   Mathematical Services Discovery

Discovering services would be an asset in the context of mathematical exploitation of web services. Ideally, when a query is sent, the destination should be known. Users familiar with given mathematical packages are likely to invoke the exact same service for each request.

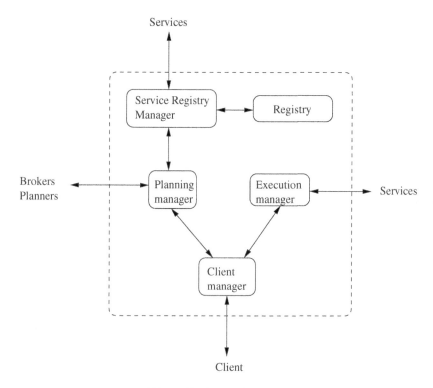

Fig. 1. Broker architecture

In other situations, it is possible that users do not know what services to invoke. A dedicated web service can then be contacted to locate appropriate mathematical servers to solve the problem. Unlike discovery of services in other areas of application, precise semantic information is essential to localize mathematical packages. For example, many mathematical algorithms may be called *solve* because they compute a solution for a given type of equation or set of equations. However, these equations may be of very different types and may require completely different services to be solved. Alone, the name of the operation implementing an algorithm can not be trusted. Complementary data on the problem solved is required for automated service discovery. That is why semantics is crucial in the description of a service – it is not realistic to simply "assume" that a mathematical package is appropriate for a given problem.

The MONET project refines the notion of *broker* in the semantic web and makes it the central component in the process of discovering and calling a mathematical service. The broker itself is viewed as a special service which typically assists clients in identifying suitable computational services for the problem they wish to solve.

Figure 1 presents the architecture of this special service. In the following paragraphs, we describe the entities that model the functionalities of the broker. Note that, at a software level, these entities may be used as distinct services or assembled into any combination. For example, the Client Manager, Planning

Manager, and Service Registry Manager could be combined into one piece of software that would handle and analyze requests to locate appropriate mathematical software.

2.1   Service Registry Manager

The Service Registry Manager (SRM) uses a Registry to store information about the functionalities registered by services. In particular, it stores information about how to contact the service. The SRM also has a role of reasoning about functionalities, exploring mathematical classifications. In order to solve mathematical, clients make queries, that are then matched with the entries in the broker's registry. The job of the SRM is to perform the matching, examining registered functionalities with respect to the problem posed by the client. It relies on semantic matching-based taxonomies used to characterize service functionalities. Reasoning at the level of the SRM is more than a simple word matching, because relations between problems are never trivial in the world of mathematics. For example, a problem A can be solved by services that advertise the "solving of A", but also by services that advertise the "solving of B" if B is a problem close enough to A. Concretely, the Registry could be implemented using an engine based on the UDDI [3] specification. Although it is still too early to decide whether this tool is sufficient for the semantics of computational mathematics, a few studies in the MONET project explored the issue of implementing mathematical service discovery. Although [4] claims that UDDI does not provide sufficient support for semantics, recent experiments proved that it is possible to add the GAMS classification [5] to the Registry Server (using UDDI v2) that can be found in the Java Web Services Developers Pack [6]. We can notice, however, that UDDI is business-oriented rather than problem-oriented. It does not seem natural to register functionalities rather than services with UDDI. Also, mathematical reasoning may be too complicated for a UDDI registry to perform.

2.2   Planning Manager

The Planning Manager allows the composition of services to solve mathematical problems. The idea is that a query received by the broker from a client may not be matched by the SRM, either because it is too complex to be solved by a single service, or simply because no service solving this problem was registered. Ideally, the Planning Manager would be able to do sophisticated reasoning about functionalities and the problem posed by the client, constructing an *execution plan* to compose services.

In practice, analyzing mathematical problems is a very difficult challenge and can only be done in specific cases. Consequently, it is not realistic to assume that the Planning Manager will be knowledgeable enough to answer every question without help. Therefore, it may consult one or more specialized services called *planners* whose purpose would be to analyze problems. Note that planners are clearly mathematical services that can be localized via a broker. Concretely, a planner may either analyze the problem or query a repository of execution plans. The latter would be the most common scenario, and such repositories are typically constructed by human intervention. The former scenario (analysis of the problem) would provide hints to the end-user rather than an execution plan. Another query – more precise – may then be built to solve the problem.

Execution plans provided by repositories are mathematical plans. That means that no service information is associated with the steps of the execution plans. It is the job of the planning manager to receive those plans and query the SRM to obtain a list of suitable services for each step. Each list is computed by service discovery according to logistical constraints expressed in the original query coming from the client. Note that the planning manager may have to do non-trivial reasoning over the constraints of the query. For example, a maximum cost or timing may be required. In this case, the planning manager must add the timings of the selected services and propose only those plans that can solve the problem in the given time. Execution plans associated with lists of suitable services would eventually be sent back to the client or to the execution manager for execution.

2.3   Execution Manager

The Execution Manager (EM) executes plans created by the Planning Manager. Even though plans are typically sent back to clients for approval and execution, our architecture allows clients to request a plan to be executed by the broker. The entity responsible for this execution (and for transaction management related to this execution) is the EM. We expect the implementation of the plans to be carried out through the use of web services orchestration (using such formalisms as BPEL4WS [7] or WSCI/BPML [8]).

For each step of the plan, the EM selects a service based on predefined or user-provided criteria (note that for each step the Planning Manager may provide several matching services). If necessary, the Execution Manager contacts services to negotiate for a handle on an instance for each mathematical service. A service may require to be managed by this entity if there is a need for external control or management of a pool of instances. This is generally managed at the location of the server itself and the Execution Manager does not have to handle this negotiation. Once the EM chose the services for each step, the orchestration document would be dynamically created and an orchestration engine could run the plan, providing transaction and security support.

2.4   Client Manager

The Client Manager handles communication with clients and hides the details of the broker. Its job is to forward clients' queries to the appropriate component. There are three destinations:

- Planning Manager for service discovery and creation of execution plans,
- Execution Manager to execute plans previously created,
- Service Manager to obtain instances of services.

3   Ontologies, Taxonomies, and Languages

The MONET project aims at using known technologies to provide a framework in which mathematical software can be exposed as web services. It also provides tools to publish such services in registries that would help clients to discover services given a query. In the context of this project, ontologies are defined to describe mathematical services and queries. These ontologies are defined in this section.

3.1   Service Description

Web services are typically defined using the Web Services Description Language [9] (WSDL). WSDL 1.2 is currently a W3C Working Draft. This language allows the interface description of various services. This description relates to the "signature" of operations rather than their semantics. As an example, we consider the following Java interface that declares an operation 'orderProduct' for a service 'Store':

```
public interface Store {
    Report orderProduct(ProductCode code,
                        int quantity,
                        CustomerInfo customer);
}
```

This interface can be transformed into a WSDL document that will map this declaration: name of the operation, parameters, returned values. A WSDL document also provides information on how to access this service. However, there is no information on what 'orderProduct' means. We only *assume* that by providing the code of the product, the quantity and necessary information for the customer, an order for the product will be placed. Semantic information would be required to make sure that this is actually what the service does.

There exists almost no attempt to classify problems in computational mathematics. In the field of numerical computation, GAMS [5] provides such a classification in the form of a decision tree, whose nodes are classes of problems and leaves reference software or libraries solving those problems. Although many packages and even strongly-typed languages have been developed, there is no classification available for symbolic computation to the authors' knowledge.

The Mathematical Problem Description Library (MPDL) (see [10]), defined by the MONET project, gathers definitions of well-defined mathematical problems. Using such a tool, service implementers can refer to a given entry and thus provide meaning to the operations they implement. The structure of an entry in the MPDL defines inputs, outputs, preconditions, and postconditions. It is also possible to provide generalization and specialization information to create relationships between problems. Objects can be formalized using OpenMath [11], MathML [12], or any other suitable language. An example of an MPDL entry is given in Section 3.3. Further experiments are required to assert that this structure is flexible enough to express most mathematical problems.

The MPDL offers a means to develop a classification expressing mathematical problems and their relationships, and is **not** the classification itself. We expect to provide an extended prototype of a classification for symbolic computation problems, within the time frame of the MONET project.

Mathematical services must associate semantics with the operations they export. Although only syntactic information is required in most applications, mathematics typically relies on precise semantics for all manipulated objects and operations. Consequently, WSDL is not enough to describe services exported by mathematical packages. The MONET project is developing an XML language called Mathematical Service Description Language [10] (MSDL) to associate semantics with operations exported by services. An MSDL document supplies two types of information related to exposed operations: semantics and syntax. The syntactic and communication part is typically covered by a reference to a WSDL document, but another formalism may be used. For the semantics, the MSDL proposes several solutions: through formalisms such as RDF, by referencing a well-known terminology (e.g. GAMS), or by referencing an entry into the Mathematical Problem Description Library. An MSDL document also allows the specification of the binding between the semantic definition of the operation and its low-level implementation represented by the WSDL document. Names are bound as well as parameters and returned values.

3.2 Queries

The client side is also an important part in the context of semantic applications on the web. A mathematical query should describe the problem instance to be solved using well-defined ontologies to refer to general problems and to provide necessary mathematical objects. Based on such information, a server can decide whether or not it can solve the problem and a broker can make appropriate reasoning to forward a query.

The MONET project defines two languages to support queries. A client should use such languages to communicate with servers and brokers (see Section 2). Queries in the MONET framework have two components: a mathematical and a logistical component. The logistical component is used to express constraints related to the query and usually includes both technical and commercial requirements that can be exploited by servers to decide whether or not they can answer the problem instance sent by the client or by brokers to decide where to send the query. An example of a query is presented below.

3.3 Characterizing Bernina's Functions

Using the languages defined by MONET, we can provide a description of the problems solved by Bernina. It is likely that these entries in the problem library will be reused by other packages that provide the same computations. Note that MONET is problem-oriented rather than software-oriented. That is, we expose specific operations that happen to be implemented by a given software package rather than expose a software package as a web service. This distinction makes sense in the context of service discovery based on semantics.

Concerning Bernina, there are many interesting algorithms to be exposed as mathematical services. There are also commodity functions which are not intended to become mathematical services but still very useful in the context of interactive use. We now show how we describe – using the MONET languages – a service implemented with Bernina. In this example, we present an MPDL entry corresponding to the solved problem and show how it is referenced in the context of an MSDL document. We also refer to the WSDL document generated for the service.

The Bernina package implements the function `Darboux`. Given a second order differential operator, the `Darboux` function computes a list of Darboux polynomials of lowest possible degree. This function solves a problem that can be referenced by the following entry in a Mathematical Problem Description Library used to describe problems related to differential operators:

```
<problem name=Darboux>
  <header/>
  <body>
    <input name=L> Differential Operator Type </input>
    <output name=dReturn> Polynomial List Type </output>
  </body>
</problem>
```

The header part is a placeholder for metadata. It may contain extra information to define the problem more precisely: bibliography referring to the problem, generalization/Specialization information, reference to a taxonomy, and so on. The body may also contain pre and post-conditions. Note that this problem is not specific to Bernina. They may be solved by another implementation, which is why the MPDL exists: to factorize such a description and to have a common taxonomy to characterize such a problem. The following excerpt from a WSDL document shows how to access the `Darboux` function:

```
<wsdl:portType name="Bernina">
   <wsdl:operation name="darboux" parameterOrder="in0">
     <wsdl:input name="darbouxRequest"
                 message="impl:darbouxRequest"/>
     <wsdl:output name="darbouxResponse"
                 message="impl:darbouxResponse"/>
   </wsdl:operation>
</wsdl:portType>
```

As explained earlier, such a document is not enough to characterize the "darboux" operation. We do not know, just by looking at the WSDL document, what computation is performed by this implementation. That is why an MSDL document both makes the link between problems described in the MPDL and the implementation shown here. The MSDL document may also provide information about the algorithm used and its properties:

```
<service name="BerninaDarboux">
  <classifications>
    <problem-reference>
        http://www.monet.org/PDL/diffop.pdl
    </problem-reference>
  </classifications>
  <implementation>
    <software>
      http://www.essi.fr/Software/SymbolicComputation/Bernina
    </software>
  </implementation>
  <service-interface-description
        sid-ref="http://www.essi.fr/Bernina/bernina.wsdl" />
  <service-binding>
    <map operation="darboux" problem-ref="Darboux" />
    <message-construction io-ref="L"
                          message-name="darbouxRequest"
                          message-part="in0" />
    <message-construction io-ref="dReturn"
                          message-name="darbouxResponse"
                          message-part="darbouxReturn" />
  </service-binding>
</service>
```

Tags in this document have the following meaning: the tag `classifications` allows referring to the entry in the MPDL. The tag `implementation` provides a unique name to refer to the implementation (note that this section also allows to provide a reference to an entry in an algorithm library). This permits a better characterization of the problem solved by this web service. The `service-interface-description` tag provides a URI to the WSDL document. Finally, `service-binding` provides the link between problem description and implementation, by mapping names and parameters.

Using both the MSDL and the WSDL documents, a client can be constructed to send queries to this service. For example, a Maple client would like $\mathrm{Darboux}(D^2 + \frac{3x^2}{16})$ to be computed. The following query would be constructed:

```
<query>
  <classifications>
    <problem-ref>
      http://www.monet.org/PDL/diffop.pdl
    </problem-ref>
  </classifications>
  <problem>
    solve Darboux(D 2 + 3*x 2/16)
  </problem>
  <constraint><free_service/></constraint>
</query>
```

The problem is not written in the actual formalism – we would typically use OpenMath to describe such a statement, but the size of the XML representation increases rapidly and becomes unreadable.

4   Implementing Mathematical Web Services

Exposing a mathematical engine as a web service requires an analysis of the existing environment of the engine. We have two cases:

- The code for the engine is available and can be modified. Also, the underlying environment includes primitives or libraries to work with web services.
- The engine is considered as a black box. We only have access to the binary version of the software and the only solution is to exploit I/O slots offered by the engine.

When the code of the application is available and web services support exists, there is no particular problem in publishing a service. The black box case is more interesting. Because we can not modify the application, it is difficult to integrate it to the web services world. The solution to this problem lies in the use of **adapters** (also called "phrasebook" in the context of OpenMath). The idea – very common in the world of interoperability – is to hide the computation engine (back-end) behind a compliant front-end. The communication between back-end and front-end is private and never exposed to the outside world. In order to make this happen, it is important to list all the ways typically used by the back-end application to communicate with the outside (standard I/O streams, files, sockets, and so on). As well, the front-end implementation of the server should be realized using a web services compliant environment. Figure 2 illustrates the use of adapters in the context calling a service (Bernina here) that solves the Darboux problem.

In the design of the solution, one should choose one of the listed communication means and make the adaptation "glue". The front-end receives standard web service input, and calls the adapter to create an input that will be understood by the back-end. This is exactly what we do for Bernina. We consider Bernina as a black box because it is written in Aldor which does not have any support for web services. Bernina can communicate through standard input and output streams, it is thus possible to plug modules to this application to organize the communication between the front-end and the back-end. In particular, if we use the MONET framework to expose Bernina as a web service, we should handle mathematical objects formatted using OpenMath. In this case, the modules will handle the translation between OpenMath and Bernina's own input format. Note that Bernina typically works with a Lisp or a Maple format. We could imagine that the Bernina web service directly understands Lisp or Maple as input data thus reducing the amount of work required to expose Bernina as a web service. We believe however that mathematical web services frameworks will rather work with XML languages, such as OpenMath.

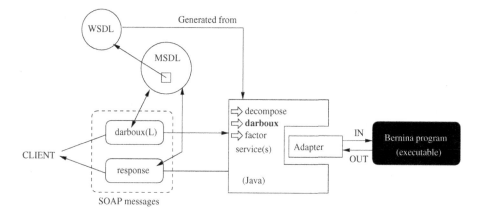

Fig. 2. Bernina as a web service

4.1 Technology

We have implemented a prototype to provide an experimental test-bed with the environment described in this paper. Although it is possible to use any number of supporting tools to create web services, certain considerations have oriented our choices.

We first remark that documents on web services clearly specify that SOAP and WSDL are only *possibilities* for working with web services. However, in practice, these technologies (SOAP in particular) are used everywhere. Consequently, we use SOAP and WSDL as a basis. This prototype is also a test-bed for the MONET project and, of course, we describe our mathematical services using MSDL. Selecting a programming language is a more complicated task than for classical e-business web services. E-business services are typically implemented on simple platforms (Windows or Linux) and using well-known environments: Java and .NET. That explains why support tools mostly exist for those two environments.

Unfortunately, mathematical packages may be implemented on any kind of platform, usually not using Java or C#. This is the case for Bernina which is implemented using the Aldor language as mentioned above. In such a situation – where no support for web services is available – the solution we found most appropriate was to rely on one of the supported languages and use the adapters technique described above. The reason is that support libraries and tools are more likely to be maintained and up-to-date. Of course, if there was maintained support for web services in the Aldor environment, we could simply get rid of the Java intermediary code, and work directly in Aldor.

For our implementation, we selected Java because this language can typically be used on various platforms and particularly Unix where many mathematical packages are developed. The link between Java and Bernina is also written in Java. Again, if support for any part of the process were to appear on the Aldor platform (in particular, OpenMath support), the Java adapter would become "lighter". We chose Tomcat [13] and the Axis library [14] for our prototype, because there is good support for Java and because these tools are simple to set up. No specific web server technology seems to be required in the context of mathematical software.

4.2   Current Status of the Prototype

Our prototype currently provides access to functionalities implemented by Bernina through MONET web services. Certain functions have been selected and exposed in an MSDL document. A Java interface was written to list Bernina's functions and a WSDL document was created using the Java2WSDL tool from Axis. The client is currently a web page, but a Maple client is being implemented at the time of writing.

Using the web client, the application contacts a broker that selects one of the available Bernina services (for experimental purposes, one service is free, another is not) to solve the problem. Input data can be provided using a Maple format and is translated into OpenMath. The result is provided as OpenMath. In this simple broker, planning is empty and sums up to invoking the Service Registry Manager to look for the appropriate services. A second broker is available that provides primitive planning by combining translation services. Once we obtain the result in the OpenMath format, it is possible to invoke services to transform the mathematical object into Maple, MathML, or SVG. The SVG translation is the most interesting as it is provided through two services. A first step is to translate the OpenMath-formatted object into Content MathML (see [15]). The resulting Content MathML is then sent to a MathML to SVG translator (see [16]). Note that we did not write these translation packages, we merely adapted them as MONET web services. The Planning Manager can find such services because queries use a format translation taxonomy, and matches inputs and outputs.

5   Conclusion and Future Work

Up to now, most users of mathematical softwares access them through fixed dedicated interfaces. Linking these softwares into their preferred environment, or calling them from another package is difficult or even impossible. Mathematical web services would solve this problem by potentially unifying all kinds of mathematical software, tools and services in a common framework where all components would be able to communicate with one another in an appropriate way. Turning a mathematical software into a mathematical web service requires to use the adequate technologies such as the ones provided by the MONET project. According to our experience with Bernina, the main problem is now to create suitable taxonomies to describe unambiguously the various mathematical problems a mathematical software can solve. Only a very few taxonomies already exists like GAMS but there are mainly related to numerical computation.

A mathematical web service based on Bernina is an interesting prototype and it would be useful to have other examples within the MONET framework to experiment with. Beside finalizing the current implementation we are in the process of writing a Maple client to use this service. The next step would be to register the Bernina web service to a real broker and to perform service discovery.

Acknowledgment. This work is partially supported by the European MONET project (IST-2001-34145). We'd like to thank Peter Sander for his useful comments and corrections.

References

1. Manuel Bronstein, *SUM-IT: A strongly-typed embeddable computer algebra library*, in Proceedings of DISCO'96, Springer LNCS 1128, 22–33.
2. Aldor.org, `http://www.aldor.org`, 2001–2003.
3. OASIS, *Universal Description, Discovery and Integration of Web Services*, `http://www.uddi.org/`.
4. Mike Dewar, David Carlisle, Olga Caprotti, *Description Schemes For Mathematical Web Services*, Electronic Workshops in Computing, Oxford, 2002.
5. National Institute of Standards and Technology, *GAMS: Guide to Available Mathematical Software*, `http://gams.nist.gov`
6. Sun Microsystems Inc, `http://java.sun.com/webservices/webservicespack.html`.
7. BEA Systems, IBM, Microsoft, SAP AG, Siebel Systems, *Business Process Execution Language for Web Services version 1.1*, Available from `http://www-106.ibm.com/developerworks/library/ws-bpel`
8. BEA Systems, Intalio, SAP AG, Sun Microsystems, *Web Service Choreography Interface (WSCI) 1.0 Specification*, Available from `http://wwws.sun.com/software/xml/developers/wsci`
9. W3C, *Web Services Description Language (WSDL) 1.1*, `http://www.w3.org/TR/wsdl.html`.
10. Stephen Buswell, Olga Caprotti, Mike Dewar, *Mathematical Service Description Language: Final Version*, The MONET Consortium, Deliverable D14. Available from `http://monet.nag.co.uk`
11. John Abbott , Angel Diaz , Robert S. Sutor, *A report on OpenMath: a protocol for the exchange of mathematical information*, In ACM SIGSAM Bulletin, volume 30, number 1, pages 21–24, 1996.
12. W3C, *W3C Math Home*, http://www.w3.org/Math.
13. The Apache Software Foundation, `http://jakarta.apache.org/tomcat`, 1999–2003.
14. The Apache Software Foundation, `http://ws.apache.org/axis`, 1999–2003.
15. Clare So, `http://www.scl.csd.uwo.ca/ clare`, 2002.
16. Dominique Broeglin, Stéphane Lavirotte, Peter Sander, *Another Approach for Displaying Mathematics on the Web: MathML Content to SVG*, in Proceedings of MathML Conference. Chicago, USA, 28–30 jun. 2002.

enTish: An Approach to Service Composition*

Stanislaw Ambroszkiewicz[1,2]

[1] Institute of Informatics, University of Podlasie
al. Sienkiewicza 51, PL-08-110 Siedlce, Poland
[2] Institute of Computer Science, Polish Academy of Sciences
al. Ordona 21, PL-01-237 Warsaw
phone ++48-22 836-28-41
sambrosz@ipipan.waw.pl
http://www.ipipan.waw.pl/mas/

Abstract. A new technology for service description and composition in open and distributed environment is proposed. The technology consists of description language (called Entish) and composition protocol called entish 1.0. They are based on software agent paradigm. The description language is the contents language of the messages that are exchanged (between agents and services) according to the composition protocol. The syntax of the language as well as the message format are expressed in XML. The language and the protocol are merely specifications. To prove that the technology does work, the prototype was implemented. A demo of the prototype is available for use and evaluation via web interfaces starting with www.ipipan.waw.pl/mas/. Related work was done by WSDL + BPEL4WS + (WS-Coordination) + (WS-Transactions), WSCI, BPML, DAML-S, SWORD, XSRL, and SELF-SERV. Our technology is based on similar principles as XSRL, however the proposed solution is different. The language Entish is fully declarative contrary to BPEL4WS and DAML-S. A request (expressed in Entish) describes the desired static situation to be realized by the composition protocol.

1 Web Services

Perhaps the most popular definition of Web services can be found in IBM's tutorial [6]:

Web services are self-contained, self-describing, modular applications that can be published, located, and invoked across the Web. Web services perform functions that can be anything from simple requests to complicated business processes ... Once a Web service is deployed, other applications (and other Web services) can discover and invoke the deployed service.

In order to realize this vision simple and ubiquitous protocols are needed. From service providers' point of view, if they can setup a web site they could join global community. From a client's point of view, if you can click, you could access services.

Web services are supposed to realize the Service-Oriented Architecture (SOA) in a global networked environment. SOA provides a standard programming model that allows software components, residing on any network, to be published, discovered, and invoked by each other as services. There are essentially three components of SOA:

---

* The work was supported partially by KBN project No. 7 T11C 040 20

B. Benatallah and M.-C. Shan (Eds.): TES 2003, LNCS 2819, pp. 168–178, 2003.

Service Provider, Service Requester (or Client), and Service Registry. The provider hosts the service and controls access to it, and is responsible for publishing a description of its service to a service registry. The requester (client) is a software component in search of a component to invoke in order to realize a request. The service registry is a central repository that facilitates service discovery by the requesters.

The following stack of protocols: SOAP, WSDL, and UDDI is positioned to become Web services standards for invocation, description, and discovery. SOAP (Simple Object Access Protocol) is a standard for applications to exchange XML-formatted messages over HTTP. WSDL (Web Service Description Language) describes the interface, protocol bindings and the deployment details of the service. UDDI (Universal Description, Discovery and Integration) provides a registry of businesses and web services. A UDDI service description consists of physical attributes such as name and address augmented by a collection of tModels, which describe additional features such as, for example, reference to WSDL document describing the service interface, and the classification of the service according to some taxonomies.

The key point of the idea of web services is service integration, that is, *"...other applications (and other Web services) can discover and invoke the deployed service..."* The service integration has several names, e.g., service composition, orchestration, choreography, process modeling, etc.. There are several approaches to service integration, each focuses on different aspects of the integration and proposes a different solution. The most popular ones are briefly described below.

BPEL4WS (BPEL for short) is a process modeling language designed to enable a service composer to aggregate Web services into an execution. There are abstract and executable processes. Abstract processes are useful for describing business protocols, while executable processes may be compiled into invokeable services. Aggregated services are modeled as directed graphs where the nodes are services and the edges represent a dependency link from one service to another. Canonical programmatic constructs like SWITCH, WHILE and PICK allow to direct an execution's path through the graph. BPEL was released along with two others specs: WS-Coordination and WS-Transaction. WS-Coordination describes how services can make use of predefined coordination contexts to subscribe to a particular role in a collaborative activity. WS-Transaction provides a framework for incorporating transactional semantics into coordinated activities. WS-Transaction uses WS-Coordination to extend BPEL to provide a context for transactional agreements between services. A composite service realized in BPEL can itself be exposed as a service, i.e., has its own WSDL interface.

DARPA project DAML-S is a DAML+OIL ontology for describing Web Services. It aims to make Web services computer-interpretable, i.e., described with sufficient information to enable automated Web service discovery, invocation, composition and execution monitoring. The DAML-S Ontology comprises ServiceProfile, ServiceModel, and ServiceGrounding. ServiceProfile is like the yellow page entry for a service. It relates and builds upon the type of content in UDDI, describing properties of a service necessary for automatic discovery, such as what the services offers, and its inputs, outputs, and its side-effects (preconditions and effects). ServiceModel describes the service's process model, i.e., the control flow and data-flow involved in using the service. It relates to BPEL and is designed to enable automated composition and execution of services. ServiceGrounding connects the process model description to communication- level protocols and message descriptions in WSDL.

Web Services Choreography Interface (WSCI) is an XML-based language for web services collaboration. It defines the overall choreography describing the messages between web services that participate in a collaborative exchange. WSCI describes only the observable behavior between web services. A single WSCI document only describes one partner's participation in a message exchange. Usually, a WSCI choreography includes a collection of WSCI documents, one for each partner in the interaction. It is interesting that there is no single controlling process managing the interaction. WSCI could be viewed as a layer on the top of WSDL. Each action represents a unit of work, which typically would map to a specific WSDL operation. Hence, WSCI would describe the interactions among these WSDL operations. The W3C recently announced a web service choreography working group that considers WSCI.

The Business Process Management Language (BPML) is a meta-language for describing business processes. The BPML specification can be loosely compared to BPEL, providing similar process flow constructs and activities. Basic activities for sending, receiving, and invoking services are available, along with structured activities that handle conditional choices, sequential and parallel activities, joins, and looping. BPML incorporated the WSCI protocol. WSCI could be used to describe the public interactions whereas the private implementations could be developed with BPML. Both BPML and WSCI share the same underlying process execution model and similar syntaxes.

SWORD [11] is a set of tools for building composite web services. A service is represented by a rule that expresses that given certain inputs, the service is capable of producing particular outputs. A simple language was design to describe inputs and outputs. A rule-based expert system is used to determine whether a desired composite service can be realized using existing (elementary) services. If so, a plan is constructed that when executed realizes the composite service.

SELF-SERV [1] is a framework for declarative web service composition using statecharts, where resulting composite services can be executed in a decentralized way. The concept of service communities is used to form alliances among a potentially large number of services performing the same operation types. The underlying execution model allows services participating in a composition, to collaborate in a peer-to-peer fashion in order to assure that the control and data flow dependencies of the composition schema (expressed by a statechart) are respected.

XSRL [12] is a formal language for expressing requests against e-marketplace registered web services. The language is an amalgamation of the Internet XML query language and AI planning constructs. XSRL includes constructs such as alternative activities, vital vs. optional activities, preconditions, postconditions, invariants, and expression operators over quantitative values that can be employed at the user-level when formulating a goal. This approach realizes the automatic generation, verification and execution of plans in order to achieve the goals. It is built on the top of BPEL.

Summing up the short descriptions presented above, a common methodological framework is needed to compare these different approaches. The next section is devoted to analyze the generic meaning of the term *service composition*.

2   Service Composition

It seems that there are two general approaches to service composition. The first one corresponds to business-to-business point of view, whereas the second one to the client's point of view. The first one is based on the assumption that services are composed, orchestrated, or choreographed in order to create sophisticated business processes, whereas the second one assumes that services are composed (typically on the fly) in order to realize clients' requests. Most of the existing technologies realize the first approach. The second approach is followed by academic projects, e.g., SWORD, XSRL, and our own project enTish. It seems that, from the business-to-business point of view, the service architecture corresponding to SOAP and WSDL is appropriate. However, in our opinion, a different service architecture is required for realizing the second approach. The reason is that clients' requests are expressed in a declarative way in a formal language, so that it is natural to propose a universal protocol for the request realization. However, also in this case the service architecture based on SOAP and WSDL may be applied as it is done in XSRL[12].

Now, let us take a client's point of view and come back to SOA. The purpose of service provider is that its services are used. So it doesn't matter if its service is used as part of service composition arranged by a broker, or the service is used directly by a client, or by an agent of the client. From a service requester (client) point of view, its purpose is that the requests are realized. So that it doesn't matter if its request is realized by a single service or by composing a number of services. It seems that service composition technology is for realizing clients' requests. Hence, the concept of request should be taken as the starting point. Similar opinion is expressed in [12] where a service request language is proposed.

If the client's request is not explicitly stated, then it must be hard-coded in the client implementation, i.e., it must be specified in an imperative (procedural) way by encoding *How to realize it?* All approaches to service composition (except SWORD and in a sense XSRL) presented briefly in the previous Section follow the imperative way to specify clients' requests, i.e., they are more or less process modeling languages. Only SWORD and XSRL try to realize the declarative way to specify the client's request, i.e., to specify formally *What to realize?*, and then to realize the request by discovering and composing services into one execution according to one fixed protocol.

The conclusion is as follows. From the client's point of view, the primary goal of service composition is to realize clients' requests. Generally, there are two ways for doing so. The first one is the imperative way, i.e., the request is not specified explicitly. It is hard-coded in the request realization process. The second way is declarative, it means that the request is specified as a formula in a formal language describing static situations, i.e., no actions can be used in the language. The declarative approach presupposes the existence of an universal protocol for request realization.

2.1   Declarative Approach to Service Composition

It seems that a declarative approach should be realized in the following two phases.

Phase 1: Given an initial situation and a goal (that constitute together a request), construct generic plans that may realize this goal starting with the initial situation.

Phase 2: Choose one generic plan and discover appropriate services, arrange them into a workflow. Present the workflow to the client along with the constrains specifying the initial situation more precisely. Once the initial situation is satisfied by the client, execute the workflow, control the execution, and realize the transaction if the execution is successful.

To realize the Phase 1, a language for describing initial situations and goals is needed, as well as reasoning for plan construction. There is a considerable work done in this area, e.g., PDDL [3], and Estimated-regression planning [2] that are extensively used in XSRL [12]. The language is supposed to be used in a distributed and heterogeneous environment so that it must be open, i.e., new concepts can be introduced in a distributive way. The semantics of the new concepts must be clear and precise, i.e., there must be fixed rules for introducing new concepts so that their semantics can be machine readable. The language should be rich enough to express the concept of service types in its generic meaning, i.e., as specification of abstract behavior of service consisting of precondition and post-condition (effect), that describe respectively the necessary condition for service invocation, and the effect of service invocation. Then, the preconditions correspond to the initial situations, whereas the effects correspond to the goals.

The second phase may be realized using a process modeling language, e.g., BPEL as it is done in XSRL. However, it seems reasonable to use one fixed protocol for all plans that may be generated in the first phase. The problem is how to represent the plans for such universal protocol. Perhaps a solutions is to represent the plans as statecharts as it is done in SELF-SERV [1].

So far we have provided an answer to the following question: *What is the composition for?* However, there are some other problems like *What is to be composed?* and *What is the result of service composition?* The problems are discussed in the following sections.

2.2   What Is the Result of Service Composition?

Let the result of service composition be called composite service. This term may be defined in several ways. Composite service may be a collection of services that collaborate in order to realize a request. Composite service may be a collection of services arranged into workflow. Composite service may be considered as a collection of operations (coming from possibly different services) arranged (orchestrated, composed, choreographed, etc.) into a single execution. It is possible do propose more definitions. The range of possible meaning of the concept "composite service" is wide; from rigid static and persistent composition to the most flexible dynamic composition arranged on-the-fly when it is needed. Another aspect is recursion, i.e., if the composite service is again a service that can be composed. Yet another aspect of composite service is the ability to reconfigure itself as to the services involved into the composition as well as to the way (schema) the composition is realized. And finally, the persistency of service composition is a crucial point here. Should composite service realize long term transaction, or rather be a temporal "one shot" transaction consisting of one execution for realizing one specific request?

Perhaps the long term transactions can be constructed (at a higher level of abstraction) out of the "one shot" compositions.

These aspects are interrelated, moreover a consistent choice of these aspects determines more or less the way the requests are realized as well as the service architecture.

It is interesting to classify the existing technologies according to these aspects. For example, BPEL provides recursive composition whereas WSCI does not. SELF-SERV composite service can reconfigure itself as to the services involved into composition, whereas SWORD realizes one-shot on-the-fly composite services.

2.3   What Is to Be Composed?

Actually, this question is about the service architecture as well as about service description. It seems that it is impossible to propose one generic service architecture that is appropriate for all composition technologies.

Since the main objective of our research is service composition, it is reasonable to consider atomic services, that is, services that perform single input/output operation. Once we have a technology for service composition, these very atomic services could be integrated into composite services.

However, from the point of view of WSDL, service is a collection of input/output operations. Hence, any application (object) with public methods exposed as operations in WSDL interface could be considered as a web service. Usually, the operations are accessible via ports using SOAP. WSDL interface can be generated from application code. It is not possible to specify (in WSDL) the abstract functions implemented by the operations, i.e., what the operations do. (Note, there was an attempt to introduce it to WSDL, see [10].) Service provider itself must classify these operations according to the taxonomies available in UDDI. Moreover, it is impossible to express in WSDL the interdependencies between operations (methods) of the same service (object).

It seems that WSDL determines a kind of service architecture that is appropriate for composition technologies that realize procedural approach like BPEL, WSCI, and BPML. It is interesting that WSCI as well as WS-Coordination, and WS-Transaction extend this architecture by augmenting a service with additional layer for realizing coordination and transactions. There is also an attempt to revise the notion of service architecture, see [5], by adding next protocol, called CS-WS (conversation support), on the top of BPEL.

There are another aspects that determine service architecture, e.g., the method used for service invocation: Should it be RPC style or message passing style? Another aspect is how to deal with data flow and control flow: Should they be separated or not? Perhaps an important aspect is the top-down versus bottom-up approach to service composition. It seems that the current paradigm for web services forces the bottom up approach: "Here's how to build web services, now let's use them for integration." The top-down approach takes a service composition (integration) method as the starting point, and then adjusts service architecture to the integration requirements.

The technology we propose tries to realize the top-down, declarative, one-shot, and on-the-fly approach to service composition.

3   Our Approach to Service Composition

We follow the idea of layered view of service architecture introduced in [5,4]. Our service architecture comprises the following three layers: Conversation layer, functionality layer, and database management (executive) layer. The database management layer is the same as in [4], it influences the real world. However, the next two layers have different meaning. The functionality layer has exactly two interrelated components: Raw application, and so called filter associated with the raw application. Raw application implements a single operation, i.e., given input resources, it produces the output resource according to the operation specification. Note, that operation has exactly one output, although it may have several inputs. The associated filter works as follows. Given constrains on the output resource, it produces the constrains on the input resources. That is, given a specification of the desired output, the filter replies with properties that must be satisfied by the input in order to produce the desired output by the raw application. It is clear that these constrains must be expressed in one common description language. The conversation layer implements a conversation protocol to arrange raw application invocation, as well as input / output resource passing to / from the raw application. The conversation protocol specifies the order for message exchange. Message contents is expressed in the description language.

Since our service architecture is different than the one corresponding to WSDL and UDDI, we must revise the concept of service description language as well as the concept of service registry. It is natural that service description language should describe the types of service input / output resources as well as attributes of these types to express constrains. Note, that the language is supposed merely to *describe* resources in terms of theirs attributes, not to construct data structures as it is done in WSDL. It is also natural to describe *what service does* in the language, i.e., the abstract function implemented by the operation the service performs. Usually, this is a job of UDDI. We include this job in our description language.

Since service has additional functionality performed by filter (i.e., service may be asked if it can produce output resources satisfying some properties), the description language should be augmented with a possibility to formulate such questions as well as answers. Moreover, the clients' requests should be expressed in the language.

We also want to describe some static properties of service composition process such as intentions, and commitments; this corresponds to the functionality of WS-Coordination.

The final requirement is that the language must be open and of distributed use. It means that names for new resource types, their attributes, and names for new functions, as well as new relations can be introduced to the language by any user, and these names are unique (e.g., URIs). This completes the requirements for the description language called Entish. Since our technology is supposed to realize the declarative approach, we need a universal protocol for realizing the requests specified in our description language.

For the simplicity (i.e., for avoiding reasoning) as well as for making the prototype implementation feasible, we assume that the requests are extremely simple; in fact they are expressed as formulas that represent abstract plans and initial situations. In the next step of our project a *distributed* reasoning for plan generation will be implemented, so that the requests will have a form of arbitrary formulas. The plan realization is done by the protocol called entish 1.0.

To prove that the requirements for the service description language and composition protocol can be satisfied we provide the prototype implementation available from http://www.ipipan.waw.pl/mas/ .

4   Walk-Through Example

The working example presented below constitutes an intuitive introduction to the description language and the composition protocol. The services described in the example are implemented and are ready for testing via the www interfaces.

A client was going to book a flight from Warsaw to Geneva; the departure was scheduled on Nov. 30, 2002. It wanted to arrange its request (task) by Nov. 15, 2002. With the help of TaskManager (TM for short), the client expressed the task in a formal language; suppose that it was the following formula:

phi =

"invoice for ticket (flight from Warsaw to Geneva, departure is Nov. 30, 2002) is delivered to TM by Nov. 15, 2002"

Then, the task formula (i.e., *phi*) was delegated to a software agent, say agent0. The task became the goal of the agent0. The agent0 set the task formula as its first intention, and was looking for a service that could realize it. First of all, the agent0 sent the query: *"agent0's intention is phi"* to a service registry called infoService in our framework. Suppose that infoService replied that there was a travel agent called FirstClass that could realize agent0's intention. Then, the agent sent again the formula *"agent0's intention is phi"* however, this time to the FirstClass. Suppose that FirstClass replied with the following commitment:

"FirstClass commits to realize phi,

if (order is delivered to FirstClass by Nov. 15, 2002 and

the order specifies the flight (i.e., from Warsaw to Geneva, departure Nov. 30,2002) and

one of the following additional specification of the order is satisfied:

(airline is Lufthansa and the price is 300 euro)

or

(airline is Swissair and the price is 330 euro)

or

(airline is LOT and the price is 280 euro))"

Let *psi* denote, the formula after *"if"* inside (...) parentheses. The formula *psi* is the precondition of the commitment. Once the agent0 received the info about the commitment, the agent0 considered the intention *phi* as arranged to be realized by FirstClass, and then the agent0 put the formula *psi* as its current intention, and looked for a service that could realize it. Let us notice that the order specified in the formula *psi* could be created only by the client via its TM, that is, the client had to decide which airline (price) should be chosen, and the complete order was supposed to include details of a credit card of the client. Hence, the agent0 sent the following message to TM: *"agent0's intention is psi"* Suppose that TM replied to the agent: *"TM commits to realize psi, if true "* The agent0 considered the intention *psi* as arranged to be realized by TM. Since the precondition of the TM commitment was the formula *"true"*, a workflow for realizing agent0's task was already constructed. Once TM created the order and sent it to FirstClass, the FirstClass would produce the invoice and send it to TM. It was supposed (in the protocol) that once a service realized a commitment, it sent the confirmation to the agent0. Once the agent0 received all confirmation, it got to know that the workflow was executed successfully. In order to complete this distributed transaction, the agent sent synchronously the final confirmation to the all services engaged in the workflow. This completes the example.

5   The Prototype Implementation

Before we go into details of the language and the protocol, let us present how the prototype works. The system resulting from the prototype implementation is fully functional. It allows providers to join their application as services as well as to formulate tasks by clients, and delegate the tasks to the system for realization.

5.1   WWW Interfaces

A demo of the prototype is available for testing and evaluation via three www interfaces starting with http://www.ipipan.waw.pl/mas/ . The first interface called *EntishDictionary* serves for introducing names for new data types, their attributes, and new functions to the language Entish. The second interface called *serviceAPI* is for joining applications (that implement the new functions) as networked services to our system. The third interface called TaskManager is devoted for a client to specify its task in Entish, and provide initial resources for the task realization. Hence, from the outside, i.e., from service providers and clients point of view, the system consists of the three interfaces: EntishDictionary, TaskManager, serviceAPI. What is inside, that is, the system engine is transparent for the service providers and clients. The engine implements the language, and the protocol that realizes the clients' tasks by discovery of appropriate services, their composition and invocation. The www interfaces are user friendly so that to use the system almost no knowledge on XML, Entish syntax, and entish 1.0 is needed.

EntishDictionary (ED for short) serves also as an ordinary dictionary, i.e., for looking at the existing ontologies as well as for explanation of names used in the language. Ontology is meant as a collection of names of resource types, their attributes, and functions defined on these types. It is supposed that they come from one application domain. Any user can introduce its own ontology. There is no conflict with names, because short names introduced by users are automatically extended to long names that are URIs. ED has also additional functionalities. It allows a service provider to create Entish formula that describes operation type performed by its application. The formula along with some additional information about the host on which the application is running is sent automatically to the system (actually to serviceServer) for registration and publication.

The second functionality of ED is that it allows a user to create task; usually it is a composition of abstract functions. The task is sent automatically to TaskManager for realization. It is important to note, that task is merely an abstract description of what is to be realized, so that it does not indicate what services could realize it. Note, that EntishDictionary realizes some functionality of UDDI concerning service classification. However, service publication and discovery is done inside the system.

Generally, there is no restriction on the type of resources that can be defined in the dictionary. However for the purpose of system demonstration we assume that resource type has flat XML format, i.e., it has several elements that are of type $\mathtt{xsd:string}$.

TaskManager is a GUI that, given a task from a user, creates and manages appropriate interfaces for delivering (by the user) initial resources needed for the task realization. Then, the task is sent to the system (actually to *agentServer*) for realization. If the system is ready to realize the task (it means that a workflow consisting of appropriate services has been already arranged), the TaskManager asks the user to provide the initial resources according to the constrains returned by the system. More sophisticated tasks can be generated directly from a repository of typical tasks provided by the TaskManager.

The interface serviceAPI provides Java classes and explanation for creating service (according to our architecture) by a service provider.

5.2   Middleware

Since the system engine is transparent for clients and service providers, it may be regarded as a *middleware*. The www interfaces were created only to facilitate the use of the middleware. The middleware is an implementation of the language Entish and the protocol entish 1.0. The language and the protocol constitute the technology we propose.

Service provider creates a service according to serviceAPI, and runs it on its host. Then, the provider registers its service to the middleware via EntishDictionary. Client creates its task via TaskManager, and the task is sent to the middleware. If the task could be realized, the middleware returns constrains on the initial resources needed for task realization. The constrains are displayed to client by TaskManager. The client creates (via GUI) initial resources according to the constrains, sends them to the middleware and waits for the final resource. What is going on inside the system is transparent to clients and service providers. From their point of view only result is important, that is, services are to be used, and tasks are to be realized.

The middleware consists of three basic elements: agentServer, serviceServer, and infoService that exchange messages according to the protocol entish 1.0. The contents language of the messages is Entish, so that these three components speak one common language. The middleware can be distributed, i.e., the components may be scattered on different hosts; several instances of the same component may be running at the same time; they may be implemented independently.

The first component, i.e., agentServer represents clients in the middleware. Once a task is delivered to the agentServer from TaskManager, a process dedicated to the task realization is created. The process is called agent, and has its own state for expressing its goal, intentions, and knowledge.

The second component, called serviceServer, represents service in the middleware. Once a service is registered to the serviceServer, a dedicated process is created that represents this service in the middleware for arranging invocation, transactions, etc. The process is equipped with its own state for expressing commitments and knowledge about the current status of conversation with agents and other services.

The third component, i.e., infoService is a global database for storing info about services, that is, what is the operation type of a service, and what is its name and the communication address.

The protocol entish 1.0 is divided into the following phases:

1. serviceServer publishes a service to infoService;
2. agent discovers services at infoService;
3. services are composed on-the-fly into a workflow by an agent;
4. workflow is executed;
5. transactional semantics is realized.

The complete documentation of our technology is available at the enTish project web site http://www.ipipan.waw.pl/mas/   The specifications of the proposed technology are in version 1.0, and were designed to be extremely simple for the purpose of understanding the idea behind them as well as for the prototype implementations. So that, several important features, not essential for the basic functionality, were skipped and left to be completed in the next version. These are for example security, and service quality. However, transactional semantics is included in the specifications.

References

1. Boualem Benatallah, Marlon Dumas, and Quan Z. Sheng. The Self-Serv Environment for Web Services Composition. IEEE Internet Computing, Jan. - Feb. 2003, pp. 40–48.
2. D. McDermott. Estimated-regression planning for interactions with Web Services. In 6th Int. Conf. on AI Planning and Scheduling. AAAI Press, 2002.
3. M. Ghallab, A. Howe, C. Knoblock, D. McDermott, A. Ram, M. Veloso, D. Weld, and D. Wilkins. PDDL The Planning Domain Definition Language. In R. Simmons, M. Veloso, and S. Smith, editors, 4th Int. Conf. on AI Planning and Scheduling, 1998.
4. F. Leymann and D. Roller. Workflow-based applications. IBM Systems Journal, Volume 36, Number 1, 1997 Application Development
   http://researchweb.watson.ibm.com/journal /sj/361/leymann.html
5. Santhosh Kumaran and Prabir Nandi. Conversational Support for Web Services: The next stage of Web services abstraction. http://www-106.ibm.com/developerworks/webservices/library/ws-conver/?dwzone=webservices
6. IBM's tutorial, http://www-4.ibm.com/software/solutions/webservices
7. Web Service Choreography Interface (WSCI), 1.0 www.w3.org/TR/wsci/
8. Web Services Choreography Working Group of W3C,
   http://www.w3.org/2002/ws/chor/
9. The Buisiness Process Management Language (BPML),www.bpmi.org
10. Sanjiva Weerawarana. WSDL 1.2: Proposed resolution to portType extensibility and service type issues. http://lists.w3.org/Archives/Public/www-ws-desc/2002Jun/att-0046/01-portTypes-2002-06-09.html
11. Shankar R. Ponnekanti and Armando Fox. SWORD: A Developer Toolkit for Building Composite Web Services. In Proc. WWW2002 Web Engineering Track,
    http://www2002.org/CDROM/alternate/786/
12. Mike Papazoglou, Marco Aiello, Marco Pistore, and Jian Yang. XSRL: A Request Language for Web Services. http://www.webservices.org/index.php/article/articleview/990/1/24/ http://www.w3.org/Addressing/

Varying Resource Consumption to Achieve Scalable Web Services

Lindsay Bradford, Stephen Milliner, and Marlon Dumas

Centre for Information Technology Innovation
Queensland University of Technology, Australia
{l.bradford,s.milliner,m.dumas}@qut.edu.au

Abstract. Web service deployment is hampered by the possibility of sudden variations in request volumes. Mechanisms exist to enhance scalability in times of heavy load when the delivered content is static. However, web services typically involve dynamic content, delivered through application servers which may have little to no support for adapting to varying loads in order to ensure timely delivery. In this paper we discuss why scaling dynamic content delivery under load is difficult, we present a technique for controlled service degradation to achieve this scalability, and we present experimental results evaluating its benefits.

1   Introduction

The vast and uncertain environment of the Internet has direct consequences for service delivery, and has the potential to derail attempts to provide economic benefits via the electronic offering of services. In particular, the tardy delivery of a service may force the provider to decrease the price or increase the quality to offset the negative effects of the poor delivery.

The delivery of software as a service across the Internet carries with it significantly more risk than that of offering functionally equivalent shrink-wrapped software. By logically centralizing the software and offering it as a service, the service provider invites direct customer dissatisfaction by transferring originally client-side risks (such as the provision of an an environment capable of meeting client demand) back upon themselves. In addition there is a significant risk of insufficient capacity for client demand: a direct consequence of the unpredictable Internet environment in which a web service operates. Web services exposed to the Internet may experience huge demand fluctuations. These changes may occur rapidly, making it impossible for a human operator to respond in a timely manner. This situation is exacerbated if a client's expectations of a service remains high regardless of the problems being experienced by the service provider.

A possible way to maintain timely delivery in cases of capacity overflow, is by dynamically varying service overhead so that performance degradation is gracefully managed and user dissatisfaction minimized. Examples of situations where service degradation can be applied include: (i) choosing not to execute code for generating advertising content; (ii) skipping non-essential validations of

B. Benatallah and M.-C. Shan (Eds.): TES 2003, LNCS 2819, pp. 179–190, 2003.
© Springer-Verlag Berlin Heidelberg 2003

XML messages; and (iii) offering delayed data (e.g. stock quotes) rather than the most up-to-date version.

As a step toward a system for controlled service degradation, this paper aims:

1. to investigate the impact of high user load (such as a flash crowd) on a given service, and
2. to determine if benefits associated with a simple method for dynamically varying service resource consumption through service degradation, outweigh the overhead introduced.

The paper specifically considers Quality of Service (QoS) measured only in terms of response time and focuses on CPU consumption, as evidence indicates that this is a bottleneck when delivering dynamic content [1].

Section 2 discusses previous work on scalability of web service provision under extreme load. Section 3 discusses our approach to measuring service adequacy. Using this approach, we discuss in section 4 our initial technique for mitigating the effects of heavy load using variable CPU consumption. Section 5 presents three experiments involving large user load on a simulated service offering and discusses the results. Section 6 concludes outlining directions for future work.

2   Background

When delivering static content such as basic HTML pages, network bandwidth is typically the bottleneck [2]. Given that static content changes infrequently, basic Internet infrastructure allows caching of the content "closer" to the user via reverse-proxy caching, web browser caching, Content Distribution Networks (CDN), etc. This allows a degree of scalability by spreading bandwidth consumption amongst a set of remotely located caches.

Resource management for bandwidth under heavy load has also been investigated and typically revolves around techniques to limit certain types of bandwidth consumption (see [3] for a comparison of popular approaches) and controlled degradation of service, for example [4].

In times of extremely heavy load, traditional caching techniques can be augmented with more active approaches to better meet demand [5]. Peer-to-Peer caching schemes [6], the use of adaptive CDNs [7] and Cooperative networking models [2] where clients act as proxy cache servers to newer clients have all been investigated as approaches to mitigate the effects of heavy request loads for static content. Regardless of the caching strategy chosen, the core target of each strategy is to maximise *cache-hits*, allowing the originating server to deliver to just a minimised number of clients that do not have access to a remote cache.

When looking to scale delivery of dynamic content offered by web services, however, the application of caching is problematic. Basic Internet infrastructure offers limited support for caching results to dynamic queries, simply because it can make no guarantees on what future response might be. Considering that the delivery of dynamic content becomes CPU bound, the target for content caching shifts to saving on content construction overhead. Dynamic content caching schemes work on the idea that some amount of the dynamic content remains static enough over time to justify the overhead of synchronizing copies with the source content as this source content changes. Data Update Propagation [1], Active Query Caching [8] and Macro-Pre-Processing of HTML [9] are examples of this approach. The applicability of dynamic content caching however, is limited as noted by Yagoub et al. [10]. Hence, the possibility of minimizing the cost of dynamic content generation during times of heavy load should be considered.

When considering the differences between static and dynamic content delivery, the bottleneck typically shifts from bandwidth to CPU. Kraiss et al. [11] note that the bottleneck for e-services resides in the application server and back-end database servers. Padmanabhan & Sripanidkulchai [2] point to the effects of September 11's tragedy on a popular news site. As dynamically generated content initially made the CPU the primary bottleneck, it was manually replaced with static content, shifting the bottleneck to network bandwidth. Challenger et al. [1] state that "a typical dynamic page may require several orders of magnitude more CPU time to serve than a typical static page of comparable size".

Graceful degradation of service in times of server-side under-capacity is not a new concept [12]. When discussing CPU as a resource however, existing discussion on techniques for resource management seem limited to queue management of a static algorithm for response generation (see [11], [13], and [14] as examples). These techniques, while useful for delivering quality service to a limited number of the total requests received, do little to increase overall service scalability. Hence, we concentrate on when a process becomes CPU bound and how judicious service overhead reduction may help us increase overall scalability.

Certain parallels exist between our proposal and the automatic Quality of Service (QoS) control mechanisms proposed by Menascé and Mason [15]. Their approach however involves modifying the configuration of the Application/Web Server, which usually cannot be done at runtime as required in case of sudden capacity overflow. In contrast, our work focuses on what the application developer may do without modifying the underlying server's configuration or API.

3   Measuring Service Adequacy

3.1   Service Time

Perhaps one of the biggest differences between web services and traditional distributed computing is the service's potential concurrent audience size and that audience's expectations for adequate service provision regardless of its own size. For services to be consumed by an end user in real-time (a user sitting and waiting for response), we define a *client_acceptable_time_limit* taking the following into consideration:

- Any human/computer interaction taking over a second is an obtrusive delay to the user [16].
- An end user's perception of service quality is strongly influenced by response time. Content makeup has little effect on user's perception of QoS [17].

- Though end users typically have a conceptual model of dynamic content delivery taking more effort than static content, these conceptual models are often grossly mismatched with the effort actually required by the server [18].
- So long as service response time is adequate, the requesting client will not bail-out waiting for it [19].

Therefore, we assume a value of 1 second as our *client_acceptable_time_limit*. We use this time limit as a worst-case response time a server should endeavour to deliver a response to its client within. This limit is a hard upper bound on performance (as opposed to say, an average over time, allowing some responses to go above the limit). We do this in recognition of user behaviour that will punish a service provider for a 4 second response the first time it happens, regardless of the fact that the past several responses were sub-second, and that an average over all the responses might definitely be within a sub-second bound.

This client acceptable time limit will no doubt vary with circumstance. We can imagine that a client may have varying requirements depending on the client's nature. A software client that is in turn a service composed of several other services may need a tighter client acceptable time limit if it is to eventually serve its composed service to some end human consumer.

The base metric we wish to collect is that of *end-to-end_response_time*, defined in [20] as *the amount of time that passes from when a client first starts sending a request to when the client completes receiving the response*. We view *end-to-end_response_time* as an attractive measure for controlled test environments, whilst acknowledging that it may be difficult (if not impossible) to collect in a real-world setting.

The choice of application server can severely restrict an application developer's options in attempting to deliver dynamic content in a user acceptable time-frame. We choose the Apache Tomcat 4.1.18 servlet engine [1] and deliberately limit ourselves to what we can achieve without modification of the Servlet engine itself. As we do not have access to the time a servlet resides on the request queue, we cannot use approaches based on length of time in queue.

3.2   Service Adequacy

We define the function *service_adequacy* between two time points (t_1 and t_2) as:

$$\frac{adequate\_responses(service\_requests(t_1, t_2))}{\#\ service\_requests(t_1, t_2)} \tag{1}$$

where *service_requests*(t_1, t_2) is the set of requests sent between times t_1 and t_2, while *adequate_responses*$(\{r : ServiceRequest\})$ is the number of requests in the supplied set that return a response within the *client_acceptable_time_limit* discussed previously.

By varying effort in dynamic content delivery, we seek to maximise the service adequacy over a period of heavy load, which in turn means generating a higher

---

[1] http://jakarta.apache.org/tomcat

number of adequate responses to requests under that load than what we would have without varying effort. This measure does not take into account any user "dissatisfaction" with a less "complete" service provision.

4   Design Considerations

We assume that for processing a given type of request, there are multiple *approaches* available, each with its own expected execution time. Approaches are statically ranked during servlet initialization in order of expected system time execution from heaviest to lightest. We also assume that a service provider would prefer to generate the most costly approach they can so long as the response is timely. Thus, in times of heavy load, we choose a less costly approach; in times of light load, we choose one more costly.

Approaches are chosen via an *approach selector* illustrated in Fig. 1. The approaches for handling a service request are placed in a group and ranked by cost. Each approach in a group is either active or inactive. Active approaches are capable of processing a service request whereas inactive ones will accept no new requests for processing. Initially all approaches in a group are active.

We define two thresholds for the activation and deactivation of approaches:

time_limit: The elapsed server time in which we desire a response to be sent for any received request. Once the reported cost of an approach breaches this limit, the approach is deactivated. The cheapest approach is not deactivated, regardless of the degree to which the limit is breached.

reactivation_threshold: Once the reported cost of an approach drops below this threshold, the next most expensive (previously deactivated) approach will be re-activated and its reported cost reset to zero.

The threshold *time_limit* differs from the *client_acceptable_time_limit* defined earlier, in that it takes no account for time outside the control of the server (such as communications overhead). The *target_processing_time* should conceivably be small enough to allow reasonable communications on top of processing time to allow overall delivery within the *client_acceptable_time_limit*. The focus of our

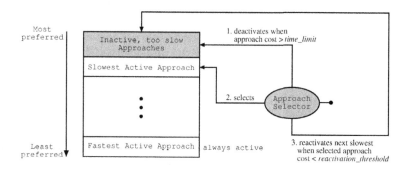

Fig. 1. The Approach Selector

research, however, is not in having the service consider network latency in its delivery so we model the time difference as a simple constant value.

Every request for a service is passed through the approach selector, implemented as a servlet filter. This filter can be plugged without requiring any alteration to the servlet engine itself. Each time that the processing of a service request is completed using a given approach, the approach selector gets the cost. If the cost has fallen below the *reactivation_threshold*, the next most expensive deactivated approach is reactivated, and its cost reset to zero. The next service request will be processed using the reactivated approach. The reported cost of a single approach is the worst elapsed time recorded of the last w calls to the approach. In the experiments presented below, we have set w at 20 for the experiment after some initial trials on the stability of approach cost reporting.

Note that for service degradation to be applicable, several versions of the application providing the service should be available: a "full" version and one or more "degraded" versions. In order to apply controlled degradation, the need for multiple versions should thus be imposed as a requirement in the application development process. In order to reduce the costs of handling this requirement in terms of analysis, design, coding, and testing, (semi-)automated support can be provided. In particular, design-level support could be introduced that would allow designers to provide meta-data about the cost and importance of various processing steps. At the coding level, special directives could be inserted in the dynamic content generation scripts (e.g. JSP, ASP, or PHP) to indicate for example not to perform a full XML message validation, or not to generate certain document portions in the degraded version of the service. As the space of possibilities is large, this issue desserves a separate treatment in future work.

5   Experiments

5.1   Simulation Environment

Our experiments are carried out on a set of eight dedicated Sun boxes running Debian Linux on an isolated 100 megabit/second LAN. The testbed relies on a single testing server and a single target server. The testing server sends broadcast UDP messages to synchronise the activity of clients in order to generate differing request patterns. The target server, a Sparc Ultra-5 with 192 Mb of memory, contains the application server and approach selection algorithm to be tested.

The remaining six boxes act as test clients. Two of these machines act simply to generate sufficient request traffic to tax the target server. These two machines have been configured to generate enough traffic to ensure the server is close to, but not actually at the point where, the server will refuse an incoming connection. The other four machines send requests and wait for responses before sending new requests. The figures reported later have been derived from the data collected on this second set of boxes.

The request processing component for each service delivery approach is an instance of a "workload simulation" servlet, pre-configured to run a set number of floating-point calculations of 3000, 1000, 500 or 100 loops. A loop of 3000 floating-point calculations is used to represent the baseline approach. A response from a service returns processing time as measured by the server.

Each experiment is conducted using two request traffic patterns. The "steady" pattern corresponds to a server under heavy, constant request pressure, as might result from the arrival of a flash crowd. The "bursty" pattern alternates periods of high arrivals of requests which go beyond server capacity, with periods of no arrivals. In future work, we look at other traffic patterns including the transition between the steady and bursty request patterns. Note that for both patterns, the total amount of requests over the period of one experiment is the same.

As a result of the non-threaded nature of the sampling clients, the number of requests that these data sampling clients can make is bound by the response times delivered by the server. Our expectation with introducing approach selection is that we should be able to reduce end-to-end response times, and allow significantly more timely service responses reported from the sampling machines than when run against the baseline.

Tests are run for one hour each to ensure the receipt of enough sampled data in the worst case. Statistics are collected for the last 50 minutes of each experiment to ensure the results are not optimistically skewed by warm-up time. We track the *end_to_end_response_time* of each client request and report the percentage that fail to fall within our *client_acceptable_time_limit*.

The time thresholds *time_limit* and *reactivation_threshold* are set at 800 and 400ms respectively. The *time_limit* threshold of 800ms was chosen as a number within our one second target with 200ms set aside to receive and transmit request and response messages. The 400ms *reactivation_threshold* was simply chosen as half of the *time_limit*.

We performed three sets of experiments. In the first experiment we run the baseline approach against both the steady and bursty request patterns. The second experiment replaces the baseline approach with our approach selection algorithm and was run against the bursty request pattern. The third experiment uses the approach selection algorithm against the steady request pattern.

Results are displayed as a histograms, with the number of responses returned to the sampling clients within a given timeframe represented as gray bars along the x axis. A line showing the cumulative percentage of responses is also supplied. Service adequacy is the percentage of responses returned within one second.

5.2   Experiment 1 – Baseline Approach for Both Request Patterns

Figure 2(a) shows that most responses were received by the sampling clients within two seconds when tested against the bursty request pattern. Via our definition of service adequacy, only around 9% of the responses received were adequate, however. The steady request pattern results in Fig. 2(b) shows that the server was taxed heavily as a result of the request traffic generated. The minimum response time recorded was slightly under 69 seconds. As a result, the baseline delivered zero service adequacy against the steady request pattern.

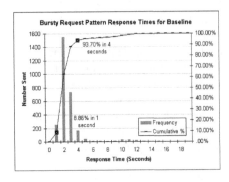
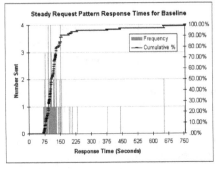

(a) Baseline: Bursty Request Pattern   (b) Baseline: Steady Request Pattern

Fig. 2. Effect of running baseline against bursty and steady request patterns

The experiments show that the request arrival pattern has a strong effect on service adequacy. By simply allowing a minute between bursts of requests, the baseline response times are 20 times better with the bursty request pattern. This is predictable given that the bursty arrival pattern allows the service to use the period of no requests between bursts to focus on response delivery, and therefore achieve some "adequate" responses. However, it is surprising that almost no request took more than 20 seconds to process under the bursty pattern, which shows that the system does perform request processing during the bursts. Note that the same total amount of requests were processed under both approaches.

5.3   Experiment 2 – Approach Selection for Bursty Pattern

Here we compare the bursty baseline presented in Fig. 2(a) (repeated in Fig. 3(a)), with approach selection in Fig. 3(b) The number of adequate responses has moved from a little under nine percent to around 48 percent. Again, most messages were received within four seconds of sending the request. However, approach selection has resulted in a much smaller worst case response time, and significantly more responses within one second. We conclude that the approach selection overhead does not outweigh its benefits.

Figure 4(a) shows the breakdown of approaches selected for the bursty request pattern. Most requests were balanced between either the most costly, or second most costly approach. Very few attempts were made to use the lightest two approaches. Figure 4(b) shows that most of the inadequate responses generated were a result of attempting the most costly approach, thereby showing a deficiency in in the approach selection algorithm. To generate better service adequacy for the bursty pattern, we would expect far less attempts at the 3000 loop algorithm and more on the 1000 and 500 loop algorithms instead (see section 6).

The results in Fig. 4(b) suggest that the decision-making algorithm for approach selection can be poor when determining when to switch between the most costly and second-most costly approaches with the bursty pattern. We believe a contributor to this result is the number of threads that can be simultaneously

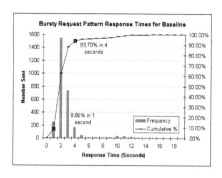 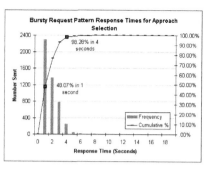

(a) Baseline   (b) Approach Selection

Fig. 3. Bursty request pattern using baseline and approach selection

running. As the number of threads running a given approach increase, it allows for larger numbers of in-progress threads that still need to complete using a given approach once that approach is deactivated. The bursty traffic pattern is likely to be compounding the issue, as we expect it to exercise the switching of approaches more frequently than the steady request pattern.

5.4 Experiment 3 – Approach Selection for Steady Pattern

In this experiment we repeat the baseline results for a steady request pattern (from Fig. 2(b)) in Fig. 5(a) and compare them against running the same pattern with approach selection in Fig. 5(b). Most responses were received between 75 and 150 seconds of transmission from the client in the baseline experiment and the worst-case response time took over 755 seconds to return. No adequate responses to baseline requests were received by the sampling clients.

In contrast to the baseline, approach selection saw over 50% of responses return in an adequate timeframe under the bursty pattern, with most responses

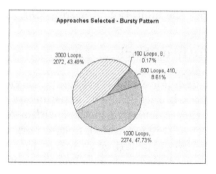 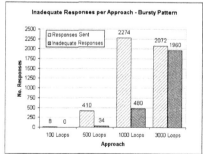

(a) Approaches Selected   (b) Inadequate Responses per Approach

Fig. 4. Breakdown of approaches selected for bursty request pattern

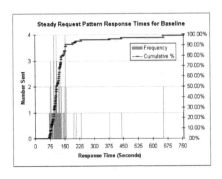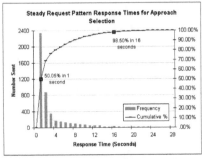

(a) Baseline   (b) Approach Selection

Fig. 5. Steady request pattern using baseline and approach selection

returned within few seconds. In addition, approach selection proved even more beneficial to response times under the steady pattern than the bursty one.

Figure 6(a) shows the breakdown of approaches selected for the steady request pattern. Most of the requests were processed using the least costly approach. This is in contrast to approach selection for the bursty request pattern, which used the 3000 and 1000 loop approaches mostly. We conclude that the accuracy of using elapsed time as a measure for determining when to switch approaches is yields better results with heavier request loads.

A relatively even distribution of attempts to use more costly approaches was recorded. Figure 6(b) shows that most of the requests processed with the least costly approach returned adequate responses, whereas, most requests attempting heavier approaches returned inadequate responses. The number of attempts at more costly approaches is surprisingly large. We theorise that a combination of the occasional break in steady request traffic, sufficient enough to retry the heaviest of approaches, and concurrent threads still running recently deactivated approaches combined to produce the numbers observed.

We have shown that despite limitations imposed by the implementation technology chosen, the principle of generating cheaper responses to a request under times of load can deliver significant performance improvement. We wish to automate the ranking of approaches to remove the limitation of hard-coding it.

6   Concluding Remarks and Future Work

The choice of cost calculation algorithm, *time_limit* and *reactivation_threshold* may also have an impact on optimal approach selection. The experiments described used a simple worst-case elapsed time calculation method with a relatively small window and time limit values that were not varied. Future work will focus on investigating the behavioural change evidenced when using the same algorithm with differing sample window sizes, varied cost sampling algorithms, differing time limit values and differing degrees of multi-threading.

We have shown that the type of request pattern has a strong effect on service provision adequacy without approach selection, and that approach selection

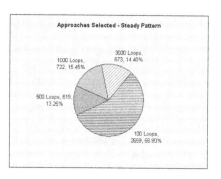

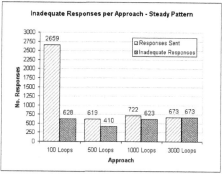

(a) Approaches Selected   (b) Inadequate Responses per Approach

Fig. 6. Breakdown of approaches selected for steady request pattern

serves to smooth the differences in response times between patterns. Though the method employed works to decrease response times and increase scalability for the request patterns tested, it produces better responses when used with heavy, constant request load. We intend to test approach selection against a wider range of request patterns to gain a better understanding of its strengths and weaknesses and help synthesize better selection algorithms. Also, we plan to study the behavioural effects of varying the two time thresholds of the proposed method, namely *reactivation_threshold* and *time_limit*, in order to undertand how they can be tuned to achieve greater scalability.

Our current experimental setup involves CPU-intensive services requiring no RAM or disk access. At present, we are working towards extending the experimental setup first to services involving frequent RAM access (e.g.to simulate XML parsing and DOM tree-traversals), and then to services involving disk access (e.g. relying on a database system).

Acknowledgments. Thanks to Alex Delis for his valuable comments on a draft of this paper.

References

1. Challenger, J., Iyengar, A., Witting, K., Ferstat, C., Reed, P.: A Publishing System for Efficiently Creating Dynamic Web Content. In: INFOCOM (2). (2000) 844–853
2. Padmanabhan, V., Sripanidkulchai, K.: The Case for Cooperative Networking (2002)
3. Lau, F., Rubin, S.H., Smith, M.H., Trajovic, L.: Distributed Denial of Service Attacks. In: IEEE International Conference on Systems, Man, and Cybernetics. Volume 3., Nashville, TN, USA (2000) 2275–2280
4. Singh, S.: Quality of service guarantees in mobile computing. Computer Communications **19** (1996)
5. Iyengar, A., Rosu, D.: Architecting Web sites for high performance. In: Scientific Programming. Volume 10. IOS Press (2002) 75–89

6. Stading, T., Maniatis, P., Baker, M.: Peer-to-Peer Caching Schemes to Address Flash Crowds. In: 1st International Peer To Peer Systems Workshop (IPTPS 2002), Cambridge, MA, USA (2002)
7. Jung, J., Krishnamurthy, B., Rabinovich, M.: Flash Crowds and Denial of Service Attacks: Characterization and Implications for CDNs and Web Sites. In: Proceedings of the International World Wide Web Conference, ACM Press New York, NY, USA (2002) 252–262
8. Luo, Q., Naughton, J.F., Krishnamurthy, R., Cao, P., Li, Y.: Active Query Caching for Database Web Servers. In Suciu, D., Vossen, G., eds.: WebDB (Selected Papers). Volume 1997 of Lecture Notes in Computer Science., Springer (2001) 92–104
9. Douglis, F., Haro, A., Rabinovich, M.: HPP: HTML Macro-Preprocessing to Support Dynamic Document Caching. In: USENIX Symposium on Internet Technologies and Systems. (1997)
10. Yagoub, K., Florescu, D., Issarny, V., Valduriez, P.: Caching Strategies for Data-Intensive Web Sites. In Abbadi, A.E., Brodie, M.L., Chakravarthy, S., Dayal, U., Kamel, N., Schlageter, G., Whang, K.Y., eds.: VLDB 2000, Proceedings of 26th International Conference on Very Large Data Bases, September 10-14, 2000, Cairo, Egypt, Morgan Kaufmann (2000) 188–199
11. Kraiss, A., Schoen, F., Weikum, G., Deppisch, U.: Towards Response Time Guarantees for e-Service Middleware. Bulletin on the Technical Committee on Data Engineering **24** (2001) 58–63
12. Hutchison, D., Coulson, G., Campbell, A.: 11. In: Quality of Service Management in Distributed Systems. Addison Wesley (1994)
13. Garg, A., Reddy, A.L.N. In: Mitigating Denial Of Service Using QoS Regulation. Volume 1270 of Lecture Notes in Computer Science. Springer (1997) 90–101
14. Leiwo, J., Zheng, Y.: A Method to Implement a Denial of Service Protection Base. In: Australasian Conference on Information Security and Privacy. Volume 1270 of Lecture Notes in Computer Science., Berlin, Germany, Springer (1997) 90–101
15. Menascé, D.A., Mason, G.: Automatic QoS Control. IEEE Internet Computing **7** (2003) 92–95
16. Miller, R.: Response Time in Man-Computer Conversational Transactions. In: Proc. AFIPS Fall Joint Computer Conference. Volume 33. (1968) 267–277
17. Ramsay, J., Barbesi, A., Peerce, J.: A psychological investigation of long retrieval times on the World Wide Web. In: Interacting with Computers, Elsevier (1998)
18. Bhatti, N., Bouch, A., Kuchinsky, A.: Integrating user-perceived quality into Web server design. Computer Networks (Amsterdam, Netherlands: 1999) **33** (2000) 1–16
19. Zona Research: The Need for Speed (1999) Whitepaper.
20. Menascé, D.A., Almeida, V.A.F.: Capacity Planning for Web Services. Prentice Hall (2001)

A Protocol for Fast Co-allocation of Shared Web Services

Jonghun Park[1] and Tao Yang[2]

[1] Dept. of Industrial Engineering
Korea Advanced Institute of Science & Technology
j.park@kaist.ac.kr
[2] School of Information Sciences & Technology
Pennsylvania State University
tyang@ist.psu.edu

Abstract. The emerging Web services are building blocks for creating highly distributed e-Business applications, allowing any services to be integrated as long as they are Web-enabled. This interoperability allows businesses to dynamically discover and aggregate a range of component services to more easily create value-added composite services. One of the problems underlying the deployment of such composite services on the Web is service co-allocation that arises when a composite service needs to ensure all the required component services to be available for execution at the same time. This paper presents a protocol, named WSCP (Web Service Co-allocation Protocol), that supports fast co-allocation of distributed Web services when they are shared by multiple independent composite Web services. Our objective is to minimize the waiting time incurred on a composite service before it successfully co-allocates its components. WSCP is inspired by two seemingly unrelated ideas in distributed computing, namely the tentative hold protocol and the backoff protocol. By efficiently combining and taking advantage of these two protocols, WSCP is able to achieve a significant improvement over existing protocols while effectively minimizing livelock.

1 Introduction

e-Service is the next stage of evolution of e-Business. With the advent of Internet-enabled service platforms such as Web services, it has become a reality to develop cross-organizational e-Business applications in the open distributed environment of the Internet. The Web services are self-contained, modular components that can be described, published, located, and invoked over the Web [1]. They can perform a specific business task and conform to particular technical standards (e.g., SOAP, WSDL, UDDI) so that each of these self-contained services can seamlessly integrate with other services. This interoperability allows businesses to dynamically discover and aggregate a range of Web services to more easily create innovative services and business processes.

Web services may be *simple* or *composite*. Composite services consist of a number of other simple or composite services. That is, Web services may have

B. Benatallah and M.-C. Shan (Eds.): TES 2003, LNCS 2819, pp. 191–202, 2003.

a recursive structure in that they can be composed of other published Web services while in turn they are also considered to be component services themselves [2]. In this regard, we refer to the services that are used by a composite service as *components*. A typical usage of the composite services is dynamic e-Business integration, which is the dynamic composition of local and remote business services to support a complex business workflow under changing business scenarios. The lifetime of such composite services may span from minutes to years. Consequently, the composite Web services will require its constituent service components to be dynamically allocated and de-allocated during their life cycle in order to deal with various contingencies such as (i) the service initialization and termination, (ii) the unexpected performance degradation or failure of the remote components, and (iii) the availability of new components.

Due to the increasing concern of quality of service in e-Business applications, service providers are likely to limit the maximum number of concurrently active service consumers to ensure the guaranteed responsiveness. We define this maximum number as *service capacity*. As a result, when the number of concurrent service consumers exceeds the capacity of a service provider, the consumers will necessarily compete for the services, and some of them may need to wait until the service becomes available. In particular, the problem becomes more challenging when composite services require to allocate multiple component services from distributed providers at the same time. The need for simultaneously co-allocating distributed services for successful execution of a composite service may arise in various application areas of service-oriented computing, including transactional Web services [3], Grid services built on OGSA [4], and brokering services such as bidding and real-time price comparison.

The problem of designing effective protocols for the service co-allocation characterized above can be addressed by introducing the two phase commit protocol (2PC) that has been extensively studied in the past [5]. A composite service that seeks to simultaneously invoke component services from multiple independent service providers can initiate 2PC prior to the actual invocations, making sure that all the component services are available for execution. Although correct, however, a direct application of 2PC to the service co-allocation problem may not provide an efficient solution. With the 2PC alone, component services are subject to frequent locks, and therefore composite services are susceptible to long waits and congestion as we discuss in the next section.

Motivated by this, this paper develops a new protocol that seeks to support fast co-allocation of distributed Web services that are shared by multiple independent composite Web services. The objective is to minimize the waiting time incurred on a composite service before it successfully co-allocates its required component services. By minimizing the waiting time of composite services, the time a composite service takes to respond to various types of requests will be reduced accordingly, and thereby quality of service of composite services can be improved [6].

Our protocol is inspired by two seemingly unrelated ideas in distributed computing, namely the tentative hold protocol (THP) [7] and the backoff protocol for contention resolution [8]. THP is an open, loosely coupled, message-based framework for the exchange of tentative commitments between service consumers and providers prior to the actual transaction. In this protocol, it is possible that multiple service consumers can place holds on the same service prior to the actual invocation, and the service providers can grant non-blocking reservations on their services, while allowing potential consumers greater flexibility in coordinating their transactions. On the other hand, the contention resolution has long been a problem in computer networks. Many different contention resolution mechanisms have been proposed, and numerous studies have been published evaluating their relative performance. One of the most widely used mechanisms is the class of backoff protocols, which dictate the duration of random delay for the next trial whenever an attempt to acquire a shared resource has failed.

By efficiently combining and taking advantage of these two ideas, the proposed protocol is able to achieve better performance than the existing solutions while at the same time being able to minimize the livelock occurrences. More specifically, the proposed protocol adds a tentative hold phase to 2PC by requiring composite services to obtain tentative holds from their respective component service providers before they initiate a 2PC transaction. The result is the reduced number of requests for locks to be placed on the component services, allowing higher service utilization and increased chance of successful co-allocation. In addition, the performance of the proposed protocol is further optimized in this paper through the introduction of a backoff protocol. Based on the observation that the existing backoff protocols can be effectively extended to accommodate the problem characteristics considered in this paper, we propose a new backoff protocol that supports efficient contention resolution among the competing service consumers.

The paper proceeds as follows. In Section 2, we describe a formal model for service co-allocation, and define the proposed Web service co-allocation protocol in terms of finite state automata. In Section 3, we present the basic idea and detailed specification of the proposed backoff protocol. Section 4 provides some experimental results that show the performance advantage of the proposed approach over the existing ones, and we conclude with some remarks for future research in Section 5.

2   Web Service Co-allocation Protocol

In this section, we first give formal definitions for the Web service co-allocation problem to be considered, discuss the issues related to the design of efficient co-allocation protocols, and finally present a formal definition of the proposed protocol.

Our model is characterized by a triple (Σ, Γ, κ), where Σ is a set of Web services, Γ is a mapping from Σ to finite subsets of 2^{Σ} such that $\Gamma(s) \subseteq 2^{\Sigma-\{s\}}$, $\forall s \in \Sigma$, and κ is a mapping from Σ to a positive integer, indicating the finite capacity of a Web service, defined by the maximum number of concurrent service consumers permitted at any time. Each Web service, $s \in \Sigma$, is assumed to be independently managed and belong to some service provider that represents a point of communication. $\Gamma(s) = \{C_1(s), \ldots, C_{\gamma(s)}(s)\}$ describes the set of possible component *co-allocation schemes* s ($\in \Sigma$) may require for its successful execution, where $\gamma(s)$ denotes the number of co-allocation schemes defined for s. Given $C_i(s) \in \Gamma(s)$, that represents a single co-allocation scheme, it is required that s co-allocates all the services defined in $C_i(s)$ as a bundle. That is, s cannot start invocation of services until all the component services in $C_i(s)$ are allocated and ready for execution. Furthermore, for $C_i(s) \in \Gamma(s)$, the number of elements in $C_i(s)$ will be called as *co-allocation size*.

From the definition, it is allowed that each composite service has more than one component composition scheme. The existence of multiple service co-allocation schemes is considered in this paper to address the dynamic service composition enabled by the availability of alternative or redundant services on the Web. That is, each co-allocation scheme defined in $\Gamma(s)$ represent a possible composition of component services that can satisfy the requirement of composite service s. It follows that $\Gamma(s) \neq \emptyset$ if s is a composite service, and $\Gamma(s) = \emptyset$ if s is a simple service that does not require allocation of other services.

In our model, we make the following assumptions: First, composite services are assumed to be dynamically instantiated and terminated by independent users or applications, and the service composition details may not be known in advance. Second, composite services are not allowed to communicate with each other for the purpose of coordinating the service co-allocation. Hence, each composite service will require a decentralized protocol. Finally, we assume that communication is reliable and there is an upperbound on the round trip time (RTT) for message transmissions, denoted by $\overline{RTT}$, but there is no requirement for ordered message delivery.

The requirement of service co-allocation can be addressed by employing the idea of 2PC protocol. The motivation of using 2PC is to ensure the atomicity of service allocation when composite services seek to co-allocate multiple services that are managed independently as a bundle. Following the definition of 2PC protocol, each service provider implements interfaces for a *prepare* method, an *abort* method, and a *commit* method. These are blocking method calls that require the caller to wait until the result is delivered. Each composite service $s \in \Sigma$ then initiates co-allocation by invoking the prepare methods of the service providers defined in $G(s) = \cup_{i=1,\ldots,\gamma(s)} C_i(s)$ to determine if there exists a set of service providers $C^*(s) \in \{C_i(s) \mid C_i(s) \in \Gamma(s), i = 1, \ldots, \gamma(s)\}$ such that all the services in $C^*(s)$ are available for commit. When service provider $t \in G(s)$ receives a request for prepare, it first locks one unit out of its service capacity, $\kappa(t)$, if there is an available unit, and replies with *yes*. Otherwise, the service provider replies with *no*. Subsequently, s will either invoke the commit methods to complete the co-allocation process if there exists a set of service providers $C^*(s)$ such that all service providers in $C^*(s)$ have replied with yes, or invoke the abort methods if no such set of service providers exists. In either case, any service provider in $G(s)$ that has replied with yes but does not belong to $C^*(s)$ must then be informed with abort to prevent indefinite service locking. We assume that s chooses a co-allocation scheme randomly when there is more than one set of providers that can be committed. In the following, we refer the co-allocation protocol characterized above as $2PCC$ (2PC with Choices).

While $2PCC$ provides a correct approach to the co-allocation of multiple services, it may not provide an efficient solution to the problem since it requires all the service components in $G(s)$ to be locked whenever a composite service s initiates co-allocation. With the frequent lock requests from many composite services, the probability of successful co-allocation will be decreased accordingly, resulting in the increased possibility of livelock in which some composite services repetitively attempt co-allocation without any success.

The starting point for development of the protocol proposed in this paper is the observation that the performance of $2PCC$ can be improved if we introduce a tentative hold phase prior to $2PCC$. With this approach, a composite service is required to obtain tentative holds from its service providers before it enters a 2PC phase. In order to support the semantics of THP, we define a *hold* method that allows a composite service to request a hold to be placed on one unit of service capacity. A hold request can be either approved or rejected according to the service provider's specific implementation of THP. When a hold is granted, the service provider will reply with *yes*, and otherwise *no*. In this paper, we use the infinite hold approach [9] in which a service provider grants a hold request as long as there is an available capacity. Accordingly, it is possible that two or more holds are placed on a single available service unit, and there is no need for a service provider to implement a method for handling a removal request for a currently placed hold. Through the introduction of THP, each composite service initiates 2PC only if it is convinced that all constituent services for a co-allocation scheme are available for execution. Therefore, it is expected that this approach will lead to less number of requests for locks than in $2PCC$.

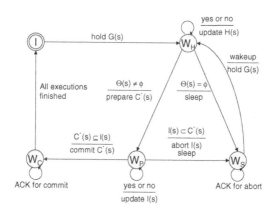

Fig. 1. Finite state automata for a composite service

In the following, we present a protocol for co-allocation of Web services in the presence of alternative co-allocation schemes, to be called $WSCP$ (Web

Service Co-allocation Protocol). The formal behavior of a composite service $s \in \Sigma$ defined in $WSCP$ is depicted in Figure 1 as a finite state automata. In an attempt to increase the speed of service co-allocation, $WSCP$ requires s to start by trying multiple co-allocation schemes in parallel, which is similar to $2PCC$. Note that, however, under $WSCP$, s makes hold requests for all the component services in the set $G(s)$ before it initiates a 2PC phase. Hence, from the definition of infinite hold policy, the available service units from the provider will not be locked for composite services. Subsequently, the results of the hold requests are recorded in the set $H(s)(\subseteq G(s))$ that contains the service components on which holds are placed successfully.

Next, s checks if any successful composition is possible by use of the components in $H(s)$. More specifically, when there exists a co-allocation scheme, $C^*(s)(\in \Gamma(s))$, such that $C^*(s) \subseteq H(s)$ and all the providers of $C^*(s)$ agreed to hold a service unit for s, s proceeds to a 2PC phase by invoking the prepare methods of the services in $C^*(s)$. If more than one such set of providers exists, s will select one randomly. The existence of $C^*(s)$ characterized above can be checked by constructing $\Theta(s) = \{C_i(s) \mid C_i(s) \in \Gamma(s) \wedge C_i(s) \subseteq H(s), i = 1, \ldots, \gamma(s)\}$ and testing if $\Theta(s) \neq \emptyset$. That is, if $\Theta(s) = \emptyset$, this implies s fails to acquire enough holds for any of co-allocation schemes, and there is no co-allocation scheme of which the providers agree to hold a service unit. Therefore, in this case, s simply enters to the backoff state so that it can try again after some random delay computed by a specific backoff protocol.

Once the prepare methods are invoked for those services defined in $C^*(s)$, the service components whose providers have agreed to commit are stored in the $I(s)$. We remark that it is possible for some service providers that have granted holds to disagree to commit since $WSCP$ employs the infinite hold policy. This is because a hold placed on a service unit is tentative and there can be more than one service consumer possessing a hold on an available service unit. If one of them initiates a 2PC by invoking the prepare method, then the service unit becomes unavailable to the others. Hence it is not possible to guarantee that a service unit that was available at the time of requesting a hold are still in hold when the prepare method is invoked.

In case that all service providers responsible for $C^*(s)$ reach an agreement to commit (i.e., $C^*(s) \subseteq I(s)$), s starts actual computation by invoking the commit methods of the service providers of $C^*(s)$. Otherwise, when the agreement for commit is not successful, s needs to invoke the abort method of the service providers defined in $I(s)$ to unlock their service units, and it goes to the backoff state for the next trial. Finally, the whole process repeats when s wakes up after the backoff time. The resulting finite state automata for a composite service s is shown in Figure 1 where W_H and W_P are the waiting states for the results of the respective method invocation, W_S and W_C are the states waiting for the next trial and execution finish, respectively. It is clear that one of the components in $WSCP$ that can affect the performance of the protocol is the backoff function. In the next section, we present in detail a new backoff protocol proposed in this paper.

3   Min-Max Backoff Protocol

The class of backoff protocols seeks to achieve contention resolution through the introduction of randomized delay time for retrials, and they can be parameterized by a non-decreasing function $f()$ [8]. When a client unsuccessfully tries to send a message, it retransmits again after T time steps, where T is selected randomly from $\{1, 2, \ldots, f(b)\}$ and b is a *failure counter* which keeps track of the number of times that the client has tried to send its message but failed. If $f(b) = (b+1)^{\Theta(1)}$, such a protocol is termed as a polynomial backoff protocol, whereas a protocol with $f(b) = 2^b$ is termed as a binary exponential backoff protocol. It has been reported that the polynomial backoff protocol is easy to implement and stable in many cases [8].

In this paper, we base our backoff protocol design on the polynomial backoff protocol to orthogonalize the component requests from independent composite services. Specifically, we view the uniform distribution $\mathcal{U}(1, f(b))$ employed by the backoff protocol as a hazard function that characterizes a composite service's retrial probability, and interpret $f(b)$ as an estimate of the overall system contention. Following the protocol definition of $WSCP$ in Section 2, whenever a composite service fails to obtain enough holds to satisfy one of its co-allocation schemes, we require the composite service to update its failure counter, indicating that its current retrial probability was too high for the system contention. In other words, for a composite service, higher the value of its failure counter, smaller is its retrial probability, which will facilitate reducing the overall contention among composite services.

The key intuition underlying the development of the proposed backoff protocol is that the failure counter can be further refined to better address the dynamics of Web service co-allocation problem. While a simple mechanism that increases the failure counter by one whenever a composite service fails its tentative hold phase will work for our purpose, it does not take into consideration of the problem characteristics of this paper. Unlike the single resource allocation system such as multiple access channels, our model consists of a set of component services shared by multiple independent composite services, each of which has co-allocation requirement possibly with multiple alternative schemes. As a result, contention will be different across the different service providers, and the success probability of a service co-allocation attempt may depend on the situation of more than one service provider. Furthermore, the existence of multiple co-allocation schemes necessitates more effective means to measure system contention since each composite service can satisfy its requirement as long as it can obtain holds for one of its co-allocation schemes.

Motivated by this, we propose a new congestion estimate perceived by a composite service. For the purpose of subsequent discussion, we consider composite service $s \in \Sigma$. Let $G(s) = \cup_{i=1,\ldots,\gamma(s)} C_i(s) = \{t_1, \ldots, t_m\} \subset \Sigma$, and also let $b_{t_j}(s), j = 1, \ldots, m$ be the failure counter defined for s with respect to component service $t_j \in G(s)$. Initially, s sets $b_{t_j}(s) = 0, \forall t_j \in G(s)$, and it updates the value of $b_{t_j}(s)$ by $b_{t_j}(s) + 1$ whenever s fails to obtain a hold from the provider of component service t_j. Furthermore, given $\gamma(s)$ different co-allocation schemes for s, we define an aggregated failure counter, $\alpha_i(s)$, for co-allocation scheme $C_i(s)$, $i = 1, \ldots, \gamma(s)$, in Equation 1 where $\phi(s)$ represents an upperbound for the value of the failure counter after which the counter is reset, and p denotes a positive constant.

$$\alpha_i(s) = \max_{j=1,\ldots,m} \{((b_{t_j}(s) \bmod \phi(s)) + 1)^p \mid t_j \in C_i(s)\} \tag{1}$$

Based on the definition of the aggregated failure counter for a single co-allocation scheme, in Equation 2 we proceed to define a function that characterizes the system congestion perceived by composite service s when there are multiple co-allocation schemes.

$$\beta(s) = \min_{i=1,\ldots,\gamma(s)} \{\alpha_i(s)\} \tag{2}$$

Finally, we propose to compute a backoff time for s, denoted by $\delta(s)$, according to the backoff function defined in Equation 3.

$$\delta(s) = \mathcal{U}(1, \beta(s)) \times \overline{RTT} \tag{3}$$

The proposed backoff protocol in Equation 3 will be referred to as (polynomial) *Min-Max* backoff. The rationale behind Equation 3 can be informally described as follows: First, we choose to use a polynomial function as a means for penalizing retrial times with respect to the congestion estimated for a single service provider. To prevent a failure counter from having excessive value, an upperbound is introduced in Equation 1. This is analogous to the truncated binary exponential backoff protocol used for Ethernet [8] in that extremely tardy processes can be avoided. However, we remark that the Min-Max backoff protocol periodically resets the failure counter as our model does not consider the termination of a composite process when the failure counter exceeds a certain threshold. Second, the employment of max function in Equation 1 is motivated from the fact that a composite service needs to consider the worst case since it needs to co-allocate the services altogether as defined in a co-allocation scheme. Finally, the min function defined in Equation 2 indicates the fact that a composite service can take advantage of the best case since its service co-allocation requirement can be satisfied as long as the services defined in one of its alternative co-allocation schemes are co-allocated.

4   Experimental Results

In this section, we examine the performance of the $WSCP$ and Min-Max backoff proposed in this paper. We first show the performance comparison results of $WSCP$ and $2PCC$ in the absence of the backoff protocol. We then consider $WSCP$, and compare the performance of the Min-Max backoff protocol to other existing alternatives such as constant backoff, quadratic polynomial backoff, and no backoff. The performance measure we consider for comparison is the average waiting time of composite services which is defined by the average of the time between the arrival and the successful co-allocation of composite services.

The performance of the service co-allocation protocols greatly depends on various environmental parameters such as overall congestion, service rate, and service usage patterns. Hence, for the purpose of experimentation, we implemented a simulator in which the following simulation parameters that affect the performance of protocols can be configured: the number of component service providers, the capacity of service providers, the number of composite services to be created along with the statistical distribution for the inter-arrival times, the largest possible co-allocation size of a composite service, the maximum number of alternative co-allocation schemes allowed for a composite service, and finally the statistical distribution for characterizing the execution time of composite services. A uniform distribution is assumed for the co-allocation size and the number of alternative co-allocation schemes. That is, if the maximum co-allocation size is equal to 9, the size of a single co-allocation requirement will be $\frac{1+9}{2} = 5$ on the average. Likewise, if the maximum number of co-allocation schemes is 3, each composite service has $\frac{1+3}{2} = 2$ co-allocation schemes on the average.

Throughout the simulation results presented in this section, we measure the performance for the situation in which 2,000 composite services are dynamically created according to an exponential distribution and compete for components available from 20 different service providers of which the capacities are all set to 5. In order to address the various deployment scenarios of Web service computing, the execution time for a composite service is assumed to follow a uniform distribution on the interval $[100, 1000]$. A single simulation run is completed when all the composite services created during the simulation successfully co-allocate their required components and finish execution. In addition, we have set $\phi(s) = 8, \forall s \in \Sigma$, and the distribution of RTT to be $\mathcal{U}(1, 200)$. That is, $\overline{RTT} = 200$. Finally, we remark that the time unit in the experimentation is defined in terms of msec.

Our first experiment compares the performance of $WSCP$ over $2PCC$ when the backoff time is set to 0. The result is shown in Figure 2 in which the mean

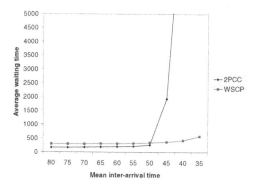

Fig. 2. Performance comparison result for 2PCC and WSCP when no backoff protocol is used

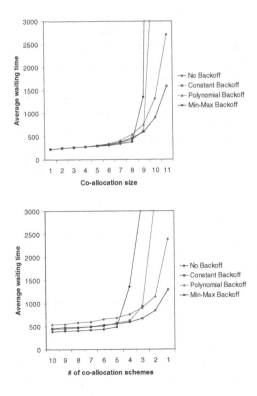

Fig. 3. Performance comparison results for various backoff protocols under $WSCP$ by varying the co-allocation size (top) and the number of co-allocation schemes (bottom)

inter-arrival time of composite Web services is varied from 80 to 35 to examine the effect of different levels of service contention. In this experiment, each composite service is configured to have up to 5 different alternative co-allocation schemes with the largest possible co-allocation size of 5. From Figure 2, it can be seen that under $2PCC$ the average waiting time grows quite quickly as the arrival rate of composite services increases. In particular, it is interesting to note that $2PCC$ performs slightly better than $WSCP$ up to some point before the contention becomes significant. This is an expected result since most composite services will be able to co-allocate their required services with a single trial when there is virtually no competition. Hence, the performance difference is solely attributed to the overhead of $WSCP$ that is introduced by adding a tentative hold phase to the 2PC. As the arrival rate of composite services increases, however, the contention for component services becomes higher, and $WSCP$ yields a significant improvement over $2PCC$. Therefore, from the observation, when the contention for the services is not negligible, $WSCP$ appears to provide an efficient and scalable solution for fast co-allocation of Web services by minimizing the unnecessary lock duration caused by pure 2PC semantics.

Next, the attempt to further optimize the performance of $WSCP$ through the adoption of the Min-Max backoff protocol in Section 3 is validated via experiments. We carried out the performance experimentation of $WSCP$ under different backoff policies by respectively changing the maximum co-allocation size and the maximum alternative co-allocation schemes. Specifically, for each experiment we investigate the performance of four backoff protocols, namely (i) the *no backoff* in which backoff time is set to 0, (ii) the *constant backoff* with the constant backoff time of $\overline{RTT}$, (iii) the *polynomial backoff* that uses a quadratic function $f(b) = (b+1)^2$ where the failure counter b is increased whenever a tentative hold phase fails, and (iv) the quadratic *Min-Max backoff* (i.e., $p = 2$) as defined in Section 3. Figure 3 compares the average waiting time results for each scenario.

In the first scenario of Figure 3 in which the impact of the maximum co-allocation size is explored when the mean inter-arrival time and the maximum number of co-allocation schemes are set to 80 and 4 respectively, the proposed Min-Max backoff protocol outperforms the others for most cases considered. It should be noted that the increased maximum co-allocation size will result in higher contention for component services. As anticipated, the performance of four backoff policies does not show significant difference up to some point since the backoff is not necessary when the overall congestion is low.

Similarly, the second scenario varies the maximum number of co-allocation schemes allowed for a composite service. For this experiment, the mean inter-arrival time is fixed to 80, and the maximum co-allocation size is to 9. From the definition, the higher number of co-allocation schemes will lead to the higher chance of successful co-allocation for a composite service owing to the increased flexibility. Hence, the average waiting time increases as the maximum number of co-allocation schemes decreases for all the backoff protocols considered. The plots in Figure 3 suggest that the Min-Max backoff achieves better performance results as the congestion increases.

For the two scenarios considered in this experimentation, it is observed that (i) the introduction of a backoff protocol can improve the performance of service co-allocation, (ii) the polynomial backoff yields better performance results than the no backoff and the constant backoff as the congestion increases, and, in particular, (ii) the proposed Min-Max backoff protocol consistently performs better than the others when the overall contention for the component services becomes non-negligible. Therefore, these results confirm that the $WSCP$ combined with the Min-Max backoff provides significant performance improvement over the existing approaches.

5   Conclusion

The recent advent of Web services has opened up the possibility of constructing a range of new e-Business applications by allowing an application to be composed from distributed Web services that are created and managed independently and autonomously. In this paper, we considered the problem of co-allocating multiple

Web services to support effective and efficient deployment of dynamic service composition. Specifically, the goal of our work was to develop a new protocol that facilitates fast co-allocation of component Web services when they are shared by independent composite Web services with possibly more than one service co-allocation scheme.

We started with an informal description of a simple protocol that employs 2PC to ensure atomicity of service co-allocation. As the first contribution of this paper, we proposed a new protocol named $WSCP$ that seeks to enhance the performance of 2PC through the introduction of tentative hold protocol which requires a composite service to obtain holds before it enters the 2PC phase. Subsequently, further improvement was pursued through the introduction of a new Min-Max backoff protocol in order to better address the problem characteristics considered in the paper.

Simulations confirmed the key intuitions underlying the design of the $WSCP$ and the Min-Max backoff protocol, and also showed that the $WSCP$ in conjunction with the Min-Max backoff protocol significantly reduces the average waiting time at the cost of small overhead introduced by the addition of tentative hold phase. Therefore, the service co-allocation protocol proposed in this paper offers a way that effectively combines two seemingly independent existing ideas, namely the tentative hold protocol and the backoff protocol. Further research is underway to finetune the proposed protocol and formally prove the performance characteristics of the proposed protocol. In particular, we seek to obtain the approximate performance bound of the polynomial Min-Max backoff protocol in terms of its corresponding pure polynomial backoff protocol.

References

1. Newcomer, E.: Understanding Web Services. Addison-Wesley (2002)
2. Yang, J., Papazoglou, M.: Web component: A substrate for Web service reuse and composition. In: Proceedings of the International Conference on Advanced Information Systems Engineering (CAISE). (2002)
3. Papazoglou, M.P.: Web services and business transactions. World Wide Web: Internet and Web Information Systems 6 (2003) 49–91
4. Tuecke, S., Czajkowski, K., Foster, I., Frey, J., Graham, S., Kesselman, C.: Grid service specification. Technical report, Open Grid Service Infrastructure WG, Global Grid Forum (2002)
5. Bernstein, P.A., Newcomer, E.: Principles of Transaction Processing. Morgan Kaufmann (1997)
6. Menascé, D.A.: QoS issues in Web services. IEEE Internet Computing (2002) 72–75
7. Roberts, J., Srinivasan, K.: Tentative hold protocol part 1: White paper. http://www.w3.org/TR/tenthold-1/ (2001)
8. Håstad, J., Leighton, T., Rogoff, B.: Analysis of backoff protocols for multiple access channels. SIAM Journal on Computing 25 (1996) 740–774
9. Park, J., Choi, K.: Design of an efficient tentative hold protocol for automated coordination of multi-business transactions. In: Proceedings of the IEEE Conference on E-Commerce. (2003)

Author Index

Lecture Notes in Computer Science

For information about Vols. 1–2722

please contact your bookseller or Springer-Verlag

Vol. 2761: R. Amadio, D. Lugiez (Eds.), CONCUR 2003 - Concurrency Theory. Proceedings, 2003. XI, 524 pages. 2003.

Vol. 2762: G. Dong, C. Tang, W. Wang (Eds.), Advances in Web-Age Information Management. Proceedings, 2003. XIII, 512 pages. 2003.

Vol. 2763: V. Malyshkin (Ed.), Parallel Computing Technologies. Proceedings, 2003. XIII, 570 pages. 2003.

Vol. 2764: S. Arora, K. Jansen, J.D.P. Rolim, A. Sahai (Eds.), Approximation, Randomization, and Combinatorial Optimization. Proceedings, 2003. IX, 409 pages. 2003.

Vol. 2765: R. Conradi, A.I. Wang (Eds.), Empirical Methods and Studies in Software Engineering. VIII, 279 pages. 2003.

Vol. 2766: S. Behnke, Hierarchical Neural Networks for Image Interpretation. XII, 224 pages. 2003.

Vol. 2768: M.J. Wilson, R.R. Martin (Eds.), Mathematics of Surfaces. Proceedings, 2003. VIII, 393 pages. 2003.

Vol. 2769: T. Koch, I. T. Sølvberg (Eds.), Research and Advanced Technology for Digital Libraries. Proceedings, 2003. XV, 536 pages. 2003.

Vol. 2773: V. Palade, R.J. Howlett, L. Jain (Eds.), Knowledge-Based Intelligent Information and Engineering Systems. Proceedings, Part I, 2003. LI, 1473 pages. 2003. (Subseries LNAI).

Vol. 2774: V. Palade, R.J. Howlett, L. Jain (Eds.), Knowledge-Based Intelligent Information and Engineering Systems. Proceedings, Part II, 2003. LI, 1443 pages. 2003. (Subseries LNAI).

Vol. 2776: V. Gorodetsky, L. Popyack, V. Skormin (Eds.), Computer Network Security. Proceedings, 2003. XIV, 470 pages. 2003.

Vol. 2777: B. Schölkopf, M.K. Warmuth (Eds.), Learning Theory and Kernel Machines. Proceedings, 2003. XIV, 746 pages. 2003. (Subseries LNAI).

Vol. 2778: P.Y.K. Cheung, G.A. Constantinides, J.T. de Sousa (Eds.), Field-Programmable Logic and Applications. Proceedings, 2003. XXVI, 1179 pages. 2003.

Vol. 2779: C.D. Walter, Ç.K. Koç, C. Paar (Eds.), Cryptographic Hardware and Embedded Systems – CHES 2003. Proceedings, 2003. XIII, 441 pages. 2003.

Vol. 2781: B. Michaelis, G. Krell (Eds.), Pattern Recognition. Proceedings, 2003. XVII, 621 pages. 2003.

Vol. 2782: M. Klusch, A. Omicini, S. Ossowski, H. Laamanen (Eds.), Cooperative Information Agents VII. Proceedings, 2003. XI, 345 pages. 2003. (Subseries LNAI).

Vol. 2783: W. Zhou, P. Nicholson, B. Corbitt, J. Fong (Eds.), Advances in Web-Based Learning – ICWL 2003. Proceedings, 2003. XV, 552 pages. 2003.

Vol. 2786: F. Oquendo (Ed.), Software Process Technology. Proceedings, 2003. X, 173 pages. 2003.

Vol. 2787: J. Timmis, P. Bentley, E. Hart (Eds.), Artificial Immune Systems. Proceedings, 2003. XI, 299 pages. 2003.

Vol. 2789: L. Böszörményi, P. Schojer (Eds.), Modular Programming Languages. Proceedings, 2003. XIII, 271 pages. 2003.

Vol. 2790: H. Kosch, L. Böszörményi, H. Hellwagner (Eds.), Euro-Par 2003 Parallel Processing. Proceedings, 2003. XXXV, 1320 pages. 2003.

Vol. 2792: T. Rist, R. Aylett, D. Ballin, J. Rickel (Eds.), Intelligent Virtual Agents. Proceedings, 2003. XV, 364 pages. 2003. (Subseries LNAI).

Vol. 2794: P. Kemper, W. H. Sanders (Eds.), Computer Performance Evaluation. Proceedings, 2003. X, 309 pages. 2003.

Vol. 2795: L. Chittaro (Ed.), Human-Computer Interaction with Mobile Devices and Services. Proceedings, 2003. XV, 494 pages. 2003.

Vol. 2796: M. Cialdea Mayer, F. Pirri (Eds.), Automated Reasoning with Analytic Tableaux and Related Methods. Proceedings, 2003. X, 271 pages. 2003. (Subseries LNAI).

Vol. 2798: L. Kalinichenko, R. Manthey, B. Thalheim, U. Wloka (Eds.), Advances in Databases and Information Systems. Proceedings, 2003. XIII, 431 pages. 2003.

Vol. 2799: J.J. Chico, E. Macii (Eds.), Integrated Circuit and System Design. Proceedings, 2003. XVII, 631 pages. 2003.

Vol. 2801: W. Banzhaf, T. Christaller, P. Dittrich, J.T. Kim, J. Ziegler (Eds.), Advances in Artificial Life. Proceedings, 2003. XVI, 905 pages. 2003. (Subseries LNAI).

Vol. 2803: M. Baaz, J.A. Makowsky (Eds.), Computer Science Logic. Proceedings, 2003. XII, 589 pages. 2003.

Vol. 2805: K. Araki, S. Gnesi, D. Mandrioli (Eds.), FME 2003: Formal Methods. Proceedings, 2003. XVII, 942 pages. 2003.

Vol. 2807: V. Matoušek, P. Mautner (Eds.), Text, Speech and Dialogue. Proceedings, 2003. XIII, 426 pages. 2003. (Subseries LNAI).

Vol. 2810: M.R. Berthold, H.-J. Lenz, E. Bradley, R. Kruse, C. Borgelt (Eds.), Advances in Intelligent Data Analysis V. Proceedings, 2003. XV, 624 pages. 2003.

Vol. 2812: G. Benson, R. Page (Eds.), Algorithms in Bioinformatics. Proceedings, 2003. X, 528 pages. 2003. (Subseries LNBI).

Vol. 2815: Y. Lindell, Composition of Secure Multi-Party Protocols. XVI, 192 pages. 2003.

Vol. 2817: D. Konstantas, M. Leonard, Y. Pigneur, S. Patel (Eds.), Object-Oriented Information Systems. Proceedings, 2003. XII, 426 pages. 2003.

Vol. 2818: H. Blanken, T. Grabs, H.-J. Schek, R. Schenkel, G. Weikum (Eds.), Intelligent Search on XML Data. XVII, 319 pages. 2003.

Vol. 2819: B. Benatallah, M.-C. Shan (Eds.), Technologies for E-Services. Proceedings, 2003. X, 203 pages. 2003.

Vol. 2820: G. Vigna, E. Jonsson, C. Kruegel (Eds.), Recent Advances in Intrusion Detection. Proceedings, 2003. X, 239 pages. 2003.

Vol. 2821: A. Günter, R. Kruse, B. Neumann (Eds.), KI 2003: Advances in Artificial Intelligence. Proceedings, 2003. XII, 662 pages. 2003. (Subseries LNAI).

Vol. 2832: G. Di Battista, U. Zwick (Eds.), Algorithms – ESA 2003. Proceedings, 2003. XIV, 790 pages. 2003.

Vol. 2834: X. Zhou, S. Jähnichen, M. Xu, J. Cao (Eds.), Advanced Parallel Processing Technologies. Proceedings, 2003. XIV, 679 pages. 2003.

Vol. 2837: N. Lavrač, D. Gamberger, H. Blockeel, L. Todorovski (Eds.), Machine Learning: ECML 2003. Proceedings, 2003. XVI, 504 pages. 2003. (Subseries LNAI).

Vol. 2838: N. Lavrač, D. Gamberger, L. Todorovski, H. Blockeel (Eds.), Knowledge Discovery in Databases: PKDD 2003. Proceedings, 2003. XVI, 508 pages. 2003. (Subseries LNAI).

Vol. 2839: A. Marshall, N. Agoulmine (Eds.), Management of Multimedia Networks and Services. Proceedings, 2003. XIV, 532 pages. 2003.